CW01651775

Whillans Tax Data 2022–23

Finance Act 2022 Edition

LexisNexis®

LexisNexis® UK & Worldwide

United Kingdom — RELX (UK) Limited trading as LexisNexis®, 1–3 Strand, London WC2N 5JR

LNUK Global — LexisNexis® encompasses authoritative legal publishing brands dating back to the 19th century including: Butterworths® in the United Kingdom, Canada and the Asia-Pacific region; Les Editions du Juris Classeur in France; and Matthew Bender® worldwide. Details of LexisNexis® locations worldwide can be found at www.lexisnexis.com

First published in 1981

Published by LexisNexis®
This is a Tolley title

A CIP Catalogue record for this book is available from the British Library.

ISBN for this volume: 9780754558514

Printed in Great Britain by Hobbs the Printers Ltd, Totton, Hampshire

Visit LexisNexis at www.lexisnexis.co.uk

Foreword

The 2022–23 Finance Act Edition of Whillans Tax Data is a compendium of essential factual information for the tax adviser covering all the main UK taxes and related matters. Comparative figures for up to six years are included in many of the tables. Statutory references are also given.

This edition includes all relevant measures in the 2022 Finance Act and other changes since the Budget edition was published in January.

Andrew Hubbard
Editor-in-chief, Taxation Magazine

Disclaimer

While every care has been taken to ensure the accuracy of this work, no responsibility for loss or damage occasioned to any person acting or refraining from action as a result of any statement in it can be accepted by the authors, editor or publisher.

Abbreviations

ACT	Advance corporation tax
AIM	Alternative Investment Market
CAA	Capital Allowances Act
CGT	Capital gains tax
Conv	Convertible
CTA	Corporation Tax Act
Cum	Cumulative
EIS	Enterprise Investment Scheme
EU	European Union
ESC	Extra-statutory concession
FA	Finance Act
FB	Finance Bill
FII	Franked investment income
HMRC	Her Majesty's Revenue and Customs
ICTA	Income and Corporation Taxes Act
IHTA	Inheritance Tax Act
IR	Inland Revenue
IRPR	Inland Revenue Press Release
ITA	Income Tax Act
ITEPA	Income Tax (Earnings and Pensions) Act
ITTOIA	Income Tax (Trading and Other Income) Act
NI	Northern Ireland
NIC	National insurance contributions
Ord	Ordinary
PAYE	Pay as you earn
PET	Potentially exempt transfer
PSA	PAYE settlement agreement
Pt	Part
RPI	Retail price index
RTI	Real time information
s	Section
Sch	Schedule
SI	Statutory Instrument
SP	Statement of Practice
SR & O	Statutory Rules and Orders
Stk	Stock
TCGA	Taxation of Chargeable Gains Act
TMA	Taxes Management Act
UK	United Kingdom
VATA	Value Added Tax Act
WDV	Written down value

2022/23 rates and allowances

Income tax

Allowances

	£
Personal allowance	12,570
Income limit (allowance reduced by ½ excess)	100,000
Transferable marriage allowance	1,260
Married couple's allowance — either partner born before 6.4.1935	9,415
Income limit (allowance reduced by ½ excess)	31,400
Minimum where income exceeds limit	3,640
Savings allowance	
Basic rate taxpayer	1,000
Higher rate taxpayer	500
Dividend allowance	2,000
Trading allowance	1,000
Property allowance	1,000
Blind person's allowance	2,600

Rates (individuals)

	Taxable income £	Rate	Dividend rate
Basic rate (note (b))	0–37,700	20%	8.75%
Higher rate	37,701–150,000	40%	33.75%
Additional rate	Over 150,000	45%	39.35%
Starting rate for savings	0–5,000	0%	

Notes

(a) See further pages 58, 59.
(b) The 2022/23 Scottish income tax rates and bands differ from those in the rest of the UK. See page 58.

National insurance contributions

Class 1		
Lower earnings limit	— per week	£123
	— per month	£533
Primary earnings threshold (6 April 2022–5 July 2022)	— per week	£190
	— per month	£823
Primary earnings threshold (6 July 2022–5 April 2023)	— per week	£242
	— per month	£1,048
Primary earnings threshold (directors)	— per week	£229
	— per month	—
Secondary earnings threshold	— per week	£175
	— per month	£758
Upper secondary earnings threshold	— per week	£967
	— per month	£4,189
Upper earnings limit	— per week	£967
	— per month	£4,189
Veterans' upper secondary threshold	— per week	£967
	— per month	£4,189
Freeport upper secondary threshold	— per week	£481
	— per month	£2,083
Employees' primary Class 1 rate (primary threshold to upper earnings limit)		13.25%
Employees' rate above upper earnings limit		3.25%
Married women's reduced rate (primary threshold to upper earnings limit)		7.1%
Married women's rate above upper earnings limit		3.25%
Employers' rate above secondary threshold/upper secondary threshold		15.05%
Class 1A rate		15.05%
Class 1B rate		15.05%
Class 2 (note (b))		
Weekly rate		£3.15
Weekly rate – share fishermen		£3.80
Weekly rate – volunteer development workers		£6.15
Small profits threshold		£6,725
Class 3 rate		£15.85
Class 4		
Lower profits limit		£11,908
Upper profits limit		£50,270
Rate from lower to upper profits limit		10.25%
Rate above upper profits limit		3.25%

Notes

(a) See further pages 87–92.
(b) For 2022–23, Class 2 NICs are not payable where an individual's profits fall between the small profits threshold and the Class 4 lower annual profits limit. The individual is treated as having paid Class 2 NICs for the purposes of benefits entitlement.

2022/23 rates and allowances

Capital gains tax

Annual exemption		£12,300
Rates		
Individuals		
Residential property and carried interest gains (note (b))	— up to basic rate limit	18%
	— above basic rate limit	28%
Other gains (note (b))	— up to basic rate limit	10%
	— above basic rate limit	20%
Settlements and personal representatives		
Residential property and carried interest gains		28%
Other gains		20%
Gains qualifying for business asset disposal relief (formerly known as entrepreneurs' relief)		10%
Gains qualifying for investors' relief		10%

Notes

(a) See further pages 18–35.
(b) For Scottish taxpayers the UK basic rate limit applies to determine the rate of capital gains tax.

Inheritance tax

£	Rate
Chargeable lifetime transfers	
0–325,000	Nil
Over 325,000	20%
Transfers on death	
0–325,000	Nil
Over 325,000	40% (36% if 10% or more of net estate is left to charity or community amateur sports club)
Residence nil rate band	
0–175,000	Nil

Note

(a) See further pages 71–76.

Corporation tax

Financial year 2022	
Rate	19%

Note

(a) See further pages 37–40.

Value added tax

Registration threshold	£85,000
Deregistration threshold	£83,000
Standard rate	20%
Reduced rate (note (b))	5%

Notes

(a) See further pages 120–128.
(b) A temporary reduced rate of 12.5% applies to VATA 1994 Sch 7A Groups 14–16 from 1 October 2021 to 31 March 2022. See page 123.

Stamp duty land tax

Land transactions

Residential property (notes (a)–(d))	**Consideration** (rates apply to consideration in each slice)	**Main rate for UK residents**	**Main rate for non-UK residents**	**Higher rate for UK residents**	**Higher rate for non-UK residents**
Effective date	**1.10.21 onwards**				
(note (a))	Up to £125,000	Nil	2%	3%	5%
	£125,001–£250,000	2%	4%	5%	7%
	£250,001–925,000	5%	7%	8%	10%
	£925,001–£1,500,000	10%	12%	13%	15%
	£1,500,001 or more	12%	14%	15%	17%

Non-residential or mixed property	**Consideration** (rates apply to consideration in each slice)	**Rate**
	Up to £150,000	Nil
	£150,001–£250,000	2%
	£250,001 or more	5%

Notes

(a) See page 112 for lease rentals and rates for first time buyers.
(b) The higher rates apply to certain purchases of residential property, including additional residential properties purchased by individuals. Transactions under £40,000 are excluded.
(c) SDLT does not apply to land transactions in Scotland or Wales. See page 111 for land and buildings transaction tax and land transaction tax.
(d) A 2% surcharge applies from 1.4.21 on purchases of residential property by non-residents (as defined for SDLT purposes only), including certain UK resident companies controlled by non-residents.

Bank interest rates

Date	Base Rate %
20 March 1985	13.5
29 March	13
2 April	13.125
12 April	12.875
19 April	12.625
12 June	12.5
15 July	12
29 July	11.5
9 January 1986	12.5
19 March	11.5
9 April	11
21 April	10.5
14 October	11
10 March 1987	10.5
18 March	10
29 April	9.5
11 May	9
7 August	10
26 October 1987	9.5
5 November	9
4 December	8.5
2 February 1988	9
17 March	8.5
11 April	8
1 May	7.5
3 June	8
6 June	8.5
22 June	9
28 June	9.5
4 July	10
18 July	10.5
26 August	12
25 November	13
24 May 1989	14
5 October	15
8 October 1990	14
14 February 1991	13.5
27 February	13

Date	Base Rate %
22 March	12.5
12 April	12
24 May	11.5
12 July	11
4 September	10.5
5 May 1992	10
16 September	12
17/18 September	10
22 September	9
16/19 October	8
13 November 1992	7
26 January 1993	6
23 November	5.5
8 February 1994	5.25
12 September	5.75
7 December	6.25
2 February 1995	6.75
13 December	6.5
19 January 1996	6.25
8 March	6
6 June	5.75
30 October	6
6 May 1997	6.25
6 June	6.5
10 July	6.75
7 August	7
6 November	7.25
4 June 1998	7.5
8 October	7.25
5 November	6.75
10 December	6.25
7 January 1999	6
4 February	5.5
8 April	5.25
10 June	5
8 September	5.25
4 November	5.5
13 January 2000	5.75

Date	Base Rate %
10 February	6
8 February 2001	5.75
5 April	5.5
10 May	5.25
2 August	5
18 September	4.75
4 October	4.5
8 November	4
6 February 2003	3.75
10 July	3.5
6 November	3.75
5 February 2004	4
6 May	4.25
10 June	4.5
5 August	4.75
4 August 2005	4.5
3 August 2006	4.75
9 November	5
11 January 2007	5.25
10 May	5.5
5 July	5.75
6 December	5.5
7 February 2008	5.25
10 April	5
8 October	4.5
6 November	3
4 December	2
8 January 2009	1.5
5 February	1
5 March	0.5
4 August 2016	0.25
2 November 2017	0.5
2 August 2018	0.75
11 March 2020	0.25
19 March	0.10
16 December 2021	0.25
3 February 2022	0.50
17 March	0.75%

Benefits in kind

Benefit provided for year		Charge/exemption for:		Reference
2016/17 onwards		All employees except as aside	'Lower-paid' ministers of religion	
Accommodation, supplies, etc. used in employment duties		Provision of accommodation, supplies or services used by an employee in performing the duties of the employment is not taxable provided that either (i) if the benefit is provided on premises occupied by the employer, any private use by the employee (or his family or household) is not significant; or (ii) in any other case, the sole purpose of providing the benefit is to enable the employee to perform those duties, any private use is not significant, and the benefit is not an 'excluded benefit' (i.e. the provision of a motor vehicle, boat or aircraft, or a benefit which involves the extension, conversion or alteration of any living accommodation or the construction, extension, conversion or alteration of a building or other structure on land adjacent to and enjoyed with living accommodation).	As aside	*ITEPA 2003, s 316*
Assets given to employees		If new, cost to employer less any part of cost made good by employee. If used, greater of (i) market value at time of transfer and (ii) where asset (other than a car or a van) first applied for the provision of a benefit after 5.4.80 and a person has been chargeable to tax on its use, market value when first so applied less amounts charged to tax for use up to and including year of transfer.	Market value	*ITEPA 2003, ss 203, 204, 206*
Board and lodging for carers		For 2016/17 onwards, the provision of board and lodging to an individual employed as a home care worker is not taxable if it is at the home of the recipient of the care and is on a reasonable scale.	n/a	*ITEPA 2003, s 306A; FA 2015, s 14*
Buses to shops		The provision of buses for journeys of 10 miles or less from the workplace to shops, etc. on a working day is not taxable.	As aside	*SI 2002 No 205*
Cheap loans				
(a)	Interest free or beneficial rates	Taxable benefit on employer-related, cheap loans is the difference between interest paid and interest payable at 'official rate' below.	Not taxable	*ITEPA 2003, ss 174, 175, 181–187*
		Exception applies		
		(i) where all the employer-related loans (or all loans not qualifying for tax relief) do not exceed £10,000;		*ITEPA 2003, s 180*
		(ii) where all the interest payable is or would be eligible for tax relief; and		*ITEPA 2003, ss 177–179*
		(iii) to ordinary commercial loans.		*ITEPA 2003, s 176*
		The 'official rate' (see note on page 8) is		
		6.4.17–5.4.20 2.50%		*SI 2017 No 305*
		6.4.20–5.4.21 2.25%		*SI 2020 No 194*
		6.4.21–5.4.22 2.00%		*SI 2021 No 249*
		6.4.22–5.4.23 2.00%		
(b)	Waiver	Amount written off	Normally taxable	*ITEPA 2003, ss 188–190*
Christmas parties and annual functions		Not taxable if cost does not exceed £150 per head per tax year and open to staff generally. Otherwise fully taxable. Expenditure may be split between more than one function.	Not taxable	*ITEPA 2003, s 264; SI 2003 No 1361*

Benefits in kind

Benefit provided for year 2016/17 onwards	Charge/exemption for: All employees except as aside	'Lower-paid' ministers of religion	Reference
Childcare provision	No liability arises (i) where the premises are not used wholly or mainly as a private dwelling and the provision is made available by the employer; (ii) where the scheme is provided under arrangements with other persons, by one or more of those persons; or (iii) in cases where (i) or (ii) does not apply, on the first £55 per week of registered or approved childcare or, where the employee joins the scheme after 5 April 2011, the first £55 per week for a basic rate taxpayer, the first £28 for a higher rate taxpayer and the first £25 for an additional rate taxpayer. The provisions in (ii) and (iii) are replaced for new claimants from 4 October 2018. Under the Government's tax-free childcare scheme, top-up payments are made equal to 25% of the amount paid for childcare of qualifying children. A maximum top-up of £2,000 each year per child (£4,000 for a disabled child) applies. No income tax or NIC liability arises in respect of the top-up payments. All eligible parents were able to join the scheme by 14 February 2018.	Not taxable	*ITEPA 2003, ss 318–318D; SI 2006 No 882; SI 2015 No 537; SI 2018 No 462*
Company cars/car fuel	See pages 84 to 86		
Company vans/van fuel	No benefit arises where a van is made available mainly for business travel and the terms on which it is made available prohibit private use other than for ordinary commuting; otherwise the benefit is £3,600 (£3,500 for 2021/22; £3,490 for 2020/21; £3,430 for 2019/20; £3,350 for 2018/19; £3,230 for 2017/18). For 2021/22 onwards the benefit is nil for zero-emission vans (£2,792 for 2020/21; £2,058 for 2019/20; £1,340 for 2018/19; £646 for 2017/18). Where the benefit charge applies and fuel for private travel is provided, there is an additional fuel benefit charge. For 2022/23 the charge is £688 (£669 for 2021/22; £666 for 2020/21; £655 for 2019/20; £633 for 2018/19; £610 for 2017/18). There is no charge for zero-emissions vans.	Not taxable	*ITEPA 2003, ss 154–164, 170; FA 2021, s 23; SI 2021 No 248; SI 2021 No 1422*
Credit tokens	Cost to employer of money, goods or services obtained less any contribution from employee (except where used to obtain certain non-taxable benefits).	As aside	*ITEPA 2003, ss 90–96, 268–270, 363*
Disabled employees	No benefit arises on the provision of or payment for transport for disabled employees for ordinary commuting. No benefit arises on the provision of equipment, services or facilities to disabled employees to help them carry out their duties of employment.	As aside	*ITEPA 2003, ss 246, 247* *SI 2002 No 1596*
Electricity for an electric car or van	No taxable benefit arises from 6 April 2018 on electricity provided in workplace charging points for electric or plug-in hybrid cars or vans used by employees.	As aside	*ITEPA 2003, s 237A*
Emergency service vehicles	No charge arises where an emergency vehicle is made available to a person employed in an emergency service (where private use is prohibited otherwise than when on call for tax years before 2017/18).	As aside	*ITEPA 2003, s 248A*
Employee shareholder agreements	No charge arises where the reasonable costs of independent advice as to the terms and effect of a proposed employee shareholder agreement (see page 20) is met by the company.	As aside	*ITEPA 2003, s 326B; FA 2013, Sch 23 paras 37, 38*
Employees' liability insurance	Not taxable	As aside	*ITEPA 2003, ss 346–350*
Expenses generally	For 2016/17 onwards, expenses payments and reimbursements are not taxable if an amount equal to or exceeding the expense would be allowed as a deduction (unless payment is under salary sacrifice arrangements). Where this does not apply, unless covered by specific exemptions elsewhere, all payments to an employee by reason of his employment in respect of expenses, including sums put at the employee's disposal and paid away by him, are taxable. Deduction is allowed for expenses the employee is obliged to incur which are either qualifying travelling expenses (broadly those necessarily incurred other than ordinary commuting or private travel) or other amounts incurred wholly, exclusively and necessarily in the performance of the duties of the employment.	Not taxable	*ITEPA 2003, ss 70–72, 289A–289E, 336–340*

Benefits in kind

Benefit provided for year	Charge/exemption for:		Reference
2016/17 onwards	**All employees except as aside**	**'Lower-paid' ministers of religion**	
Eye tests and corrective appliances	Not taxable provided that provision is required under health and safety legislation and is available as required to employees generally.	As aside	*ITEPA 2003, s 320A; FA 2006, s 62*
Fixed rate expenses	See pages 61 and 62		
Homeworkers	Equipment provided by the employer solely to enable the employee to carry out their employment duties is exempt provided there is insignificant private use. A temporary exemption applied for 2020/21 and 2021/22 where an employee purchases equipment enabling them to work from home as a result of the coronavirus (COVID-19) pandemic and claims reimbursement from the employer.	As aside	*ITEPA 2003, ss 316, 316A; SI 2020 No 524; SI 2020 No 525; SI 2021 No 225*
	Employer contributions to additional household costs not taxable where employee works at home. Supporting evidence required if contributions exceed £6 per week from 6 April 2020 (previously £4) (or £26 per month for monthly paid employees (previously £18)). This exemption can apply where an employee is required to work from home as a result of the coronavirus pandemic.		
Incidental overnight expenses	Not taxable where employee stays away from home on business and payment from employer does not exceed £5 per night in the UK or £10 per night overseas.	As aside	*ITEPA 2003, ss 240, 241*
Living accommodation (a) Representative	Employees – no liability where (i) necessary for proper performance of duties; (ii) customary to provide employee with accommodation; or (iii) special threat to employee's security Directors – (a) full-time working director whose interest in the company does not exceed 5%, as for employees above; (b) other directors, not taxable when (iii) above applies; otherwise as for beneficial below.	Not taxable	*ITEPA 2003, ss 99, 100*
(b) Beneficial	Annual rental value (or actual rent if greater) less any sums made good by the employee. For leases of ten years or less commencing or extended after 21 April 2009, a premium is treated as actual rent spread over the lease term. Where the cost of providing accommodation exceeds £75,000 (and the charge under *ITEPA 2003, s 105* is not calculated on the full open market rental value), there is an additional charge at an annual rate, equivalent to the excess over £75,000 at the official rate for cheap loans (see above) at the beginning of the year of assessment (less any rent paid in excess of the benefit under *s 105*).	As aside	*ITEPA 2003, ss 102–105B* *ITEPA 2003, ss 106, 107*
	Where there is multiple occupation in a period, the total amount charged cannot exceed that chargeable if the property was available to one person throughout.		*ITEPA 2003, s 108*
	An exemption applies in respect of occupation of an overseas property owned by a company that is owned by individuals and whose only activities are incidental to its ownership of the property, provided that the property is the company's only or main asset and is not funded by a connected company.		*ITEPA 2003, ss 100A, 100B*
Living expenses			
(a) Company's property			
(i) Representative	Cost to company subject to a maximum of 10% of net earnings	Normally not taxable	*ITEPA 2003, ss 313–315*
(ii) Beneficial	Normally cost to employer	Normally not taxable	
(b) Own accommodation	Normally cost to employer	Normally as aside	
Long service awards	Not taxable provided at least 20 years' service and cost to employer does not exceed £50 for each year of service. No similar award must have been made in the previous 10 years.	As aside	*ITEPA 2003, s 323; SI 2003 No 1361*

Benefits in kind

Benefit provided for year	Charge/exemption for:		Reference
2016/17 onwards	All employees except as aside	'Lower-paid' ministers of religion	
Meal allowances during business travel	An amount paid or reimbursed to an employee in respect of meals in the course of qualifying travel (broadly, travel other than ordinary commuting or private travel) is not taxable provided that the amount does not exceed: (i) £5 where the duration of the qualifying travel in that day is at least 5 hours (ii) £10 where it is at least 10 hours (iii) £25 where it is at least 15 hours and is still ongoing at 8pm An additional meal allowance of up to £10 is not taxable where a meal allowance within (i) or (ii) above is paid and the qualifying travel is ongoing at 8pm.	As aside	*ITEPA 2003, s 289A(2A); SI 2015 No 1948, Reg 2*
Medical check-ups	One screening and one check-up each year not taxable.	As aside	*ITEPA 2003, s 320B*
Medical insurance	Premium paid on behalf of employee taxable unless for treatment outside UK whilst employee performing his duties abroad.	Not taxable	*ITEPA 2003, s 325*
Medical treatment	Not taxable up to an annual cap of £500 per employee when an employer meets the cost of recommended medical treatment. Treatment is recommended for this purpose if provided in accordance with a recommendation from an occupational health service to help an employee return to work after absence due to ill-health or injury.	As aside	*ITEPA 2003, s 320C; SI 2014 No 3226*
Medical: Coronavirus (COVID-19) tests	Coronavirus test kits provided to employees by their employers are not a taxable benefit in 2020/21 and 2021/22.	As aside	*FA 2021, s 26*
Miners' free coal	Miners' free coal and coal allowances in lieu are not taxable.	As aside	*ITEPA 2003, s 306*
Mobile telephones	Loan of one mobile phone to employee not taxable. Exemption covers making the telephone available (without any transfer of property), line rental, and calls (business and private).	Not taxable	*ITEPA 2003, s 319*
Parking spaces	Parking spaces at or near place of work for cars, bicycles, motorcycles and vans not taxable.	Not taxable	*ITEPA 2003, s 237*
Pension advice	Not taxable if available to all employees and benefit does not exceed £500 per tax year (£150 before 6 April 2017). From 6 April 2017 relief extended to include advice on general financial and tax issues relating to pensions.	As aside	*SI 2002 No 205; ITEPA 2003, s 308C*
	Payments by employers for independent advice to employees on conversion and transfers of pension benefits not taxable.	As aside	*ITEPA 2003, s 308B*
Public transport strikes	The provision of travel, accommodation and subsistence during public transport disruption caused by industrial action is not taxable.	As aside	*ITEPA 2003, s 245*
Relocation expenses	Qualifying removal expenses and benefits up to £8,000 per move in connection with job-related residential moves are not taxable. Included are expenses of disposal, acquisition, abortive acquisition, transporting belongings, travelling and subsistence, bridging loans and duplicate expenses.	As aside	*ITEPA 2003, ss 271–289*
Salary sacrifice and flexible benefit arrangements	From 2017/18 the range of benefits that attract income tax and NIC advantages when provided as part of optional remuneration arrangements is limited but savings can still be achieved on employer pension contributions and advice, employer-provided childcare, cycle to work schemes, and ultra-low emission company cars. Any arrangements in place before 6 April 2017 could continue unaffected until 5 April 2018 (with a further extension until 5 April 2021 for existing longer term agreements covering cars, living accommodation and school fees).	As aside	*ITEPA 2003, ss 69A, 69B*
Scholarships	Cost of any scholarship awarded (i) out of a trust fund etc. not satisfying a 25% distribution test; or (ii) because of employee's employment.	Not taxable	*ITEPA 2003, ss 211–215*
Sports and recreational facilities	Not taxable	Not taxable	*ITEPA 2003, ss 261–263*
Subscriptions and fees	Not taxable where paid to professional bodies where employee has a contractual or professional requirement to be a member of the body.	As aside	*ITEPA 2003, ss 343–345*
Third party entertaining	Not taxable where provided by a party unconnected with the employer and not for services provided in connection with employment.	As aside	*ITEPA 2003, s 265*

Benefits in kind

Benefit provided for year	Charge/exemption for:		Reference
2016/17 onwards	All employees except as aside	'Lower-paid' ministers of religion	
Third party small gifts	Gifts of goods and non-cash vouchers up to £250 during the tax year not taxable where provided by a party unconnected with the employer and not for services provided in connection with employment.	As aside	*ITEPA 2003, ss 270, 324; SI 2003 No 1361*
Training/counselling	Certain employee training costs, work-related training, and counselling services provided by employers are not taxable.	As aside	*ITEPA 2003, ss 250–260, 310–312*
Transport to home	Transport and occasional late night journeys from work to home or following a failure of a car-sharing arrangement are not taxable.	As aside	*ITEPA 2003, s 248*
Travel expenses of councillors	For 2016/17 onwards an exemption applies to reimbursed travel expenses incurred by local authority councillors.	As aside	*ITEPA 2003, ss 235A, 295A*
Trivial benefits	From 6 April 2016, benefits meeting the following conditions are not taxable; the benefit is not cash or a cash voucher; the cost of providing it does not exceed £50; the benefit is not provided under salary sacrifice arrangements, under any other contractual obligation or in recognition of particular services.	As aside	*ITEPA 2003, ss 323A–323C*
	There is an annual limit of £300 for office holders of close companies and family members of such office holders.		
Use of employer's assets (other than cars and vans)	Land at annual rental value; other assets at 20% of market value when first lent or rental charge to employer if higher. From 2017/18 the benefit is reduced by periods during which the asset is unavailable for private use by the employee or his family/household, or where the asset is shared by two or more employees. No benefit arises in respect of	Not taxable	*ITEPA 2003, ss 203–205B*
	(i) use of computer equipment for private home use where equipment first made available before 6 April 2006 (provided use not restricted to directors and senior staff and cash equivalent of benefit does not exceed £500);		*ITEPA 2003, s 320; FA 2006, s 61*
	(ii) use of works buses with a passenger seating capacity of at least 9 provided for employees (or their children) to travel to and from work;		*ITEPA 2003, s 242*
	(iii) bicycles and cycling safety equipment made available for employees to get between home and work. The qualifying journeys condition (ie travel between home and work) is treated as met from 16 March 2020 to 5 April 2022 where equipment was first provided before 21 December 2020.		*ITEPA 2003, s 244; FA 2021, s 25*
	No benefit arises on purchase by employee at market value of computer or bicycle previously on loan.		*FA 2005, s 17*
Vouchers			
(a) Cash vouchers	Amount for which voucher can be exchanged	Cashable value	*ITEPA 2003, ss 73–81, 95, 96*
(b) Non-cash vouchers	Cost to employer less any contribution from employee (except where used to obtain certain non-taxable benefits)	Cost to employer	*ITEPA 2003, ss 82–88, 95, 96, 268–270A, 362*
(c) Luncheon vouchers	Taxable	As aside	*ITEPA 2003, s 89; FA 2012, Sch 39 para 50*
(d) Transport vouchers	Cost to employer less any contribution from employee	As aside	*ITEPA 2003, ss 82–86*
Vulnerable persons schemes	No charge arises where an employer pays or reimburses an employee's registration fee to the Protection of Vulnerable Groups Scheme or pays or reimburses fees for subscribing to the Disclosure and Barring Service's update service or fees for criminal records certificates applied for when an update service subscription is applied for.	As aside	*ITEPA 2003, s 326A; SI 2013 No 1133*
Welfare counselling	Not taxable (but excluding medical treatment and advice on finance (other than debt problems), tax, leisure or recreation, and legal advice).	As aside	*SI 2000 No 2080*
Workplace meals	Subsidised meals provided for staff generally at the workplace are not taxable. This exemption does not apply if entitlement arises under salary sacrifice or flexible benefits arrangements.	As aside	*ITEPA 2003, s 317*

Note

(a) The official rate is set in advance for the whole of the following tax year, subject to review if the typical mortgage rates *fall* sharply during a tax year (IRPR 6/00, 25 January 2000).

Capital allowances

Business premises renovation

Expenditure after	Allowance	Reference
Initial allowance		
10 April 2007	100%	*CAA 2001, ss 360A–360Z4* *FA 2005, s 92, Sch 6*

Notes

(a) Business premises renovation allowances are **abolished** for expenditure incurred on or after 6 April 2017 (1 April 2017 for corporation tax).

(b) Allowances were available only for renovation or conversion of business properties that had been vacant for at least a year and were situated in any of the disadvantaged areas of the UK designated as Enterprise Areas. For expenditure incurred on or after 6 April 2014 (1 April 2014 for corporation tax purposes) allowances were not available if another form of EU State aid had been, or would be, received.

(c) Where the initial allowance was not claimed or not claimed in full, a writing-down allowance of 25% on the cost was given.

Dredging

Expenditure after	Allowance	Reference
Writing-down allowance (on cost)		
5 November 1962	4%	*CAA 2001, s 487*

Know-how

Expenditure after	Allowance	Reference
Writing-down allowance		
31 March 1986	25% (on tax wdv)	*CAA 2001, s 458*

Mineral extraction

Expenditure after	Allowance	Reference
Writing-down allowance		
After 31 March 1986	25% (on tax wdv); 10% on minerals and mineral rights	*CAA 2001, s 418*

Note

(a) A 100% first-year allowance is available for certain expenditure incurred after 16 April 2002 wholly for the purposes of a North Sea Oil ring-fence trade or on plant and machinery for use in such a trade. *CAA 2001, s 416D*

Motor cars suitable for private use

Not normally eligible for annual investment or first-year allowances (but see page 11, note (b))

Expenditure after	Allowance
Writing-down allowance	
5 April 2009 (31 March 2009 for CT)	
—chargeable periods ending after 5.4.12 (31.3.12 for CT)	18% where CO_2 emissions do not exceed the limit in note (b); otherwise 6% for chargeable periods beginning on or after 6 April 2019 (1 April 2019 for CT) (previously 8%) (see note (a))

Notes

(a) Expenditure incurred after 5 April 2009 (31 March 2009 for corporation tax) is allocated either to the main pool, or where the 6% or 8% rate applies, to the special rate pool, unless there is private use of the car. [*CAA 2001, ss 104A, 104AA*]. For chargeable periods beginning before 6 April 2019 and ending on or after that date (or, for corporation tax purposes, beginning before 1 April 2019 and ending on or after that date) a hybrid rate of WDAs applies, calculated by time apportionment of the 8% and 6% rates.

(b) The emission limit is 50g/km for expenditure incurred on or after 6 April 2021 (for income tax purposes) or 1 April 2021 (for corporation tax purposes). For expenditure incurred before 6 April 2021 (1 April 2021 for corporation tax purposes) the limit is 110g/km, for expenditure incurred before 1 April 2018 the limit is 130g/km, for expenditure incurred before 6 April 2013 (1 April 2013 for corporation tax purposes) the limit is 160g/km. [SI 2021 No 120].

Patent rights

Expenditure after	Allowance	Reference
Writing-down allowance		
31 March 1986	25% (on tax wdv)	*CAA 2001, s 472*

Research and development

Expenditure after	Allowance	Reference
Allowance in year 1		
5 November 1962	100%	*CAA 2001, s 441*

Capital allowances

Structures and buildings allowance

[*CAA 2001, Part 2A; SI 2019 No 1087; FA 2020, s 29; FA 2021, s 114, Sch 22; FA 2022, s 13*]

	Annual rate on or after	Annual rate before	Allowance
General			
Income tax	6 April 2020		3%
	28 October 2018	6 April 2020	2%
Corporation tax	1 April 2020		3%
	28 October 2018	1 April 2020	2%
Freeport tax sites (note (b))			
Income tax	Date of tax designation of site		10%
Corporation tax	Date of tax designation of site		10%

Notes

(a) Applies on a straight-line basis to qualifying construction expenditure on new non-residential structures and buildings (but not land) where contract for construction is entered into after 28 October 2018. Relief applies to UK and overseas structures and buildings, including new conversions or renovations, where the business is within the charge to UK tax. Where a chargeable period spans 1 or 6 April 2020 the rate of 2% will apply for days before the relevant date and 3% for the days after.

(b) The annual rate for Freeport tax sites applies where the first contract for construction is entered into on or after the date the tax site is designated, and the building or structure must be brought into qualifying use before 1 October 2026. See *SI 2021 Nos 1193, 1194, 1195* and *1389* and *SI 2022 Nos 184, 185* and *186* for details of the current freeport tax sites.

Plant and machinery

Annual investment allowance [*CAA 2001, ss 51A–51N; FA 2019, s 32, Sch 13; FA 2021, s 15; FA 2022, s 12*]

Qualifying expenditure incurred on or after 6 April 2008 (1 April 2008 for corporation tax purposes) up to the annual maximum incurred in a chargeable period qualifies for the annual investment allowance at **100%**.

	Expenditure after	Expenditure before	Maximum allowance
Income tax	31 March 2023		£200,000
	31 December 2018	1 April 2023	£1,000,000
	31 December 2015	1 January 2019	£200,000
	5 April 2014	1 January 2016	£500,000
Corporation tax	31 March 2023		£200,000
	31 December 2018	1 April 2023	£1,000,000
	31 December 2015	1 January 2019	£200,000
	31 March 2014	1 January 2016	£500,000

Notes

(a) Transitional rules apply to all of the changes in the maximum allowance for chargeable periods which straddle the dates of the changes.

(b) The annual maximum is proportionately increased or decreased where the chargeable period is longer or shorter than a year. A group of companies (defined as for company law purposes) can only receive a single maximum amount. This restriction also applies to certain related businesses or companies. Expenditure on cars and that qualifying for structures and buildings allowance does not qualify.

First-year allowances		Expenditure after	before	Rate
(a)	Energy-saving equipment			
	— for IT purposes (note (a))	31.3.01	6.4.20	100%
	— for CT purposes (note (a))	31.3.01	1.4.20	100%
(b)	Certain cars (note (b))	16.4.02	1.4.25	100%
(c)	Certain refuelling equipment (note (c))	16.4.02	1.4.25	100%
(d)	Environment-friendly equipment			
	— for IT purposes (note (d))	31.3.03	6.4.20	100%
	— for CT purposes (note (d))	31.3.03	1.4.20	100%
(e)	Zero-emission goods vehicles			
	— for IT purposes (note (e))	5.4.10	6.4.25	100%
	— for CT purposes (note (e))	1.4.10	1.4.25	100%
(f)	Equipment for use in designated areas of enterprise zones (note (f))	31.3.12		100%
(g)	Electric charge-point equipment			
	— for IT purposes (note (h))	22.11.16	6.4.23	100%
	— for CT purposes (note (h))	22.11.16	1.4.23	100%
(h)	Equipment for use in designated freeport tax sites (note (i))	Date of tax designation of site	1.10.26	100%
(i)	Super-deduction and temporary FYA (note (j))			
	main rate assets	31.3.21	1.4.23	130%
	special rate assets	31.3.21	1.4.23	50%

Notes

(a) The allowance is withdrawn for expenditure on or after 6 April 2020 (1 April 2020 for corporation tax). 100% FYAs were available for expenditure on designated energy-saving plant or machinery, in accordance with the Energy Technology Criteria and Product Lists. 100% FYAs were available even if the assets were leased or let on hire. [*CAA 2001, ss 45A–45C; SI 2019 No 501*]. See List E on page 13.

(b) Expenditure in the period attracts a FYA of 100% on new (not second-hand) cars first registered after 16 April 2002 which are either electrically-propelled or emit not more than 0g/km of CO_2 for expenditure incurred on or after 1 April 2021 (50g/km for expenditure incurred before 1 April 2021, 75g/km for expenditure incurred before 1 April 2018; 95g/km for expenditure before 1 April 2015; 110g/km for expenditure before 1 April 2013; 120g/km for expenditure before 1 April 2008). For expenditure incurred after 31 March 2013 cars provided for leasing do not qualify. [*CAA 2001, ss 45D, 46; SI 2015 No 60; SI 2016 No 984; SI 2021 No 120*].

(c) Expenditure in the period attracts a FYA of 100% on new plant or machinery for use in a refuelling station for the refuelling of vehicles with natural gas, hydrogen fuel or (for expenditure on or after 1 April 2008) biogas. [*CAA 2001, s 45E; SI 2015 No 60; SI 2017 No 1304*].

(d) The allowance is withdrawn for expenditure on or after 6 April 2020 (1 April 2020 for corporation tax). Expenditure incurred on designated environmentally-friendly plant and machinery attracted a FYA of 100%. Details of the qualifying technologies and products were published in the Water Technology Criteria and Products List. [*CAA 2001, s 45H; SI 2019 No 499*]. See List F on page 13.

(e) Expenditure in the period attracts a FYA of 100% on new (not second-hand) vehicles which cannot produce carbon dioxide emissions when driven and which are of a design primarily suited to the conveyance of goods or burden. This is limited to expenditure of 85 million euros per undertaking (as defined) over the eight years. [*CAA 2001, ss 45DA, 212T; F(No 3)A 2010, Sch 7 paras 3, 6; FA 2015, s 45; SI 2017 No 1304*]. For expenditure incurred on or after 6 April 2015 (1 April 2015 for corporation tax), the FYA is limited to businesses that do not claim another State aid in respect of the same expenditure. The FYA also cannot be claimed if such aid is paid on or after that date towards expenditure on a van incurred before that date (and allowances already given are withdrawn).

(f) Expenditure incurred by a trading company in the period ending on the later of 31 March 2021 or eight years from the date the area is (or is treated as) designated, attracts a FYA of 100% on new (not second-hand) plant or machinery which represents investment and not replacement expenditure and which is not transport or transport equipment for use in a transport business. This is limited to expenditure of 125 million euros per investment project. The asset must not be held for use in an area outside of the designated assisted area for a period of five years. [*CAA 2001, ss 45K–45N; FA 2012, Sch 11 para 3; SI 2020 No 260*]. The designated assisted areas are listed in *SI 2014 No 3183*, *SI 2015 No 2047*, *SI 2016 No 751* and *SI 2018 No 485*.

(g) For expenditure incurred on or after 1 April 2008 and before 1 April 2020, a company can surrender a tax loss attributable to FYAs within categories (a) or (d) above in exchange for a cash payment from the Government. The cash payment is equal to a percentage of the loss surrendered, subject to an upper limit of the greater of £250,000 and the company's PAYE and NIC liability for the period concerned. For chargeable periods beginning before 1 April 2018 the percentage was fixed at 19%. For chargeable periods beginning on or after 1 April 2018 the percentage is 2/3 of the corporation tax rate chargeable. [*CAA 2001, s 262A, Sch A1; SI 2013 No 464*].

(h) Expenditure in the period attracts a FYA of 100% on new (not second-hand), unused electric charge-point equipment installed solely for the purpose of charging electric vehicles. [*CAA 2001, s 45EA*].

(i) For expenditure incurred by companies in the period on unused (not second hand) plant or machinery for use primarily in designated tax sites within freeports. See *SI 2021 Nos 1193*, *1194*, *1195* and *1389* and *SI 2022 Nos 184*, *185* and *186* for details of the current freeport tax sites. [*CAA 2001, ss 45P–45R; FA 2021, Sch 22, FA 2022, s 13*].

(j) For qualifying expenditures incurred from 1 April 2021 up to and including 31 March 2023, companies can claim in the period of investment: (a) a super-deduction providing allowances of 130% on unused (not second hand) plant and machinery investments that ordinarily qualify for 18% main rate writing down allowances; (b) a first year allowance of 50% on unused (not second hand) plant and machinery investments that ordinarily qualify for 6% special rate writing down allowances. [*FA 2021, ss 9–14*].

Writing-down allowances (WDAs)

		Rate
(a)	General (expenditure after 26.10.70)	
	— chargeable periods ending after 5.4.12 (31.3.12 for CT)	18%
(b)	Special rate expenditure	
	— chargeable periods ending after 5.4.19 (31.3.19 for CT) (see note (a))	6%
	— chargeable periods ending after 5.4.12 and before 6.4.19 (after 31.3.12 and before 31.3.19 for CT)	8%

Notes

(a) WDAs are calculated on a reducing balance basis. When the rate changes during a chargeable period a hybrid rate of WDAs applies, calculated by time apportionment of the new and old rates. For chargeable periods beginning on or after 6 April 2008 (1 April 2008 for CT purposes), a WDA of up to £1,000 can be claimed in respect of the main pool and/or the special rate pool where the unrelieved expenditure in the pool concerned is £1,000 or less.

(b) The special rate applies to expenditure on:

- long-life assets (see also note (c));
- integral features of a building and thermal insulation of a building incurred on or after 6 April 2008 (1 April 2008 for CT purposes) (see also note (d));
- expenditure on long life assets incurred before 6 April 2008 (1 April 2008 for CT purposes) but not allocated to a pool until a chargeable period beginning on or after that date;
- expenditure on certain motor cars incurred on or after 6 April 2009 (1 April 2009 for CT purposes) (see page 10);
- expenditure on cushion gas incurred on or after 1 April 2010; and
- expenditure on solar panels incurred on or after 6 April 2012 (1 April 2012 for CT purposes).

The rate also applies to long-life assets pooled before 6/1 April 2008 for chargeable periods ending on or after 5 April 2008 (31 March 2008 for CT purposes), subject to transitional rules. [*CAA 2001, s 104A; FA 2008, s 83; FA 2019, s 31*].

The special rate for ring fence trades is 10%.

(c) Long-life assets are plant and machinery with an expected working life when new of at least 25 years where expenditure on long-life assets is more than £100,000 p.a. It does not apply to plant and machinery which is: (i) second-hand where the rate applied to the vendor because the original expenditure pre-dated these rules; (ii) in a building used wholly or mainly as, or for purposes ancillary to, a dwelling-house, retail shop, showroom, hotel or office; (iii) cars; or (iv) sea-going ships and railway assets purchased before 1 January 2011.

For companies, the £100,000 *de minimis* limit is divided by one plus the number of related 51% group companies (if any). [*CAA 2001, ss 90–104, Sch 3 para 20*].

(d) Integral features of a building are:

- electrical systems;
- cold water systems;
- space or water heating systems;
- powered ventilation systems;
- air cooling or purification, and any floor or ceiling comprised in such systems;
- lifts;
- escalators and moving walkways; and
- external solar shading.

[*CAA 2001, ss 33A, 33B*].

Expenditure on

(a) the provision of a building (including assets incorporated, or normally incorporated, in the building),

(b) the provisions of certain structures and assets or works involving the alteration of land, and

(c) the acquisition of any interest in land

does not qualify for plant and machinery allowances. [*CAA 2001, ss 21, 22, 24*].

Subject to certain conditions, these provisions do not apply to

(i) thermal insulation of buildings; personal security; integral features; software and rights to software; films; or

(ii) expenditure on assets in List C.

See List A for assets treated as buildings and not qualifying as plant or machinery. [*CAA 2001, ss 21, 23*].

See List B for other assets specifically excluded from being plant or machinery. [*CAA 2001, ss 22, 23*].

See List C for assets not excluded from being plant or machinery. [*CAA 2001, s 23*].

See List D for activities which are qualifying activities for plant and machinery allowances. [*CAA 2001, s 15*].

See List E for classes of plant and machinery specified in the Energy Technology Criteria List.

See List F for classes of plant and machinery specified in the Water Technology Criteria List.

List G, reproduced by kind permission of Edward Magrin FTII, is a list of expenditure which *should*, subject to business use, be regarded as plant or machinery. The list has been compiled from case law (UK and foreign), court, tribunal and Commissioners' decisions and HMRC practice. It is not exhaustive.

See also HMRC Brief 3/10 which includes a list of items specific to the pig industry which may qualify as plant or machinery.

Whether expenditure on items within List C or List D qualifies for capital allowances will depend upon the facts of the case as applied to existing case law.

List A Assets treated as buildings

(1) Walls, floors, ceilings, doors, gates, shutters, windows and stairs.

(2) Mains services, and systems, for water, electricity and gas.

(3) Waste disposal systems.

(4) Sewerage and drainage systems.

(5) Shafts or other structures in which lifts, hoists, escalators and moving walkways are installed.

(6) Fire safety systems.

List B Excluded structures and other assets

(1) A tunnel, bridge, viaduct, aqueduct, embankment or cutting.

(2) A way, hard standing (such as a pavement), road, railway, tramway, a park for vehicles or containers, or an airstrip or runway.

(3) An inland navigation, including a canal or basin or a navigable river.

(4) A dam, reservoir or barrage, including any sluices, gates, generators and other equipment associated with the dam, reservoir or barrage.

(5) A dock, harbour, wharf, pier, marina or jetty or any other structure in or at which vessels may be kept, or merchandise or passengers may be shipped or unshipped.

(6) Any dike, sea wall, weir or drainage ditch.

(7) Any structure not within items 1 to 6 other than

- (a) a structure (but not a building) within the meaning of 'industrial building',
- (b) a structure in use for the purposes of an undertaking for the extraction, production, processing or distribution of gas, and
- (c) a structure in use for the purposes of a trade which consists in the provision of telecommunication, television or radio services.

List C Assets not excluded from being plant or machinery

Note that items 1 to 15 do not include any assets whose principle purpose is to insulate or enclose the interior of a building, or to provide an interior wall, floor or ceiling intended to remain permanently in place.

(1) Machinery (including devices for providing motive power) not within any other item in this list.

(2) Gas and sewerage systems provided mainly

- (a) to meet the particular requirements of the qualifying activity, or
- (b) to serve particular plant or machinery used for the purposes of the qualifying activity.

(3) Manufacturing or processing equipment; storage equipment (including cold rooms); display equipment; and counters, checkouts and similar.

(4) Cookers, washing machines, dishwashers, refrigerators and similar equipment; washbasins, sinks, baths, showers, sanitary ware and similar equipment; and furniture and furnishings.

(5) Hoists.

(6) Sound insulation provided mainly to meet the particular requirements of the qualifying activity.

(7) Computer, telecommunication and surveillance systems (including their wiring or other links).

(8) Refrigeration or cooling equipment.

(9) Fire alarm systems; sprinkler and other equipment for extinguishing or containing fires.

(10) Burglar alarm systems.

(11) Strong rooms in bank or building society premises; safes.

(12) Partition walls, where moveable and intended to be moved in the course of the qualifying activity.

(13) Decorative assets provided for the enjoyment of the public in hotel, restaurant or similar trades.

(14) Advertising hoardings; signs, displays and similar.

(15) Swimming pools (including diving boards, slides and structures on which such boards or slides are mounted).

(16) Any glasshouse constructed so that the required environment (namely, air, heat, light, irrigation and temperature) for the growing of plants is provided automatically by means of devices forming an integral part of its structure.

(17) Cold stores.

(18) Caravans provided mainly for holiday lettings.

(19) Buildings provided for testing aircraft engines run within the buildings.

(20) Moveable buildings intended to be moved in the course of the qualifying activity.

(21) The alteration of land for the purpose only of installing plant or machinery.

(22) The provision of dry docks.

(23) The provision of any jetty or similar structure provided mainly to carry plant or machinery.

(24) The provision of pipelines or underground ducts or tunnels with a primary purpose of carrying utility conduits.

(25) The provision of towers to support floodlights.

(26) The provision of

- (a) any reservoir incorporated into a water treatment works, or
- (b) any service reservoir of treated water for supply within any housing estate or other particular locality.

(27) The provision of

- (a) silos provided for temporary storage, or

(b) storage tanks.
(28) The provision of slurry pits or silage clamps.
(29) The provision of fish tanks or fish ponds.
(30) The provision of rails, sleepers and ballast for a railway or tramway.
(31) The provision of structures and other assets for providing the setting for any ride at an amusement park or exhibition.
(32) The provision of fixed zoo cages.

List D Qualifying Activities

Each of the following is a qualifying activity for the purposes of plant and machinery allowances but to the extent only that the profits or gains from the activity are, or (if there were any) would be, chargeable to tax.

(a) A trade.
(b) An ordinary UK property business.
(c) A UK or EEA furnished holiday lettings business.
(d) An ordinary overseas property business.
(e) A profession or vocation.
(f) A concern listed in *ITTOIA, s 12(4), CTA 2009, s 39(4)* (mines, transport undertakings etc).
(g) The management of an investment company.
(h) Special leasing of plant or machinery i.e. the hiring out of plant or machinery otherwise than in the course of another qualifying activity.
(i) An employment or office.

Where a person's qualifying activity falls within (b), (d) or (h) above, plant or machinery for use in a dwelling house is not qualifying expenditure. [*CAA 2001, s 35*].

Where a qualifying activity falls within (i) above, expenditure is qualifying expenditure only if the plant or machinery is necessarily provided for use in the performance of the duties of the employment or office. [*CAA 2001, ss 36, 80*].

List E Energy-saving plant and machinery

The Energy Technology Criteria List specifies the following technology classes as eligible for first-year allowances as energy-saving equipment. The allowance is withdrawn for expenditure on or after 6 April 2020 (1 April 2020 for corporation tax). See page 11 note (a).

(1) Combined heat and power.
(2) Lighting.
(3) Pipework insulation.
(4) Boilers.
(5) Motors and drives.
(6) Refrigeration
(7) Heat pumps.
(8) Radiant and warm air heaters.
(9) Compressed air equipment.
(10) Solar thermal systems.
(11) Automatic monitoring and targeting equipment.
(12) Air to air energy recovery equipment.
(13) Heating, ventilation and air conditioning equipment.
(14) Uninterruptible power supplies.
(15) High speed hand air dryers.
(16) (For expenditure incurred on or after 2 July 2015) waste heat to electricity conversion equipment.

The equipment must meet the energy-saving criteria set out in that List and, in the case of classes (4) to (17), must be of a type specified in (and not removed from) or which has been accepted for inclusion in, the Energy Technology Product List. [*CAA 2001, s 45A; SI 2018 No 268; SI 2019 No 501*].

For expenditure incurred on or after 6 April 2012 (1 April 2012 for corporation tax purposes) FYAs are not available for expenditure on plant or machinery which generates electricity or heat, or produces biogas or biofuels, that attract tariff payments under the feed-in tariffs scheme or renewable heat incentive scheme introduced by the Department of Energy and Climate Change. This restriction applies to expenditure incurred on or after 6 April 2014 (1 April 2014) for combined heat and power equipment installations.

List F Environmentally-friendly plant and machinery

The Water Technology Criteria List specifies the following technology classes as eligible for first-year allowances as environmentally-friendly equipment. The allowance is withdrawn for expenditure on or after 6 April 2020 (1 April 2020 for corporation tax). See page 11 note (d).

(1) Meters and monitoring equipment.
(2) Flow controllers.
(3) Leakage detection equipment.
(4) Efficient toilets.
(5) Efficient taps.
(6) Rainwater harvesting equipment.
(7) Water reuse systems.
(8) Cleaning in place equipment.
(9) Efficient showers.
(10) Efficient washing machines.
(11) (Up to 19 February 2019) small scale slurry and sludge dewatering equipment.
(12) (Up to 19 February 2019) vehicle wash waste reclaim units.
(13) Water efficient industrial cleaning equipment.
(14) Water management equipment for mechanical seals.
(15) Greywater recovery and reuse equipment.

The equipment must meet the environmental criteria set out in that List and must be of a type specified in (and not removed from) or which has been accepted for inclusion in, the Water Technology Product List. [*CAA 2001, s 45H; SI 2003 No 2076; SI 2019 No 499*].

Capital allowances items qualifying as plant or machinery

List G items which can qualify as plant or machinery based on case law, HMRC practice etc.

Acid chambers

Acoustic treatment of e.g. room ducts (specialised installations)

Advertising signs, billboards, hoardings and roller boards

Aerials

Air compressors and services

Air conditioning including ducting and vents

Air lines

Alterations to a building re: plant installation e.g. ventilating ducts

Amusement slides

Annealing ovens

Aquarium tanks

Arc and gas welding plant

Architects and professional fees related to a number of items including plant (part may qualify)

Armco barriers

Art works at a museum etc.

Artificial manure manufacturing plant

Bacon curing plant

Baffles

Baker's plant

Ball feeders and specialist tennis equipment

Banana ripening plant

Baths

Battery chargers

Beehives

Bicycle holders

Biscuit making plant

Bitumen laminating plant

Blast furnace

Blast tunnels

Blinds, curtains, blind boxes and pelmets

Boat shed jetties

Bobbin tamping machines

Boiler plants and auxiliaries

Boilers

Bowling alleys including ball return tracks, gutters, pit signals and terminals

Bowser tanks

Brewing plant including pipes, condenser and expansion

Brick elevators (portable)

Brick kilns

Bullet resistant screens

Burglar alarms

Buzz bars

Cable TV provision and ducting

Cable, both overhead and underground

Cable car systems

Calorifiers

Cameras

Canopy – where certain conditions met e.g. serves purpose of advertising

Canteen fittings and equipment

Capital contribution to a sewerage authority in the UK

Car park illumination

Carpets and other loose floor coverings

Car wash apparatus and housing

Cash dispensers

Casting pit

Cat walks

Catalysts (granuals)

Cathode filling machines

Ceilings – false, but only when performing a function distant from setting e.g. an integral part of a ventilation or air conditioning system

Central dictation systems

Charcoal burning kilns

Checkouts

Chillers

Cleaning cradles (including tracks and anchorages)

Clock installations

Coal carbonising apparatus

Coal hulks

Coffee making machines

Compressed air plant and piping

Computers and associated attachments together with specialised flooring and ceilings

Conduit for security alarm systems

Construction costs of erecting plant on site

Contribution to plant purchased by others (certain conditions must be met)

Conveyor installations and equipment

Cooking baths

Cooking, conveying and servicing equipment

Cooler rooms

Cooling furnaces

Cooling-water systems for (i) drinking and (ii) air-conditioning

Counters and fittings

Court floors – indoor and outdoor (certain cases only)

Cradles and fire balconies (demountable)

Crane gantries and towers

Curing barns e.g. tobacco and peanuts

Cyclic reforming apparatus

Dam (certain situations where not made of earth)

Dark rooms (demountable)

Derricks

Designs and blueprints

Dips for sheep and cattle

Dispensers

Disposal units with all live feeds, wastes and flues

Distillery plant and brewery apparatus including casks

Distribution systems

Documents hoist and other hoists and doors

Door closers

Draglines and buckets

Drilling plant

Drop hammers

Dry dock

Dry riser installation

Dryers

Capital allowances items qualifying as plant or machinery

Dumbwaiters
Dust extraction equipment
Dyehouse – specially designed
Dynamos
Electric dodgems
Electric fences
Electrically operated doors
Electrically operated roller shutters
Electrical sub-stations and generators
Electrical wiring closely related to an accepted piece of plant e.g. to smoke detectors
Electrical wiring and sockets in connection with particular trades e.g. TV shops and departments where the numbers of sockets are more than is normal for the size of the shop or department
Electronic scoring equipment
Electronic timing devices
Emergency lighting
Escalators and travelators
Excavating costs re: plant installation
Exchange losses when linked to capital expenditure
Extinguishers
Fairground and similar amusements
Fans
Fascia lettering
Fermentation chambers
Fire blankets and alarms
Fire protection systems and sprinklers
Fires
Fire safety equipment to comply with the requirements of a fire authority
Fish farming equipment
Fish ponds at garden centres and fish farms
Fitted desks, writing tables and screens
Fixed site caravans in a motor village
Flight simulators and trainers
Floating docks, pontoons and marinas
Floodlighting
Floor covering
Flooring (demountable)
Flooring (raised but only where incorporating special features necessary for trade)
Foreign currency fluctuation relating to expenditure (in certain cases)
Forges
Freezer rooms and chambers
Furnaces
Gamma irradiation apparatus
Gangways
Gantries
Gas bells
Gas installations after incoming main
General control and supervisory systems
Generators
Glasshouse (if of sophisticated design with e.g. a computer system monitoring and controlling such matters as temperature, humidity, ventilation and screens)
Goods and bullion lifts and doors
Grain silos
Gramophones and juke boxes
Grill work (removable)
Gymnasium equipment
Hand dryers
Heating installations, fittings, pipes and radiators
Hoists
Holding bay for oxygen steelmaking installation
Hoses and hose reels
Hot water services and related plumbing
Humidification buildings (specialist)
Hydraulic elevated platforms and hoists e.g. for car parking trade
Hydraulic presses
Ice making apparatus
Immersion and instant water heaters
Incinerators
Installation costs re: plant
Intercom installations
Internal signs
Kennels (moveable)
Kitchen equipment
Knives and lasts
Launches for ships
Laundry equipment and services
Letter-boxes
Lifts and lift shafts
Light fittings and lamps (certain trades e.g. hotels re ambience)
Lighting protection systems
Livestock pens and cages
Loudspeakers
Lockers
Locks (certain situations)
Loose floor coverings and doormats
Loose furniture
LPG cylinders
Mannequin display figures
Mechanical hand dryers
Mechanical gates
Mechanical vehicle barriers
Mechanical ventilation systems
Merry-go-rounds
Mezzanine storage platforms (moveable)
Milking machinery and refrigeration storage facilities
Mining machinery
Mirrors
Mobile phones
Model steam trains, permanent way and other equipment for carrying passengers
Moveable partitions (where required by trade)
Murals (certain trades e.g. hotels re ambience)
Museums – items displayed
Name plates
Navigation apparatus (both on and offshore)
Offshore accommodation modules and helidecks
Oil rigs, well linings and platforms
Organic peroxides expansion cell block
Ornaments (certain trades e.g. hotels re ambience)

Capital allowances items qualifying as plant or machinery

Outside tennis fencing
Ovens
Paper combining plant
Passenger lifts and doors
Payment for cancellation of options (in certain cases)
PBX
Personnel – location and call systems
Photofinish equipment
Pictures (certain trades e.g. hotels re ambience)
Pig unit (purpose built), automatic feeding etc.
Pipelines
Planetarium and space theatre domes
Plant housing (special circumstances)
Pneumatic tube conveying systems
Poles, cables, conductors and switch boards for the distribution of electricity
Portable toilet
Portakabins, huts of a nomadic type moved from site to site (e.g. the construction industry)
Pottery – works equipment and kiln
Poultry house – specially designed
Power cables
Power installations
Powering barrel mills
Prawn farming ponds
Professional fees specially related to an item of plant acquired
Projecting signs
Protective structures closely related to accepted items of plant
Public address and piped music systems
Pulleys
Pumps
Purifiers
Racking, cupboards and shelving (removable)
Radar installations
Radiators
Radio, television and data receivers
Radio, television and data transmission installations
Railway track including sleepers and ballast
Refinery
Refrigerated fruit juice dispensers
Refrigeration installations and cold stores
Refrigeration plant
Refuse collecting and disposal systems (including chutes and incinerators)
Reinforcing plant
Reticulation services installed in a factory if certain conditions are met
Retorts and associated structures
Revolving mechanical doors
Rock crushing machines
Roller shutter doors
Roofing – cost of strengthening roofs to support plant such as cranes and hoists
Safes, night safes and enclosures
Safety equipment and screens
Salmon farming apparatus
Sanitary installations such as lavatories, urinals and pans together with pipeline fittings
Sauna and jacuzzi
Screens and fire safety curtains – cinemas
Screens in a window display (moveable)
Sculptures (certain trades e.g. hotels re ambience)
Seats
Security assets and devices
Security gates to cash loading area (removable)
Security screens and lobbies
Sewer pipes in relation to e.g. factory or a large hotel
Shafts
Showers and baths
Shutters (mechanical)
Silage storage bunkers
Silos e.g. slurry blending and mixing and cement storage
Skating surface – synthetic
Skidpans and special surface tracks
Sleeping units for workers which are portable and taken from site to site
Slicing and wrapping machines
Smelters
Smoke detectors and heat detectors
Soda water fountains
Soft furnishings
Software purchased at the same time as the hardware re a computer system
Software with a life of more than 2 years
Solar energy systems
Special acoustical or suspended ceilings (in certain cases)
Special buildings which cannot be used as ordinary buildings e.g. boiler house, concrete shells housing plant, wind tunnels and anechoic chambers
Special foundations or reinforced flooring for plant
Special housing around plant
Special lighting related to the trade
Splashbacks (where not part of a wholly-tiled wall or floor)
Sports stadia expenditure re a safety certificate
Spray booth
Sprinkler systems
Squash courts – directly related to certain trading activities e.g. amusement park
Staff lockers
Stage lights and scenery
Stand (racecourse and similar trades (but only if certain conditions are met))
Starting gantries and stalls
Steam and other trains, permanent way and other equipment for carrying passengers or goods
Steam vats
Storage racks
Storage tanks and bins
Stoves
Stream services and condensate return systems
Strong rooms (demountable)
Strong room doors
Swimming pools directly related to certain trading activities e.g. amusement or caravan park
Switchboards
Switchgear

Tanks (for brine, cream etc.)
Tapestries (certain trades e.g. hotels re ambience)
Tea and coffee dispensers
Telegraph poles
Telephone booths and kiosks
Telephone equipment and conduits
Teleprinters
Telex systems
Tennis courts – directly related to certain trading activities e.g. amusement or caravan park
Testing tanks
Thermal insulation re industrial buildings
Ticket issuing and collecting machines
Toll booths
Totalisator equipment
Towel dispensers
Towel rails
Traffic control apparatus
Tramway rails
Transformers
Transportation costs of plant
Trellis
Trickle irrigation equipment in glasshouses
Trolley parks
Turnstiles
Turntables
Vacuum cleaning installations
Vats e.g. for cyanide
Vaults
Vents
Vibration control
Video equipment
WC partitions (if demountable venestra type)
Wall decor (certain trades e.g. hotels re ambience)
Wash basins including drains
Water slide and associated equipment
Water softening installations
Water tower
Water treatment and filtration
Weighbridge
Welfare facilities
Wells
Wet and dry risers
Wharves – certain situations
Winches
Wind tunnels
Windmills
Window display lighting e.g. shops
Window displays (moveable)
Window panels, lighting and sockets for a shop front
Wiring and trunking to accepted items of plant
X-ray apparatus
Zoo cages (fixed)

Capital gains tax

Annual exempt amount

(a) Individuals, personal representatives for the year of death and following two years and trusts for disabled person (as defined) [*TCGA 1992, s 1K, Sch 1C*]

2022/23	£12,300	*FA 2021, s 40*
2021/22	£12,300	*FA 2021, s 40*
2020/21	£12,300	*SI 2020 No 333*
2019/20	£12,000	*FA 2019, Sch 1*
2018/19	£11,700	*SI 2018 No 244*
2017/18	£11,300	*SI 2017 No 377*
2016/17	£11,100	*FA 2014, s 9*

In respect of qualifying trusts above, where one person creates more than one settlement, the exemption above is divided by the number of settlements created after 9 March 1981, subject to a minimum of 10% of the annual exemption.

An individual who claims to use the remittance basis for a tax year is not entitled to the capital gains tax annual exemption for that year. This does not apply if the individual's unremitted foreign income and gains for the year are less than £2,000.

The annual exempt amount will remain at the 2022/23 level up to and including 2025/26.

(b) Settlements other than trusts covered in (a) above [*TCGA 1992, s 1K, Sch 1C*]

2022/23	£6,150	*FA 2021, s 40*
2021/22	£6,150	*FA 2021, s 40*
2020/21	£6,150	*SI 2020 No 333*
2019/20	£6,000	*FA 2019, Sch 1*
2018/19	£5,850	*SI 2018 No 244*
2017/18	£5,650	*SI 2017 No 377*
2016/17	£5,550	*FA 2014, s 9*

In respect of settlements made after 6 June 1978, where one person creates more than one settlement, the exemption above is divided by the number of settlements created, subject to a minimum of 10% of the annual exemption for individuals.

The annual exempt amount will remain at the 2022/23 level up to and including 2025/26.

Annual rates [*TCGA 1992, s 1H; formerly TCGA 1992, s 4*]

Gains are chargeable as follows

2016/17–2022/23	*Individuals*: treating gains as the top slice of taxable income (subject to business asset disposal relief (formerly known as entrepreneurs' relief) and investors' relief (see page 20)): Residential property and carried interest gains (see below): 18% up to basic rate limit; 28% above basic rate limit Gains other than residential property and carried interest gains: 10% up to basic rate limit; 20% above basic rate limit *Settlements and personal representatives* (subject to business asset disposal relief (formerly known as entrepreneurs' relief) and investors' relief (see page 20)): Residential property and carried interest gains (see below): 28% Gains other than residential property and carried interest gains: 20%
2015/16	*Individuals*: treating gains as the top slice of taxable income: 18% up to basic rate limit; 28% above basic rate limit (subject to business asset disposal relief (formerly known as entrepreneurs' relief) (see page 20)) *Settlements and personal representatives*: 28% (subject to business asset disposal relief (formerly known as entrepreneurs' relief) (see below))

Residential property and carried interest gains from 2019/20 are gains on the disposal of residential property (where not exempt) and gains in respect of carried interest. From 2016/17 to 2018/19 they were known as upper rate gains.

High value disposals of dwellings by companies. The rate of capital gains tax for gains made by companies on or after 6 April 2013 and before 6 April 2019 on disposals of dwellings subject to the annual tax on enveloped dwellings is 28%.

Non-resident CGT on UK residential property. The rate of capital gains tax for gains made by non-resident companies on or after 6 April 2015 and before 6 April 2019 on disposals of UK residential property interests is 20%. The normal rates apply to individuals subject to the charge.

Basic rate limit. For Scottish taxpayers the Scottish basic rate limit (see page 59) does not apply to determine the rate of capital gains tax payable.

Business asset disposal relief (formerly known as entrepreneurs' relief) [*TCGA 1992, ss 169H–169S; FA 2013, Sch 24; FA 2015, ss 41–44; FA 2016, ss 83–85, Sch 13; FA 2019, s 39, Sch 16; FA 2020, s 23, Sch 3*]

Business asset disposal relief (formerly known as entrepreneurs' relief) applies to disposals by an individual on or after 6 April 2008 of:

- all or part of a trade carried on alone or in partnership;
- assets of such a trade following cessation;
- shares or securities in the individual's 'personal trading company' (as defined); or
- for disposals on or after 6 April 2013, shares acquired on or after 6 April 2012 on the exercise of an enterprise management incentives option.

Personal trading company is broadly one in which the individual holds at least 5% of ordinary share capital, 5% of voting rights, and, additionally for disposals after 28 October 2018, by virtue of their shareholding, at least 5% of the distributable profits and 5% of assets available for distribution to equity holders on a winding up, and / or is beneficially entitled to at least 5% of the proceeds on the disposal of all the company's ordinary share capital. Where the shareholding is diluted below 5% as a result of a new share issue after 5 April 2019, an election can be made to allow relief for gains up to that time, subject to conditions.

Where a disposal of shares or of an interest in the assets of a partnership qualifies for relief, an associated disposal of assets owned by the individual and used by the company or partnership also qualifies for relief. For disposals on or after 18 March 2015, the taxpayer must either dispose of at least 5% of the company's shares, dispose of a 5% share of the assets of the partnership or dispose of the whole of his interest in the partnership having held at least a 5% interest in the assets of the partnership for a continuous period of at least three years in the eight years before disposal of the asset. For disposals of assets acquired on or after 13 June 2016, the disposal must be of an asset or assets which the individual has owned throughout the three years ending with the date of disposal.

Trustees can claim relief where a qualifying beneficiary has an interest in the business concerned.

The relief is available where the relevant conditions are met throughout a period of two years (one year for disposals before 6 April 2019, and for cessations of a business or trading company status before 29 October 2018). The relief operates by charging qualifying net gains to CGT at 10% and is subject to a lifetime limit of gains of £1 million for qualifying disposals made on or after 11 March 2020, though specific rules may apply for contracts exchanged before 11 March but not completed until after that date and for certain reorganisations and share exchanges made before 11 March (£10 million for disposals before 11 March 2020; £5 million for disposals before 6 April 2011; £2 million for disposals before 23 June 2010; £1 million for disposals before 6 April 2010), but disposals before 6 April 2008 do not normally count towards the limit. Relief given to trustees counts towards the limit of the qualifying beneficiary.

A gain on a disposal made on or after 3 December 2014 which qualifies for relief can be deferred under the enterprise investment scheme or social investment relief scheme without loss of entitlement to the relief. The relief can be claimed when the deferred gain becomes chargeable. There are also transitional rules to allow relief to be claimed in certain circumstances where a gain made before 6 April 2008 is deferred and becomes chargeable on or after that date.

Business expansion scheme [*TCGA 1992, s 150*]

In respect of shares issued after 18 March 1986 and before 1 January 1994 a disposal of scheme shares is exempt provided the scheme relief has been given and not withdrawn and other conditions are satisfied.

Charities, etc, gifts to [*TCGA 1992, s 257; FA 2012, Sch 14*]

Disposals (not at arm's length) to charities, community amateur sports clubs or bodies within *IHTA 1984, Sch 3* by way of gift or at a consideration not exceeding allowable expenditure are deemed to be made for a consideration giving neither a gain nor a loss. See also page 63.

Under the cultural gifts scheme, taxpayers who donate pre-eminent objects, or collections of objects, to the nation may qualify for a tax reduction. Individuals qualify for a reduction in capital gains tax (and/or income tax) liability equal to 30% of the value of the objects. For corporation tax purposes the reduction is up to 20% of the value. The cultural gifts scheme is administered by the Arts Council.

Chattels (other than currency) [*TCGA 1992, s 45, s 262*]

Maximum exempt proceeds

1989/90 onwards	£6,000

Marginal relief applies to limit any gain to five-thirds of the excess over the above maximum. For the purposes of loss relief, a disposal for less than the maximum is deemed to be made for that maximum.

Chattels which are wasting assets are exempt whatever the consideration received, but this exemption is restricted or eliminated to the extent that the asset has been or could have been the subject of a capital allowance. For disposals on or after 6 April 2015 (1 April 2015 for corporation tax purposes), the exemption is also eliminated where the asset has become plant as a result of its use for the purposes of a trade, profession or vocation carried on by a person other than the owner and it would not otherwise have been a wasting asset.

Child trust funds [*SI 2004 No 1450*]

No tax is chargeable on the account provider, his nominee or the child on gains on account investments. The child is treated as having sold all the account investments, and as having reacquired them in his personal capacity, for their market value, immediately before attaining the age of 18. See also page 63.

Dwelling houses [*TCGA 1992, ss 222–226B; FA 2015, Schs 7, 9*]

A proportion of the gain accruing to an individual on the disposal of a dwelling house which has been his main residence is exempt given by the fraction

$$\frac{\text{length of the period of ownership after 31.3.82 during which the dwelling-house was the individual's only or main residence (but in any case inclusive of the last 9 months)}}{\text{the length of the period of ownership after 31.3.82}}$$

For disposals before 6 April 2020, the last 18 months of ownership were included in the numerator in the fraction. For disposals before 6 April 2014, the last 36 months of ownership were included in the numerator in the fraction. The 36-month period continues to apply where the property is disposed of by an individual who is, or whose spouse or civil partner is, a disabled person or a long-term resident in a care home, provided that neither holds an interest in any other dwelling house.

Certain periods of absence during which the individual had no other residence available for relief (including any period or periods not exceeding three years) are included in the denominator provided both before and after the period there was a time when the dwelling house was the individual's only or main residence.

For disposals on or after 6 April 2015, a property is treated as not being occupied as a residence for a tax year when it is located in a territory in which neither the person making the disposal nor their spouse or civil partner is tax resident and they do not stay overnight at the property at least 90 times during the year.

Where the dwelling house has been let at any time as residential accommodation, the gain otherwise chargeable by reason of the letting is exempt up to the lower of £40,000 and the amount of the gain otherwise exempt under these provisions. For disposals after 5 April 2020 the relief is only available if the owner is in shared-occupancy with the tenant. Where a gain on a disposal of UK residential property is chargeable to CGT the taxpayer must, subject to some specific exceptions, make a special return to HMRC within 60 days after the date of completion of sale and pay the tax (30 days where the date of completion is before 27 October 2021).

Non-resident CGT charge on UK residential property. Gains on disposals on or after 6 April 2015 and before 6 April 2019 of UK residential property by non-UK residents (including both individuals and certain companies) are chargeable to CGT. Broadly, only the gain accruing from that date is charged. Individuals and trustees may be able to obtain main residence relief. The taxpayer must in most cases make a special return to HMRC within 30 days after the date of completion of sale using the online NRCGT return form.

Employee-ownership trusts [*TCGA 1992, ss 236H–236S; FA 2014, s 290, Sch 37*]

A disposal by a person other than a company of shares in a trading company or parent company of a trading group to the trustees of a settlement is treated as being made at no gain/no loss if the settlement is for the benefit of all the employees of the company or group and the settlement acquires a controlling interest in the company during the tax year in which the disposal is made.

Employee shareholder shares [*FA 2013, Sch 23; FA 2016, ss 87, 88; FA 2017, s 13*]]

A special employment status, known as 'employee shareholder' status, was introduced by *Growth and Infrastructure Act 2013, s 31*, but tax relief is abolished for employee shareholder agreements entered into on or after 1 December 2016 (or 2 December 2016 in cases where the potential employee shareholder receives professional advice in relation to the share offer on 23 November 2016 before 1.30pm). Employee shareholders are issued or allotted at least £2,000 worth of shares in consideration of an employee shareholder agreement. For arrangements entered into before the abolition date, and subject to conditions, a gain on the first disposal of shares worth up to £50,000 on acquisition is exempt from CGT. The exemption applies to shares received through the adoption of employee shareholder status on or after 1 September 2013. The normal share identification rules do not apply to employee shareholder shares. If an employee disposes of part of a holding of shares which includes employee shareholder shares, the employee can determine what proportion of the shares disposed of are employee shareholder shares (subject to the total number of such shares held). A lifetime limit of £100,000 applies to gains on the disposal of shares acquired under employee shareholder agreements entered into on or after 17 March 2016. See also page 64.

Enterprise investment scheme [*TCGA 1992, ss 150A–150D, Schs 5B, 5BA*]

A disposal of shares on which EIS income tax relief has been given and not withdrawn is exempt. Any loss (net of income tax relief) on a disposal of EIS shares may be relieved against income or capital gains. A chargeable gain arising on disposal of any assets can be deferred by a subscription for shares under the EIS made one year before or three years after the disposal. Deferral is possible regardless of whether or not the EIS investment qualifies for income tax relief or the subscriber is connected with the company, but is restricted to cash subscriptions for new eligible shares in qualifying companies. See also page 64.

Gifts [*TCGA 1992, ss 165–169G, 260, Sch 7*]

Where an individual makes a disposal not at arm's length (e.g. a gift) of a qualifying business asset, then, on a joint claim by the transferor and transferee, the unrelieved gain of the transferor is held over and the transferee's acquisition cost is reduced by a similar amount. Where any consideration exceeds the allowable expenditure, the held-over gain is the unrelieved gain less the excess. Qualifying business assets are:

(a) assets used for the purposes of the trade, profession or vocation carried on by the transferor or his personal company; and

(b) shares or securities of a trading company which is the transferor's personal company or whose shares etc are not listed. (Transfers of shares or securities *to a company* are excluded.)

Where a transferor makes a disposal not at arm's length of any asset which is a chargeable transfer under *IHTA 1984*, similar hold-over rules apply as above.

Government securities ('gilts') [*TCGA 1992, s 115*]

Disposals by individuals and trustees are exempt.

Indexation [*TCGA 1992, ss 53–57, 109*]

Indexation allowance is available up to December 2017 for disposals by companies (but not individuals, trustees and personal representatives) and is computed by multiplying each item of allowable expenditure by an indexation factor equal to

$$\frac{RD - RI}{RI} \text{ where}$$

RD = the RPI for month of disposal (or December 2017 if earlier);

RI = the RPI for the later of March 1982 or month expenditure incurred (but no later than March 1998 for individuals etc.)

Indexation allowance is 'frozen' from 1 January 2018, so for disposals on or after this date the allowance is calculated up to December 2017. It can only be used to reduce or extinguish a gain and cannot increase or create a capital loss. The allowance for an asset held on 31 March 1982 is calculated by reference to its market value on that date rather than its cost. It can be claimed on the original cost if this is to the company's advantage. See page 104 for RPI values and pages 24–35 for indexation factors for disposals on or after 1.1.16.

Individual savings accounts ('ISAs') [*SI 1998 No 1870*]

Investors are entitled to exemption from capital gains tax on their investments. There is no lock-in period and withdrawals may be made at any time without loss of tax relief. Where investments are withdrawn *in specie*, the investor is deemed to have made a disposal and reacquisition at market value. See also page 65.

Investors' relief [*TCGA 1992, ss 169VA–169VY; FA 2016, s 86, Sch 14*]

Investors' relief applies to disposals by an individual of ordinary shares in an unlisted trading company or unlisted holding company of a trading group if:

- the shares were subscribed for by the individual for new consideration on or after 17.3.16;
- the individual held the shares for at least three years beginning on or after 6.4.16; and
- (subject to certain limited exceptions) neither the individual nor any connected person was an officer or employee of the company in the period of ownership.

The relief operates by charging the qualifying gains to CGT at 10%. Relief is subject to a lifetime limit of gains of £10 million.

Trustees can claim relief where an eligible beneficiary has an interest in settled property which includes the qualifying shares.

Lease depreciation table [*TCGA 1992, Sch 8 para 1(3)–(6)*]

This table relates to leases of land which have 50 years or less to run (short leases)

Years	Percentage	Years	Percentage	Years	Percentage
50 or more	100	33	90.280	16	64.116
49	99.657	32	89.354	15	61.617
48	99.289	31	88.371	14	58.971
47	98.902	30	87.330	13	56.167
46	98.490	29	86.226	12	53.191
45	98.059	28	85.053	11	50.038
44	97.595	27	83.816	10	46.695
43	97.107	26	82.496	9	43.154
42	96.593	25	81.100	8	39.399
41	96.041	24	79.622	7	35.414
40	95.457	23	78.055	6	31.195
39	94.842	22	76.399	5	26.722
38	94.189	21	74.635	4	21.983
37	93.497	20	72.770	3	16.959
36	92.761	19	70.791	2	11.629
35	91.981	18	68.697	1	5.983
34	91.156	17	66.470	0	0

The fraction of expenditure (original cost and additional expenditure being treated separately) which is not allowed is calculated from the table above as follows

$$\frac{P(1) - P(3)}{P(1)} \text{ or } \frac{P(2) - P(3)}{P(2)}$$

where the percentages for the duration of the lease are

P(1) at acquisition

P(2) at the time of any additional expenditure

P(3) at disposal

If the duration of the lease is not an exact number of years, the percentage is that for the whole number of years plus one-twelfth of the difference between that and the next higher number for each odd month, counting an odd fourteen days or more as one month.

Miscellaneous

The following is a summary of other important exemptions from capital gains tax not covered separately in this section.

(a) **Betting, lottery etc.** Winnings from betting or lotteries of games with prizes are not chargeable gains, and no chargeable gain accrues on the disposal of rights to such winnings obtained by participating. [*TCGA 1992, s 51(1)*].

(b) **Damages and compensation.** Sums received as compensation or damages for any wrong or injury suffered by an individual in his person or in his profession or vocation are not chargeable gains. [*TCGA 1992, s 51(2)*]. Compensation from foreign governments for assets confiscated, destroyed or expropriated is, subject to conditions, exempt. [*TCGA 1992, s 268B*].

(c) **Debts.** A debt, other than a debt on a security, disposed of by the original creditor or his personal representative or legatee is exempt. [*TCGA 1992, s 251(1)*].

(d) **Decorations.** A decoration for valour or gallantry is exempt unless acquired by the vendor for money or money's worth. [*TCGA 1992, s 268*].

(e) **Foreign currency** acquired for an individual's (or his dependant(s)) personal expenditure outside the UK is exempt. [*TCGA 1992, s 269*]. All gains on withdrawals of money from foreign currency bank accounts by individuals, trustees and personal representatives are exempt.

(f) **Insurance policies.** A gain on the disposal of the rights conferred by a non-life insurance policy is exempt, subject to a restriction in certain cases where the policy is for loss or depreciation of assets which could themselves give rise to a chargeable gain. [*TCGA 1992, s 204*].

(g) **Motor cars etc.** [*TCGA 1992, s 263*].

(h) **Qualifying corporate bonds** are exempt. [*TCGA 1992, s 115*].

(i) **Renewables obligations certificates.** A gain on the disposal by an individual of a certificate issued under *Electricity Act 1989, s 32B* is, subject to conditions, exempt. [*TCGA 1992, s 263AZA*].

(j) **Right to receive interest on deposit of victim of Nazi persecution.** A gain on the disposal of a right to receive interest eligible for income tax exemption under *ITTOIA 2005, s 756A* is not a chargeable gain. [*TCGA 1992, s 268A*].

(k) **Savings certificates, schemes and accounts etc.** No chargeable gain arises on the disposal of savings certificates and non-marketable securities issued under *National Loans Acts 1939* and *1968*. [*TCGA 1992, s 121*].

(l) **Settlements.** With certain exceptions, no chargeable gain accrues on the disposal of an interest created by or arising under a settlement by the original beneficiary or any other person. [*TCGA 1992, s 76*].

(m) **Substantial shareholdings of companies.** A gain on a disposal by a company of shares is exempt if, subject to further conditions, throughout a continuous twelve-month period beginning not more than six years before the disposal (two years for disposals before 1 April 2017), the company held a substantial shareholding (broadly, at least a 10% interest) in the company whose shares are the subject of the disposal. [*TCGA 1992, Sch 7AC*].

Capital gains tax

Negligible value securities

HMRC have accepted that certain quoted securities have become of negligible value within *TCGA 1992, s 24(2)*. The effect is that, on a claim, the claimant is treated as having sold, and immediately reacquired, the shares for a consideration equal to the amount specified in the claim. The following is a list of securities so accepted in recent years.

Company	Security	Effective date
Afren Plc	Ord	31/07/15
Carillion plc	All	15/01/18
Conviviality PLC	All	2017 to 2018
Debenhams plc	Ord	13/06/19
GLOBO Plc	Ord	10/11/15
Intu Properties plc	All	8/10/20
Weatherly International plc	Ord 5p	29/07/18

Payment of tax

Under self-assessment, CGT liability is generally taken into account in arriving at the final payment (or repayment) of IT and CGT due on 31 January following the tax year. From 6 April 2019 for disposals of UK land by non-residents and by UK residents in the overseas part of a split tax year, CGT is due 60 days after the date of completion of sale (30 days for disposals that completed before 27 October 2021). From 6 April 2020 the 60-day/30-day limit also applies to disposals of UK residential property by UK residents. See page 68 which includes details of certain relaxations relating to COVID-19.

CGT payable by a non-resident on a disposal of UK residential property before 6 April 2019 was due within 30 days after date of completion of sale, unless the taxpayer was subject to self-assessment.

Personal representatives (HMRC Statement of Practice SP 2/04)

HMRC have agreed that expenditure based on the following scale may be added to the market values of assets at the date of death (as an estimate of the legal and accountancy costs in preparing the inheritance tax account and obtaining probate etc.) in computing chargeable gains on disposal.

Gross value of estate	Allowable expenditure
(a) Up to £50,000	1.8% of probate value of assets sold
(b) £50,001–£90,000	£900 — divided among all the assets in the estate in proportion to their probate values
(c) £90,001–£400,000	1% of probate value of assets sold
(d) £400,001–£500,000	£4,000 — divided as in (b) above
(e) £500,001–£1,000,000	0.8% of probate value of assets sold
(f) £1,000,001–£5,000,000	£8,000 — divided as in (b) above
(g) Over £5,000,000	0.16% of probate value of assets sold (maximum £10,000)

Rebasing to 31 March 1982 [*TCGA 1992, ss 35, 36*]

Gains and losses on disposals after 5 April 1988 of assets held on 31 March 1982 are computed by reference to their 31 March 1982 value rather than original cost. However, for disposals by companies, a gain or loss cannot be greater than would have been the case if the rules relating to pre-6 April 1988 disposals had applied, unless a global election is made for 31 March 1982 value to apply irrevocably to all assets held on that date.

Rollover relief (replacement of business assets) [*TCGA1992, ss 152–160*]

A person disposing of a qualifying asset used exclusively for the purposes of a trade who uses the proceeds to purchase other qualifying assets so used may claim to defer the CGT payable by deducting the otherwise chargeable gain from the cost of new assets. Qualifying assets are

(a) land and buildings occupied and used for the purposes of the trade;
(b) fixed plant and machinery;
(c) ships, aircraft and hovercraft;
(d) satellites, space stations and spacecraft;
(e) goodwill;
(f) milk and potato quotas;
(g) ewe and suckler cow premium quotas;
(h) fish quotas;
(i) Lloyd's syndicate capacity;
(j) payment entitlement under the single payment scheme; and
(k) (where the disposal of the old asset or the acquisition of the new asset is on or after 20 December 2013) payment entitlement under the basic payment scheme.

Partial relief is available where not all the disposal proceeds are applied in acquiring new qualifying assets. As regards companies only, items (e) to (k) do not apply.

Seed enterprise investment scheme [*TCGA 1992, ss 150E–150G, Sch 5BB; FA 2012, Sch 6 paras 2–5; FA 2013, s 57*]

A disposal of shares on which SEIS income tax relief has been given and not withdrawn is exempt. Chargeable gains arising on disposals of any assets can be deferred by a subscription for shares under the SEIS made in the same year provided the SEIS investment qualifies for income tax relief (and such relief is claimed). From 2013/14 onwards the deferral relief applies to half of the reinvested amount, giving a maximum of £50,000 relief. See also page 67.

Capital gains tax

Share identification rules [*TCGA 1992, ss 104–106A; FA 2008, Sch 2*]

For disposals by individuals, trustees or personal representatives, shares and securities of the same class in the same company are normally identified with acquisitions in the following order:

- acquisitions on the same day as the disposal;
- acquisitions within 30 days after the day of disposal;
- shares comprised in a single pool incorporating all other shares of the same class, whenever acquired.

The 30-day rule does not apply where the person making the disposal is, or is treated as, neither resident nor ordinarily resident in the UK at the time of acquisition.

Special identification rules apply to shares (or securities) to which enterprise investment scheme relief, seed enterprise investment scheme relief, venture capital trust scheme relief, social investment relief or community investment tax relief is attributable, to shares in respect of which relief has been given (and not withdrawn) under the business expansion scheme, employee shareholder shares, share incentive plan shares and relevant enterprise management incentives shares.

For the purposes of corporation tax on chargeable gains, disposals of shares etc. are identified with acquisitions in the following order:

- same day acquisitions;
- acquisitions within the previous nine days on a first in/first out basis;
- the pool of shares acquired after 31 March 1982;
- any shares held at 31 March 1982;
- any shares acquired on or before 6 April 1965 on a last in/first out basis;
- (if shares disposed of still not fully matched) subsequent acquisitions.

Social investment relief [*TCGA 1992, ss 255AJ–255E, Sch 8B; FA 2014, Sch 12; FA 2021, s 20*]

A disposal of an asset to which SI income tax relief has been given and not withdrawn is exempt if the asset is held for at least three years. A chargeable gain arising on or after 6 April 2014 and before 6 April 2023 on disposal of any assets can be deferred by an investment which qualifies for SI income tax relief and which is made within the period from one year before to three years after the disposal. See also page 66.

Venture capital trusts [*TCGA 1992, ss 151A, 151B, Sch 5C*]

An individual's disposals of shares in VCTs are exempt from capital gains tax provided the shares were not *acquired* in excess of the permitted investment limit for any tax year. See page 67.

Capital gains indexation allowances for companies (January 2016 – December 2017)

Month of acquisition	2016 Jan	Feb	Mar	Apr	May	June	July	Aug	Sept	Oct	Nov	Dec	2017 Jan	Feb	Mar	Apr	May	June	July	Aug	Sept	Oct	Nov	Dec
1982																								
Mar	2.258	2.273	2.287	2.290	2.299	2.312	2.316	2.328	2.334	2.333	2.342	2.362	2.342	2.379	2.390	2.406	2.420	2.428	2.435	2.458	2.463	2.465	2.472	2.501
Apr	2.194	2.208	2.222	2.226	2.234	2.247	2.250	2.263	2.269	2.268	2.276	2.292	2.276	2.312	2.323	2.339	2.353	2.360	2.368	2.390	2.395	2.397	2.403	2.432
May	2.171	2.185	2.199	2.203	2.211	2.223	2.227	2.239	2.245	2.244	2.253	2.272	2.253	2.288	2.299	2.315	2.329	2.336	2.343	2.366	2.370	2.373	2.379	2.407
June	2.162	2.177	2.190	2.194	2.202	2.214	2.218	2.230	2.236	2.235	2.244	2.263	2.244	2.279	2.290	2.306	2.319	2.327	2.334	2.356	2.361	2.363	2.370	2.398
July	2.161	2.176	2.189	2.193	2.201	2.213	2.217	2.229	2.235	2.234	2.243	2.262	2.243	2.278	2.289	2.305	2.318	2.326	2.333	2.355	2.360	2.362	2.369	2.397
Aug	2.160	2.175	2.188	2.192	2.200	2.212	2.216	2.228	2.234	2.233	2.242	2.261	2.242	2.277	2.288	2.304	2.317	2.325	2.332	2.354	2.359	2.361	2.367	2.396
Sept	2.162	2.177	2.190	2.194	2.202	2.214	2.218	2.230	2.236	2.235	2.244	2.263	2.244	2.279	2.290	2.306	2.319	2.327	2.334	2.356	2.361	2.363	2.370	2.398
Oct	2.146	2.161	2.174	2.178	2.186	2.199	2.202	2.214	2.220	2.219	2.228	2.247	2.228	2.263	2.274	2.290	2.303	2.310	2.318	2.340	2.344	2.347	2.353	2.381
Nov	2.131	2.145	2.159	2.162	2.171	2.183	2.186	2.199	2.205	2.203	2.212	2.231	2.212	2.247	2.258	2.274	2.287	2.294	2.301	2.323	2.328	2.330	2.336	2.364
Dec	2.137	2.151	2.164	2.168	2.177	2.189	2.192	2.204	2.211	2.209	2.218	2.237	2.218	2.253	2.264	2.280	2.293	2.300	2.307	2.329	2.334	2.337	2.343	2.371
1983																								
Jan	2.133	2.147	2.161	2.164	2.173	2.185	2.188	2.201	2.207	2.205	2.214	2.233	2.214	2.249	2.260	2.276	2.289	2.296	2.303	2.325	2.330	2.332	2.339	2.366
Feb	2.119	2.134	2.147	2.151	2.159	2.171	2.175	2.187	2.193	2.192	2.200	2.219	2.200	2.235	2.246	2.262	2.275	2.282	2.289	2.311	2.316	2.318	2.324	2.352
Mar	2.114	2.128	2.141	2.145	2.153	2.165	2.169	2.181	2.187	2.186	2.194	2.214	2.194	2.229	2.240	2.256	2.269	2.276	2.283	2.305	2.310	2.312	2.318	2.346
Apr	2.071	2.085	2.098	2.101	2.110	2.122	2.125	2.137	2.143	2.142	2.150	2.169	2.150	2.184	2.195	2.211	2.224	2.231	2.238	2.259	2.264	2.266	2.272	2.300
May	2.058	2.072	2.085	2.088	2.097	2.109	2.112	2.124	2.130	2.129	2.137	2.156	2.137	2.171	2.182	2.197	2.210	2.217	2.224	2.246	2.250	2.253	2.259	2.286
June	2.050	2.065	2.078	2.081	2.089	2.101	2.105	2.116	2.122	2.121	2.129	2.148	2.129	2.164	2.174	2.189	2.202	2.210	2.217	2.238	2.243	2.245	2.251	2.278
July	2.034	2.048	2.061	2.065	2.073	2.084	2.088	2.100	2.106	2.104	2.113	2.131	2.113	2.147	2.157	2.172	2.185	2.192	2.199	2.220	2.225	2.228	2.233	2.260
Aug	2.021	2.035	2.047	2.051	2.059	2.071	2.074	2.086	2.092	2.091	2.099	2.117	2.099	2.133	2.143	2.158	2.171	2.178	2.185	2.206	2.211	2.213	2.219	2.246
Sept	2.007	2.021	2.034	2.037	2.046	2.057	2.061	2.072	2.078	2.077	2.085	2.104	2.085	2.119	2.129	2.144	2.157	2.164	2.171	2.192	2.197	2.199	2.205	2.232
Oct	1.997	2.011	2.023	2.027	2.035	2.046	2.050	2.062	2.067	2.066	2.074	2.093	2.074	2.108	2.118	2.133	2.146	2.153	2.160	2.181	2.185	2.188	2.194	2.220
Nov	1.986	2.000	2.013	2.016	2.024	2.036	2.039	2.051	2.057	2.055	2.063	2.082	2.063	2.097	2.107	2.122	2.135	2.142	2.149	2.170	2.174	2.177	2.182	2.209
Dec	1.978	1.992	2.005	2.008	2.016	2.028	2.031	2.043	2.049	2.047	2.055	2.074	2.055	2.089	2.099	2.114	2.127	2.134	2.141	2.161	2.166	2.168	2.174	2.200
1984																								
Jan	1.980	1.994	2.007	2.010	2.018	2.030	2.033	2.045	2.050	2.049	2.057	2.076	2.057	2.091	2.101	2.116	2.129	2.136	2.142	2.163	2.168	2.170	2.176	2.202
Feb	1.968	1.982	1.994	1.998	2.006	2.017	2.021	2.032	2.038	2.037	2.045	2.063	2.045	2.078	2.088	2.103	2.116	2.123	2.130	2.150	2.155	2.157	2.163	2.189
Mar	1.958	1.972	1.985	1.988	1.996	2.008	2.011	2.022	2.028	2.027	2.035	2.053	2.035	2.068	2.078	2.093	2.106	2.113	2.120	2.140	2.145	2.147	2.153	2.179
Apr	1.920	1.933	1.945	1.949	1.957	1.968	1.971	1.983	1.988	1.987	1.995	2.013	1.995	2.028	2.038	2.053	2.065	2.072	2.079	2.099	2.103	2.106	2.111	2.137
May	1.909	1.922	1.935	1.938	1.946	1.957	1.960	1.972	1.977	1.976	1.984	2.002	1.984	2.017	2.027	2.041	2.054	2.060	2.067	2.087	2.092	2.094	2.100	2.126
June	1.901	1.915	1.927	1.930	1.938	1.950	1.953	1.964	1.970	1.969	1.976	1.994	1.976	2.009	2.019	2.034	2.046	2.053	2.059	2.080	2.084	2.086	2.092	2.118
July	1.905	1.918	1.930	1.934	1.942	1.953	1.956	1.967	1.973	1.972	1.980	1.998	1.980	2.012	2.022	2.037	2.049	2.056	2.063	2.083	2.088	2.090	2.095	2.121
Aug	1.878	1.891	1.903	1.906	1.914	1.925	1.929	1.940	1.945	1.944	1.952	1.970	1.952	1.984	1.994	2.009	2.021	2.028	2.034	2.054	2.059	2.061	2.067	2.092
Sept	1.872	1.885	1.897	1.901	1.909	1.920	1.923	1.934	1.940	1.938	1.946	1.964	1.946	1.978	1.988	2.003	2.015	2.022	2.028	2.048	2.053	2.055	2.061	2.086
Oct	1.854	1.867	1.880	1.883	1.891	1.902	1.905	1.916	1.922	1.920	1.928	1.946	1.928	1.960	1.970	1.984	1.997	2.003	2.010	2.030	2.034	2.036	2.042	2.067
Nov	1.846	1.859	1.871	1.874	1.882	1.893	1.896	1.907	1.913	1.911	1.919	1.937	1.919	1.951	1.961.	1.975	1.987	1.994	2.001	2.020	2.025	2.027	2.032	2.058
Dec	1.848	1.861	1.873	1.876	1.884	1.895	1.899	1.910	1.915	1.914	1.922	1.939	1.922	1.954	1.963	1.978	1.990	1.996	2.003	2.023	2.027	2.029	2.035	2.060

Capital gains indexation allowances for companies (January 2016 – December 2017)

Month of acquisition	2016 Jan	Feb	Mar	Apr	May	June	July	Aug	Sept	Oct	Nov	Dec	2017 Jan	Feb	Mar	Apr	May	June	July	Aug	Sept	Oct	Nov	Dec
1985																								
Jan	1.838	1.851	1.863	1.866	1.874	1.885	1.888	1.899	1.904	1.903	1.911	1.929	1.911	1.943	1.953	1.967	1.979	1.986	1.992	2.012	2.016	2.019	2.024	2.049
Feb	1.815	1.828	1.840	1.843	1.851	1.862	1.865	1.876	1.881	1.880	1.888	1.905	1.888	1.919	1.929	1.943	1.955	1.962	1.968	1.988	1.992	1.994	2.000	2.025
Mar	1.789	1.802	1.814	1.817	1.824	1.835	1.838	1.849	1.854	1.853	1.861	1.878	1.861	1.892	1.902	1.916	1.928	1.934	1.941	1.960	1.964	1.967	1.972	1.997
Apr	1.731	1.743	1.755	1.758	1.765	1.776	1.779	1.790	1.795	1.794	1.801	1.818	1.801	1.832	1.841	1.855	1.867	1.873	1.879	1.898	1.903	1.905	1.910	1.934
May	1.718	1.731	1.742	1.746	1.753	1.763	1.767	1.777	1.782	1.781	1.789	1.805	1.789	1.819	1.829	1.842	1.854	1.860	1.866	1.885	1.889	1.892	1.897	1.921
June	1.712	1.725	1.737	1.740	1.747	1.758	1.761	1.771	1.776	1.775	1.783	1.799	1.783	1.813	1.822	1.836	1.848	1.854	1.860	1.879	1.883	1.885	1.891	1.915
July	1.718	1.730	1.742	1.745	1.752	1.763	1.766	1.776	1.782	1.781	1.788	1.805	1.788	1.818	1.828	1.841	1.853	1.859	1.866	1.884	1.889	1.891	1.896	1.920
Aug	1.710	1.723	1.734	1.738	1.745	1.755	1.758	1.769	1.774	1.773	1.780	1.797	1.780	1.811	1.820	1.834	1.845	1.852	1.858	1.877	1.881	1.883	1.888	1.912
Sept	1.712	1.724	1.736	1.739	1.746	1.757	1.760	1.770	1.776	1.775	1.782	1.799	1.782	1.812	1.822	1.835	1.847	1.853	1.859	1.878	1.883	1.885	1.890	1.914
Oct	1.707	1.720	1.731	1.735	1.742	1.752	1.756	1.766	1.771	1.770	1.778	1.794	1.778	1.808	1.817	1.831	1.842	1.849	1.855	1.874	1.878	1.880	1.885	1.909
Nov	1.698	1.711	1.722	1.725	1.733	1.743	1.746	1.756	1.762	1.761	1.768	1.785	1.768	1.798	1.808	1.821	1.833	1.839	1.845	1.864	1.868	1.870	1.875	1.899
Dec	1.695	1.707	1.718	1.722	1.729	1.739	1.742	1.753	1.758	1.757	1.764	1.781	1.764	1.795	1.804	1.817	1.829	1.835	1.841	1.860	1.864	1.866	1.872	1.895
1986																								
Jan	1.689	1.701	1.713	1.716	1.723	1.734	1.737	1.747	1.752	1.751	1.758	1.775	1.758	1.789	1.798	1.811	1.823	1.829	1.835	1.854	1.858	1.860	1.866	1.889
Feb	1.679	1.691	1.703	1.706	1.713	1.724	1.727	1.737	1.742	1.741	1.748	1.765	1.748	1.778	1.788	1.801	1.813	1.819	1.825	1.844	1.848	1.850	1.855	1.879
Mar	1.675	1.688	1.699	1.702	1.710	1.720	1.723	1.733	1.739	1.738	1.745	1.761	1.745	1.775	1.784	1.797	1.809	1.815	1.821	1.840	1.844	1.846	1.851	1.875
Apr	1.650	1.662	1.673	1.676	1.684	1.694	1.697	1.707	1.712	1.711	1.718	1.735	1.718	1.748	1.757	1.771	1.782	1.788	1.794	1.813	1.817	1.819	1.824	1.847
May	1.645	1.657	1.668	1.672	1.679	1.689	1.692	1.702	1.707	1.706	1.713	1.730	1.713	1.743	1.752	1.766	1.777	1.783	1.789	1.807	1.812	1.814	1.819	1.842
June	1.646	1.659	1.670	1.673	1.680	1.690	1.693	1.704	1.709	1.708	1.715	1.731	1.715	1.745	1.754	1.767	1.778	1.784	1.791	1.809	1.813	1.815	1.820	1.844
July	1.654	1.666	1.678	1.681	1.688	1.698	1.701	1.711	1.716	1.715	1.723	1.739	1.723	1.752	1.762	1.775	1.786	1.792	1.799	1.817	1.821	1.823	1.828	1.852
Aug	1.646	1.658	1.669	1.672	1.679	1.690	1.693	1.703	1.708	1.707	1.714	1.731	1.714	1.744	1.753	1.766	1.778	1.784	1.790	1.808	1.812	1.814	1.819	1.843
Sept	1.633	1.645	1.656	1.659	1.666	1.676	1.680	1.690	1.695	1.694	1.701	1.717	1.701	1.730	1.740	1.753	1.764	1.770	1.776	1.794	1.799	1.801	1.806	1.829
Oct	1.629	1.641	1.652	1.655	1.662	1.672	1.675	1.686	1.691	1.690	1.697	1.713	1.697	1.726	1.735	1.748	1.760	1.766	1.772	1.790	1.794	1.796	1.801	1.825
Nov	1.606	1.619	1.630	1.633	1.640	1.650	1.653	1.663	1.668	1.667	1.674	1.690	1.674	1.703	1.712	1.725	1.736	1.742	1.749	1.767	1.771	1.773	1.778	1.801
Dec	1.598	1.610	1.621	1.624	1.631	1.641	1.644	1.654	1.659	1.658	1.665	1.681	1.665	1.694	1.703	1.716	1.727	1.733	1.739	1.757	1.762	1.764	1.769	1.792
1987																								
Jan	1.588	1.600	1.611	1.614	1.621	1.631	1.634	1.644	1.649	1.648	1.655	1.671	1.655	1.684	1.693	1.706	1.717	1.723	1.729	1.747	1.751	1.753	1.758	1.781
Feb	1.578	1.590	1.601	1.604	1.611	1.621	1.624	1.633	1.638	1.637	1.644	1.660	1.644	1.673	1.682	1.695	1.706	1.712	1.718	1.736	1.740	1.742	1.747	1.770
Mar	1.573	1.584	1.595	1.598	1.605	1.615	1.618	1.628	1.633	1.632	1.639	1.655	1.639	1.668	1.677	1.690	1.701	1.707	1.713	1.731	1.735	1.737	1.742	1.764
Apr	1.542	1.554	1.565	1.568	1.575	1.584	1.587	1.597	1.602	1.601	1.608	1.624	1.608	1.637	1.645	1.658	1.669	1.675	1.681	1.698	1.702	1.704	1.709	1.732
May	1.540	1.552	1.562	1.565	1.572	1.582	1.585	1.595	1.600	1.599	1.605	1.621	1.605	1.634	1.643	1.656	1.666	1.672	1.678	1.696	1.700	1.702	1.707	1.729
June	1.540	1.552	1.562	1.565	1.572	1.582	1.585	1.595	1.600	1.599	1.605	1.621	1.605	1.634	1.643	1.656	1.666	1.672	1.678	1.696	1.700	1.702	1.707	1.729
July	1.542	1.554	1.565	1.568	1.575	1.584	1.587	1.597	1.602	1.601	1.608	1.624	1.608	1.637	1.645	1.658	1.669	1.675	1.681	1.698	1.702	1.704	1.709	1.732
Aug	1.535	1.547	1.557	1.560	1.567	1.577	1.580	1.590	1.595	1.594	1.600	1.616	1.600	1.629	1.638	1.650	1.661	1.667	1.673	1.690	1.694	1.696	1.701	1.724
Sept	1.527	1.539	1.550	1.553	1.560	1.569	1.572	1.582	1.587	1.586	1.593	1.608	1.593	1.621	1.630	1.643	1.653	1.659	1.665	1.683	1.687	1.688	1.693	1.716
Oct	1.515	1.527	1.537	1.540	1.547	1.557	1.560	1.569	1.574	1.573	1.580	1.596	1.580	1.608	1.617	1.630	1.640	1.646	1.652	1.670	1.673	1.675	1.680	1.703
Nov	1.503	1.515	1.525	1.528	1.535	1.544	1.547	1.557	1.562	1.561	1.568	1.583	1.568	1.596	1.604	1.617	1.628	1.633	1.639	1.657	1.661	1.662	1.667	1.690
Dec	1.505	1.517	1.528	1.530	1.537	1.547	1.550	1.560	1.564	1.563	1.570	1.586	1.570	1.598	1.607	1.620	1.630	1.636	1.642	1.659	1.663	1.665	1.670	1.692

Capital gains indexation allowances for companies (January 2016 – December 2017)

Month of acquisition	2016 Jan	Feb	Mar	Apr	May	June	July	Aug	Sept	Oct	Nov	Dec	2017 Jan	Feb	Mar	Apr	May	June	July	Aug	Sept	Oct	Nov	Dec
1988																								
Jan	1.505	1.517	1.528	1.530	1.537	1.547	1.550	1.560	1.564	1.563	1.570	1.586	1.570	1.598	1.607	1.620	1.630	1.636	1.642	1.659	1.663	1.665	1.670	1.692
Feb	1.496	1.507	1.518	1.521	1.527	1.537	1.540	1.550	1.554	1.554	1.560	1.576	1.560	1.588	1.597	1.609	1.620	1.626	1.632	1.649	1.653	1.655	1.660	1.682
Mar	1.486	1.498	1.508	1.511	1.518	1.527	1.530	1.540	1.545	1.544	1.550	1.566	1.550	1.578	1.587	1.599	1.610	1.616	1.622	1.639	1.643	1.645	1.649	1.671
Apr	1.446	1.457	1.468	1.471	1.477	1.487	1.490	1.499	1.504	1.503	1.509	1.525	1.509	1.537	1.545	1.558	1.568	1.574	1.579	1.596	1.600	1.602	1.607	1.629
May	1.437	1.448	1.459	1.461	1.468	1.477	1.480	1.490	1.494	1.493	1.500	1.515	1.500	1.527	1.536	1.548	1.558	1.564	1.570	1.587	1.590	1.592	1.597	1.619
June	1.428	1.439	1.449	1.452	1.459	1.468	1.471	1.480	1.485	1.484	1.491	1.506	1.491	1.518	1.526	1.538	1.549	1.554	1.560	1.577	1.581	1.583	1.587	1.609
July	1.425	1.437	1.447	1.450	1.456	1.466	1.469	1.478	1.483	1.482	1.488	1.503	1.488	1.515	1.524	1.536	1.546	1.552	1.558	1.575	1.578	1.580	1.585	1.606
Aug	1.399	1.410	1.420	1.423	1.429	1.438	1.441	1.450	1.455	1.454	1.461	1.475	1.461	1.487	1.496	1.508	1.518	1.524	1.529	1.546	1.550	1.551	1.556	1.577
Sept	1.387	1.399	1.409	1.411	1.418	1.427	1.430	1.439	1.444	1.443	1.449	1.464	1.449	1.476	1.484	1.496	1.506	1.512	1.518	1.534	1.538	1.540	1.544	1.565
Oct	1.363	1.374	1.384	1.387	1.394	1.403	1.405	1.415	1.419	1.418	1.425	1.439	1.425	1.451	1.459	1.471	1.481	1.487	1.492	1.509	1.512	1.514	1.519	1.540
Nov	1.353	1.364	1.374	1.376	1.383	1.392	1.395	1.404	1.408	1.407	1.414	1.428	1.414	1.440	1.448	1.460	1.470	1.475	1.481	1.497	1.501	1.503	1.507	1.528
Dec	1.346	1.357	1.367	1.370	1.376	1.385	1.388	1.397	1.402	1.401	1.407	1.422	1.407	1.433	1.442	1.453	1.463	1.469	1.474	1.490	1.494	1.496	1.500	1.521
1989																								
Jan	1.332	1.342	1.352	1.355	1.361	1.370	1.373	1.382	1.386	1.386	1.392	1.406	1.392	1.418	1.426	1.438	1.448	1.453	1.459	1.475	1.478	1.480	1.485	1.505
Feb	1.315	1.326	1.335	1.338	1.344	1.353	1.356	1.365	1.369	1.369	1.375	1.389	1.375	1.401	1.409	1.420	1.430	1.436	1.441	1.457	1.461	1.462	1.467	1.487
Mar	1.305	1.315	1.325	1.328	1.334	1.343	1.346	1.354	1.359	1.358	1.364	1.378	1.364	1.390	1.398	1.410	1.419	1.425	1.430	1.446	1.450	1.451	1.456	1.476
Apr	1.264	1.275	1.284	1.287	1.293	1.302	1.304	1.313	1.318	1.317	1.323	1.337	1.323	1.348	1.356	1.367	1.377.	1.382	1.388	1.403	1.407	1.409	1.413	1.433
May	1.250	1.261	1.270	1.273	1.279	1.288	1.290	1.299	1.303	1.303	1.309	1.323	1.309	1.334	1.342	1.353	1.363	1.368	1.373	1.389	1.392	1.394	1.398	1.418
June	1.243	1.253	1.263	1.265	1.271	1.280	1.282	1.291	1.295	1.295	1.301	1.315	1.301	1.326	1.334	1.345	1.354	1.360	1.365	1.380	1.384	1.386	1.390	1.410
July	1.241	1.251	1.261	1.263	1.269	1.278	1.281	1.289	1.294	1.293	1.299	1.313	1.299	1.324	1.332	1.343	1.352	1.358	1.363	1.378	1.382	1.384	1.388	1.408
Aug	1.235	1.245	1.255	1.257	1.263	1.272	1.275	1.283	1.288	1.287	1.293	1.307	1.293	1.318	1.326	1.337	1.346	1.351	1.357	1.372	1.376	1.377	1.382	1.402
Sept	1.220	1.230	1.239	1.242	1.248	1.256	1.259	1.268	1.272	1.271	1.277	1.291	1.277	1.302	1.310	1.321	1.330	1.335	1.340	1.356	1.359	1.361	1.365	1.385
Oct	1.203	1.213	1.222	1.225	1.231	1.239	1.242	1.250	1.254	1.254	1.260	1.273	1.260	1.284	1.292	1.303	1.312	1.317	1.323	1.338	1.341	1.343	1.347	1.367
Nov	1.184	1.194	1.203	1.206	1.212	1.220	1.223	1.231	1.235	1.235	1.241	1.254	1.241	1.265	1.273	1.284	1.293	1.298	1.303	1.318	1.322	1.323	1.327	1.347
Dec	1.178	1.189	1.198	1.200	1.206	1.215	1.217	1.226	1.230	1.229	1.235	1.248	1.235	1.259	1.267	1.278	1.287	1.292	1.297	1.312	1.316	1.317	1.322	1.341
1990																								
Jan	1.166	1.176	1.185	1.187	1.193	1.202	1.204	1.213	1.217	1.216	1.222	1.235	1.222	1.246	1.254	1.264	1.274	1.279	1.284	1.299	1.302	1.304	1.308	1.327
Feb	1.153	1.163	1.172	1.175	1.181	1.189	1.191	1.200	1.204	1.203	1.209	1.222	1.209	1.233	1.240	1.251	1.260	1.265	1.270	1.285	1.289	1.290	1.295	1.314
Mar	1.132	1.142	1.151	1.153	1.159	1.167	1.170	1.178	1.182	1.181	1.187	1.200	1.187	1.211	1.218	1.229	1.238	1.243	1.248	1.263	1.266	1.268	1.272	1.291
Apr	1.069	1.078	1.087	1.090	1.095	1.103	1.106	1.114	1.118	1.117	1.122	1.135	1.122	1.145	1.153	1.163	1.172	1.177	1.181	1.196	1.199	1.201	1.205	1.223
May	1.051	1.060	1.069	1.071	1.077	1.085	1.087	1.095	1.099	1.098	1.104	1.116	1.104	1.127	1.134	1.144	1.153	1.158	1.162	1.177	1.180	1.181	1.185	1.204
June	1.043	1.052	1.061	1.063	1.069	1.077	1.079	1.087	1.091	1.090	1.096	1.108	1.096	1.118	1.125	1.136	1.144	1.149	1.154	1.168	1.171	1.173	1.177	1.195
July	1.041	1.050	1.059	1.062	1.067	1.075	1.077	1.085	1.089	1.088	1.094	1.106	1.094	1.117	1.124	1.134	1.143	1.147	1.152	1.166	1.170	1.171	1.175	1.193
Aug	1.020	1.030	1.038	1.041	1.046	1.054	1.056	1.064	1.068	1.067	1.073	1.085	1.073	1.095	1.102	1.112	1.121	1.126	1.130	1.144	1.148	1.149	1.153	1.171
Sept	1.002	1.011	1.019	1.022	1.027	1.035	1.037	1.045	1.049	1.048	1.053	1.066	1.053	1.076	1.083	1.093	1.101	1.106	1.111	1.125	1.128	1.129	1.133	1.151
Oct	0.986	0.995	1.004	1.006	1.012	1.019	1.021	1.029	1.033	1.032	1.038	1.050	1.038	1.060	1.067	1.077	1.085	1.090	1.094	1.108	1.111	1.113	1.117	1.134
Nov	0.991	1.000	1.008	1.011	1.016	1.024	1.026	1.034	1.038	1.037	1.042	1055	1.042	1.065	1.072	1.082	1.090	1.095	1.099	1.113	1.116	1.118	1.122	1.139
Dec	0.992	1.002	1.010	1.012	1.018	1.025	1.028	1.035	1.039	1.038	1.044	1056	1.044	1.066	1.073	1.083	1.092	1.096	1.101	1.115	1.118	1.119	1.123	1.141

Capital gains indexation allowances for companies (January 2016 – December 2017)

Month of acquisition	2016												2017											
	Jan	Feb	Mar	Apr	May	June	July	Aug	Sept	Oct	Nov	Dec	Jan	Feb	Mar	Apr	May	June	July	Aug	Sept	Oct	Nov	Dec
1991																								
Jan	0.988	0.997	1.005	1.008	1.013	1.021	0.123	1.031	1.035	1.034	1.039	1.051	1.039	1.061	1.068	1.078	1.087	1.091	1.096	1.110	1.113	1.114	1.118	1.136
Feb	0.977	0.986	0.995	0.997	1.002	1.010	1.012	1.020	1.024	1.023	1.028	1.040	1.028	1.050	1.057	1.067	1.076	1.080	1.085	1.099	1.102	1.103	1.107	1.125
Mar	0.970	0.979	0.987	0.989	0.995	1.002	1.005	1.012	1.016	1.015	1.021	1.033	1.021	1.043	1.049	1.059	1.068	1.072	1.077	1.091	1.094	1.095	1.099	1.116
Apr	0.944	0.953	0.962	0.964	0.969	0.977	0.979	0.986	0.990	0.989	0.995	1.007	0.995	1.017	1.023	1.033	1.041	1.046	1.050	1.064	1.067	1.068	1.072	1.089
May	0.939	0.948	0.956	0.958	0.963	0.971	0.973	0.981	0.984	0.984	0.989	1.001	0.989	1.010	1.017	1.027	1.035	1.040	1.044	1.058	1.061	1.062	1.066	1.083
June	0.930	0.939	0.947	0.949	0.955	0.962	0.964	0.972	0.975	0.975	0.980	0.992	0.980	1.001	1.008	1.018	1.026	1.031	1.035	1.048	1.051	1.053	1.057	1.074
July	0.934	0.943	0.951	0.954	0.959	0.966	0.969	0.976	0.980	0.979	0.984	0.996	0.984	1.006	1.013	1.022	1.031	1.035	1.040	1.053	1.056	1.058	1.061	1.078
Aug	0.930	0.939	0.947	0.949	0.955	0.962	0.964	0.972	0.975	0.975	0.980	0.992	0.980	1.001	1.008	1.018	1.026	1.031	1.035	1.048	1.051	1.053	1.057	1.074
Sept	0.923	0.932	0.940	0.942	0.947	0.955	0.957	0.964	0.968	0.967	0.973	0.984	0.973	0.994	1.001	1.010	1.019	1.023	1.027	1.041	1.044	1.045	1.049	1.066
Oct	0.916	0.925	0.933	0.935	0.940	0.947	0.950	0.957	0.961	0.960	0.965	0.977	0.965	0.987	0.993	1.003	1.011	1.016	1.020	1.033	1.036	1.038	1.041	1.058
Nov	0.909	0.917	0.926	0.928	0.933	0.940	0.942	0.950	0.954	0.953	0.958	0.970	0.958	0.979	0.986	0.996	1.004	1.008	1.013	1.026	1.029	1.030	1.034	1.051
Dec	0.907	0.916	0.924	0.926	0.931	0.939	0.941	0.948	0.952	0.951	0.957	0.968	0.957	0.978	0.985	0.994	1.002	1.007	1.011	1.024	1.027	1.029	1.032	1.049
1992																								
Jan	0.909	0.917	0.926	0.928	0.933	0.940	0.942	0.950	0.954	0.953	0.958	0.970	0.958	0.979	0.986	0.996	1.004	1.008	1.013	1.026	1.029	1.030	1.034	1.051
Feb	0.899	0.908	0.916	0.918	0.923	0.930	0.933	0.940	0.944	0.943	0.948	0.960	0.948	0.969	0.976	0.985	0.993	0.998	1.002	1.015	1.018	1.020	1.023	1.040
Mar	0.893	0.902	0.910	0.912	0.917	0.925	0.927	0.934	0.938	0.937	0.942	0.954	0.942	0.963	0.970	0.980	0.988	0.992	0.996	1.010	1.012	1.014	1.018	1.034
Apr	0.865	0.873	0.881	0.883	0.888	0.896	0.898	0.905	0.909	0.908	0.913	0.924	0.913	0.934	0.940	0.950	0.957	0.962	0.966	0.979	0.982	0.983	0.987	1.004
May	0.858	0.866	0.874	0.877	0.882	0.889	0.891	0.898	0.902	0.901	0.906	0.917	0.906	0.927	0.933	0.943	0.950	0.955	0.959	0.972	0.975	0.976	0.980	0.996
June	0.858	0.866	0.874	0.877	0.882	0.889	0.891	0.898	0.902	0.901	0.906	0.917	0.906	0.927	0.933	0.943	0.950	0.955	0.959	0.972	0.975	0.976	0.980	0.996
July	0.865	0.873	0.881	0.883	0.888	0.896	0.898	0.905	0.909	0.908	0.913	0.924	0.913	0.934	0.940	0.950	0.957	0.962	0.966	0.979	0.982	0.983	0.987	1.004
Aug	0.863	0.872	0.880	0.882	0.887	0.894	0.896	0.904	0.907	0.906	0.911	0.923	0.911	0.932	0.939	0.948	0.956	0.960	0.965	0.978	0.981	0.982	0.986	1.002
Sept	0.857	0.865	0.873	0.875	0.880	0.887	0.890	0.897	0.900	0.900	0.905	0.916	0.905	0.925	0.932	0.941	0.949	0.953	0.958	0.971	0.973	0.975	0.978	0.995
Oct	0.850	0.858	0.866	0.868	0.873	0.881	0.883	0.890	0.893	0.893	0.898	0.909	0.898	0.919	0.925	0.934	0.942	0.946	0.951	0.964	0.966	0.968	0.971	0.988
Nov	0.853	0.861	0.869	0.871	0.876	0.883	0.885	0.893	0.896	0.895	0.901	0.912	0.901	0.921	0.928	0.937	0.945	0.949	0.953	0.966	0.969	0.971	0.974	0.991
Dec	0.859	0.868	0.876	0.878	0.883	0.890	0.892	0.899	0.903	0.902	0.907	0.919	0.907	0.928	0.935	0.944	0.952	0.956	0.960	0.973	0.976	0.978	0.981	0.998
1993																								
Jan	0.877	0.885	0.893	0.896	0.901	0.908	0.910	0.917	0.921	0.920	0.925	0.937	0.925	0.946	0.953	0.962	0970	0.975	0.979	0.992	0.995	0.996	1.000	1.017
Feb	0.865	0.873	0.881	0.883	0.888	0.896	0.898	0.905	0.909	0.908	0.913	0.924	0.913	0.934	0.940	0.950	0.957	0.962	0.966	0.979	0.982	0.983	0.987	1.004
Mar	0.858	0.866	0.874	0.877	0.882	0.889	0.891	0.898	0.902	0.901	0.906	0.917	0.906	0.927	0.933	0.943	0.950	0.955	0.959	0.972	0.975	0.976	0.980	0.996
Apr	0.841	0.849	0.857	0.859	0.864	0.871	0.873	0.881	0.884	0.883	0.888	0.900	0.888	0.909	0.915	0.925	0.932	0.937	0.941	0.954	0.957	0.958	0.962	0.978
May	0.834	0.843	0.850	0.853	0.858	0.865	0.867	0.874	0.877	0.877	0.882	0.893	0.882	0.902	0.909	0.918	0.926	0.930	0.934	0.947	0.950	0.951	0.955	0.971
June	0.835	0.844	0.852	0.854	0.859	0.866	0.868	0.875	0.879	0.878	0.883	0.894	0.883	0.904	0.910	0.919	0.927	0.931	0.935	0.948	0.951	0.952	0.956	0.972
July	0.839	0.848	0.856	0.858	0.863	0.870	0.872	0.879	0.883	0.882	0.887	0.898	0.887	0.908	0.914	0.923	0.931	0.935	0.940	0.952	0.955	0.957	0.960	0.977
Aug	0.832	0.840	0.848	0.850	0.855	0.862	0.864	0.871	0.875	0.874	0.879	0.890	0.879	0.900	0.906	0.915	0.923	0.927	0.931	0.944	0.947	0.948	0.952	0.968
Sept	0.824	0.832	0.840	0.842	0.847	0.854	0.856	0.863	0.867	0.866	0.871	0.882	0.871	0.891	0.898	0.907	0.915	0.919	0.923	0.936	0.939	0.940	0.944	0.960
Oct	0.825	0.834	0.841	0.843	0.848	0.855	0.858	0.865	0.868	0.867	0.872	0.884	0.872	0.893	0.899	0.908	0.916	0.920	0.925	0.937	0.940	0.941	0.945	0.961
Nov	0.828	0.836	0.844	0.846	0.851	0.858	0.860	0.867	0.871	0.870	0.875	0.886	0.875	0.895	0.902	0.911	0.919	0.923	0.927	0.940	0.943	0.944	0.948	0.964
Dec	0.824	0.832	0.840	0.842	0.847	0.854	0.856	0.863	0.867	0.866	0.871	0.882	0.871	0.891	0.898	0.907	0.915	0.919	0.923	0.936	0.939	0.940	0.944	0.960

Capital gains indexation allowances for companies (January 2016 – December 2017)

Month of acquisition	2016 Jan	Feb	Mar	Apr	May	June	July	Aug	Sept	Oct	Nov	Dec	2017 Jan	Feb	Mar	Apr	May	June	July	Aug	Sept	Oct	Nov	Dec
1994																								
Jan	0.832	0.840	0.848	0.850	0.855	0.862	0.864	0.871	0.875	0.874	0.879	0.890	0.879	0.900	0.906	0.915	0.923	0.927	0.931	0.944	0.947	0.948	0,952	0.968
Feb	0.821	0.830	0.837	0.840	0.844	0.852	0.854	0.861	0.864	0.863	0.868	0.880	0.868	0.889	0.895	0.904	0.912	0.916	0.920	0.933	0.936	0.937	0.941	0.957
Mar	0.816	0.825	0.832	0.834	0.839	0.846	0.848	0.855	0.859	0.858	0.863	0.874	0.863	0.884	0.890	0.899	0.907	0.911	0.915	0.928	0.931	0.932	0.935	0.952
Apr	0.795	0.803	0.811	0.813	0.818	0.825	0.827	0.834	0.837	0.836	0.841	0.852	0.841	0.861	0.868	0.877	0.884	0.888	0.893	0.905	0.908	0.909	0.913	0.929
May	0.789	0.797	0.804	0.806	0.811	0.818	0.820	0.827	0.831	0.830	0.835	0.846	0.835	0.855	0.861	0.870	0.878	0.882	0.886	0.898	0.901	0.903	0.906	0.922
June	0.789	0.797	0.804	0.806	0.811	0.818	0.820	0.827	0.831	0.830	0.835	0.846	0.835	0.855	0.861	0.870	0.878	0.882	0.886	0.898	0.901	0.903	0.906	0.922
July	0.797	0.806	0.813	0.815	0.820	0.827	0.829	0.836	0.840	0.839	0.844	0.855	0.844	0.864	0.870	0.879	0.887	0.891	0.895	0.908	0.910	0.912	0.915	0.931
Aug	0.789	0.797	0.804	0.806	0.811	0.818	0.820	0.827	0.831	0.830	0.835	0.846	0.835	0.855	0.861	0.870	0.878	0.882	0.886	0.898	0.901	0.903	0.906	0.922
Sept	0.785	0.793	0.801	0.803	0.808	0.814	0.817	0.823	0.827	0.826	0.831	0.842	0.831	0.851	0.857	0.866	0.874	0.878	0.882	0.894	0.897	0.899	0.902	0.918
Oct	0.782	0.791	0.798	0.800	0.805	0.812	0.814	0.821	0.824	0.824	0.829	0.840	0.829	0.848	0.855	0.864	0.871	0.875	0.879	0.892	0.895	0.896	0.899	0.915
Nov	0.781	0.789	0.797	0.799	0.804	0.811	0.813	0.820	0.823	0.822	0.827	0.838	0.827	0.847	0.853	0.862	0.870	0.874	0.878	0.891	0.893	0.895	0.898	0.914
Dec	0.773	0.781	0.788	0.790	0.795	0.802	0.804	0.811	0.814	0.814	0.818	0.829	0.818	0.838	0.845	0.853	0.861	0.865	0.869	0.882	0.884	0.886	0.889	0.905
1995																								
Jan	0.773	0.781	0.788	0.790	0.795	0.802	0.804	0.811	0.814	0.814	0.818	0.829	0.818	0.838	0.845	0.853	0.861	0.865	0.869	0.882	0.884	0.886	0.889	0.905
Feb	0.762	0.770	0.777	0.779	0.784	0.791	0.793	0.800	0.803	0.803	0.807	0.818	0.807	0.827	0.833	0.842	0.850	0.854	0.858	0.870	0.873	0.874	0.877	0.893
Mar	0.755	0.763	0.770	0.772	0.777	0.784	0.786	0.793	0.796	0.795	0.800	0.811	0.800	0.820	0.826	0.835	0.842	0.846	0.850	0.862	0.865	0.866	0.870	0.885
Apr	0.737	0.745	0.752	0.754	0.759	0.766	0.768	0.774	0.778	0.777	0.782	0.793	0.782	0.801	0.807	0.816	0.823	0.828	0.832	0.844	0.846	0.848	0.851	0.866
May	0.730	0.738	0.745	0.747	0.752	0.759	0.761	0.767	0.771	0.770	0.775	0.785	0.775	0.794	0.800	0.809	0.816	0.820	0.824	0.836	0.839	0.840	0.844	0.859
June	0.728	0.736	0.743	0.745	0.750	0.756	0.758	0.765	0.768	0.768	0.772	0.783	0.772	0.792	0.798	0.806	0.814.	0.818	0.822	0.834	0.836	0.838	0.841	0.856
July	0.736	0.744	0.751	0.753	0.758	0.765	0.767	0.773	0.777	0.776	0.781	0.791	0.781	0.800	0.806	0.815	0.822	0.826	0.830	0.842	0.845	0.846	0.850	0.865
Aug	0.726	0.734	0.742	0.744	0.748	0.755	0.757	0.764	0.767	0.767	0.771	0.782	0.771	0.791	0.797	0.805	0.813	0.817	0.821	0.833	0.835	0.837	0.840	0.855
Sept	0.718	0.726	0.734	0.736	0.740	0.747	0.749	0.756	0.759	0.758	0.763	0.774	0.763	0.782	0.788	0.797	0.804	0.808	0.812	0.824	0.827	0.828	0.831	0.847
Oct	0.728	0.736	0.743	0.745	0.750	0.756	0.758	0.765	0.768	0.768	0.772	0.783	0.772	0.792	0.798	0.806	0.814	0.818	0.822	0.834	0.836	0.838	0.841	0.856
Nov	0.728	0.736	0.743	0.745	0.750	0.756	0.758	0.765	0.768	0.768	0.772	0.783	0.772	0.792	0.798	0.806	0.814	0.818	0.822	0.834	0.836	0.838	0.841	0.856
Dec	0.717	0.725	0.733	0.735	0.739	0.746	0.748	0.754	0.758	0.757	0.762	0.772	0.762	0.781	0.787	0.796	0.803	0.807	0.811	0.823	0.825	0.827	0.830	0.845
1996																								
Jan	0.723	0.731	0.738	0.740	0.745	0.752	0.754	0.760	0.764	0.763	0.768	0.778	0.768	0.787	0.793	0.802	0.809	0.813	0.817	0.829	0.832	0.833	0.836	0.852
Feb	0.715	0.723	0.730	0.732	0.737	0.744	0.746	0752	0.755	0.755	0.759	0.770	0.759	0.779	0.785	0.793	0.801	0.805	0.808	0.820	0.823	0.824	0.828	0.843
Mar	0.708	0.716	0.723	0.725	0.730	0.737	0.739	0.745	0.749	0.748	0.752	0.763	0.752	0.772	0.778	0.786	0.793	0.797	0.801	0.813	0.816	0.817	0.820	0.836
Apr	0.696	0.704	0.711	0.713	0.718	0.724	0.726	0.733	0.736	0.735	0.740	0.750	0.740	0.759	0.765	0.773	0.780	0.784	0.788	0.800	0.803	0.804	0.807	0.822
May	0.693	0.700	0.708	0.710	0.714	0.721	0.723	0.729	0.733	0.732	0.736	0.747	0.736	0.755	0.761	0.770	0.777	0.781	0.785	0.797	0.799	0.801	0.804	0.819
June	0.692	0.699	0.707	0.708	0.713	0.720	0.722	0.728	0.731	0.731	0.735	0.746	0.735	0.754	0.760	0.769	0.776	0.780	0.784	0.795	0.798	0.799	0.803	0.818
July	0.698	0.706	0.713	0.715	0.720	0.726	0.728	0.735	0.738	0.738	0.742	0.753	0.742	0.761	0.767	0.776	0.783	0.787	0.791	0.802	0.805	0.806	0.810	0.825
Aug	0.690	0.698	0.705	0.707	0.712	0.718	0.720	0.727	0.730	0.730	0.734	0.745	0.734	0.753	0.759	0.767	0.775	0.779	0.782	0.794	0.797	0.798	0.801	0.816
Sept	0.683	0.691	0.698	0.700	0.704	0.711	0.713	0.719	0.722	0.722	0.726	0.737	0.726	0.745	0.751	0.759	0.767	0.770	0.774	0.786	0.789	0.790	0.793	0.808
Oct	0.683	0.691	0.698	0.700	0.704	0.711	0.713	0.719	0.722	0.722	0.726	0.737	0.726	0.745	0.751	0.759	0.767	0.770	0.774	0.786	0.789	0.790	0.793	0.808
Nov	0.682	0.689	0.697	0.699	0.703	0.710	0.712	0.718	0.721	0.721	0.725	0.736	0.725	0.744	0.750	0.758	0.765	0.769	0.773	0.785	0.788	0.789	0.792	0.807
Dec	0.676	0.684	0.691	0.693	0.698	0.704	0.706	0.712	0.716	0.715	0.720	0.730	0.720	0.738	0.744	0.753	0.760	0.764	0.767	0.779	0.782	0.783	0.786	0.801

Capital gains indexation allowances for companies (January 2016 – December 2017)

Month of acquisition	2016 Jan	Feb	Mar	Apr	May	June	July	Aug	Sept	Oct	Nov	Dec	2017 Jan	Feb	Mar	Apr	May	June	July	Aug	Sept	Oct	Nov	Dec
1997																								
Jan	0.676	0.684	0.691	0.693	0.698	0.704	0.706	0.712	0.716	0.715	0.720	0.730	0.720	0.738	0.744	0.753	0.760	0.764	0.767	0.779	0.782	0.783	0.786	0.801
Feb	0.670	0.677	0.685	0.686	0.691	0.697	0.699	0.706	0.709	0.708	0.713	0.723	0.713	0.732	0.737	0.746	0.753	0.757	0.761	0.772	0.775	0.776	0.779	0.794
Mar	0.665	0.673	0.680	0.682	0.687	0.693	0.695	0.701	0.705	0.704	0.708	0.719	0.708	0.727	0.733	0.741	0.748	0.752	0.756	0.768	0.770	0.772	0.775	0.790
Apr	0.656	0.663	0.671	0.672	0.677	0.683	0.685	0.692	0.695	0.694	0.699	0.709	0.699	0.717	0.723	0.731	0.738	0.742	0.746	0.758	0.760	0.761	0.765	0.779
May	0.649	0.657	0.664	0.666	0.670	0.677	0.679	0.685	0.688	0.688	0.692	0.702	0.692	0.711	0.716	0.725	0.732	0.736	0.739	0.751	0.753	0.755	0.758	0.772
June	0.643	0.651	0.658	0.660	0.664	0.670	0.672	0.679	0.682	0.681	0.686	0.696	0.686	0.704	0.710	0.718	0.725	0.729	0.733	0.744	0.747	0.748	0.751	0.766
July	0.643	0.651	0.658	0.660	0.664	0.670	0.672	0.679	0.682	0.681	0.686	0.696	0.686	0.704	0.710	0.718	0.725	0.729	0.733	0.744	0.747	0.748	0.751	0.766
Aug	0.633	0.640	0.647	0.649	0.654	0.660	0.662	0.668	0.671	0.671	0.675	0.685	0.675	0.693	0.699	0.707	0.714	0.718	0.722	0.733	0.736	0.737	0.740	0.755
Sept	0.625	0.632	0.639	0.641	0.645	0.652	0.653	0.660	0.663	0.662	0.667	0.677	0.667	0.685	0.691	0.699	0.706	0.709	0.713	0.724	0.727	0.728	0.731	0.746
Oct	0.623	0.630	0.637	0.639	0.643	0.650	0.651	0.658	0.661	0.660	0.665	0.675	0.665	0.683	0.688	0.697	0.703	0.707	0.711	0.722	0.725	0.726	0.729	0.744
Nov	0.622	0.629	0.636	0.638	0.642	0.648	0.650	0.657	0.660	0.659	0.664	0.674	0.664	0.682	0.687	0.695	0.702	0.706	0.710	0.721	0.724	0.725	0.728	0.742
Dec	0.618	0.625	0.632	0.634	0.638	0.644	0.646	0.653	0.656	0.655	0.659	0.669	0.659	0.678	0.683	0.691	0.698	0.702	0.706	0.717	0.719	0.721	0.724	0.738
1998																								
Jan	0.623	0.630	0.637	0.639	0.643	0.650	0.651	0.658	0.661	0.660	0.665	0.675	0.665	0.683	0.688	0.697	0.703	0.707	0.711	0.722	0.725	0.726	0.729	0.744
Feb	0.614	0.622	0.629	0.631	0.635	0.641	0.643	0.649	0.653	0.652	0.656	0.666	0.656	0.674	0.680	0.688	0.695	0.699	0.702	0.714	0.716	0.717	0.721	0.735
Mar	0.609	0.617	0.624	0.626	0.630	0.636	0.638	0.644	0.647	0.647	0.651	0.661	0.651	0.669	0.675	0.683	0.690	0.693	0.697	0.708	0.711	0.712	0.715	0.729
Apr	0.592	0.599	0.606	0.608	0.612	0.618	0.620	0.626	0.629	0.629	0.633	0.643	0.633	0.651	0.656	0.664	0.671	0.675	0.678	0.689	0.692	0.693	0.696	0.710
May	0.583	0.590	0.597	0.599	0.603	0.609	0.611	0.617	0.620	0.620	0.624	0.634	0.624	0.642	0.647	0.655	0.662	0.665	0.669	0.680	0.683	0.684	0.687	0.701
June	0.584	0.591	0.598	0.600	0.604	0.610	0.612	0.618	0.621	0.621	0.625	0.635	0.625	0.643	0.648	0.656	0.663	0.666	0.670	0.681	0.684	0.685	0.688	0.702
July	0.588	0.595	0.602	0.604	0.608	0.614	0.616	0.622	0.625	0.625	0.629	0.639	0.629	0.647	0.652	0.660	0.667	0.671	0.674	0.685	0.688	0.689	0.692	0.706
Aug	0.581	0.588	0.595	0.597	0.601	0.607	0.609	0.615	0.618	0.618	0.622	0.632	0.622	0.640	0.645	0.653	0.660	0.663	0.667	0.678	0.681	0.682	0.685	0.699
Sept	0.574	0.582	0.588	0.590	0.594	0.600	0.602	0.608	0.611	0.611	0.615	0.625	0.615	0.633	0.638	0.646	0.653	0.656	0.660	0.671	0.673	0.675	0.678	0.692
Oct	0.573	0.581	0.587	0.589	0.593	0.599	0.601	0.607	0.610	0.610	0.614	0.624	0.614	0.632	0.637	0.645	0.652	0.655	0.659	0.670	0.672	0.674	0.677	0.691
Nov	0.574	0.582	0.588	0.590	0.594	0.600	0.602	0.608	0.611	0.611	0.615	0.625	0.615	0.633	0.638	0.646	0.653	0.656	0.660	0.671	0.673	0.675	0.678	0.692
Dec	0.574	0.582	0.588	0.590	0.594	0.600	0.602	0.608	0.611	0.611	0.615	0.625	0.615	0.633	0.638	0.646	0.653	0.656	0.660	0.671	0.673	0.675	0.678	0.692
1999																								
Jan	0.584	0.591	0.598	0.600	0.604	0.610	0.612	0.618	0.621	0.621	0.625	0.635	0.625	0.643	0.648	0.656	0.663	0.666	0.670	0.681	0.684	0.685	0.688	0.702
Feb	0.581	0.588	0.595	0.597	0.601	0.607	0.609	0.615	0.618	0.618	0.622	0.632	0.622	0.640	0.645	0.653	0.660	0.663	0.667	0.678	0.681	0.682	0.685	0.699
Mar	0.577	0.584	0.591	0.593	0.597	0.603	0.605	0.611	0.614	0.614	0.618	0.628	0.618	0.636	0.641	0.649	0.656	0.659	0.663	0.674	0.676	0.678	0.681	0.695
Apr	0.567	0.574	0.581	0.582	0.587	0.593	0.594	0.600	0.604	0.603	0.607	0.617	0.607	0.625	0.630	0.638	0.645	0.648	0.652	0.663	0.665	0.666	0.669	0.683
May	0.563	0.570	0.577	0.579	0.583	0.589	0.591	0.597	0.600	0.599	0.603	0.613	0.603	0.621	0.626	0.634	0.641	0.644	0.648	0.659	0.661	0.662	0.665	0.679
June	0.563	0.570	0.577	0.579	0.583	0.589	0.591	0.597	0.600	0.599	0.603	0.613	0.603	0.621	0.626	0.634	0.641	0.644	0.648	0.659	0.661	0.662	0.665	0.679
July	0.568	0.575	0.581	0.583	0.588	0.594	0.595	0.601	0.604	0.604	0.608	0.618	0.608	0.626	0.631	0.639	0.646	0.649	0.653	0.664	0.666	0.667	0.671	0.684
Aug	0.564	0.571	0.578	0.579	0.584	0.590	0.592	0.598	0.601	0.600	0.604	0.614	0.604	0.622	0.627	0.635	0.642	0.645	0.649	0.660	0.662	0.663	0.666	0.680
Sept	0.557	0.564	0.571	0.573	0.577	0.583	0.585	0.591	0.594	0.593	0.597	0.607	0.597	0.615	0.620	0.628	0.635	0.638	0.642	0.653	0.655	0.656	0.659	0.673
Oct	0.554	0.562	0.568	0.570	0.574	0.580	0.582	0.588	0.591	0.590	0.595	0.604	0.595	0.612	0.617	0.625	0.632	0.635	0.639	0.650	0.652	0.653	0.656	0.670
Nov	0.552	0.560	0.566	0.568	0.572	0.578	0.580	0.586	0.589	0.588	0.593	0.602	0.593	0.610	0.615	0.623	0.630	0.633	0.637	0.648	0.650	0.651	0.654	0.668
Dec	0.547	0.554	0.561	0.562	0.567	0.573	0.574	0.580	0.583	0.583	0.587	0.597	0.587	0.604	0.610	0.617	0.624	0.628	0.631	0.642	0.644	0.646	0.649	0.662

Capital gains indexation allowances for companies (January 2016 – December 2017)

Month of acquisition	2016 Jan	Feb	Mar	Apr	May	June	July	Aug	Sept	Oct	Nov	Dec	2017 Jan	Feb	Mar	Apr	May	June	July	Aug	Sept	Oct	Nov	Dec
2000																								
Jan	0.553	0.561	0.567	0.569	0.573	0.579	0.581	0.587	0.590	0.589	0.594	0.603	0.594	0.611	0.616	0.624	0.631	0.634	0.638	0.649	0.651	0.652	0.655	0.669
Feb	0.545	0.552	0.559	0.561	0.565	0.571	0.573	0.579	0.581	0.581	0.585	0.595	0.585	0.602	0.608	0.616	0.622	0.626	0.629	0.640	0.642	0.644	0.647	0.660
Mar	0.537	0.544	0.550	0.552	0.556	0.562	0.564	0.570	0.573	0.572	0.577	0.586	0.577	0.594	0.599	0.607	0.613	0.617	0.621	0.631	0.634	0.635	0.638	0.651
Apr	0.521	0.529	0.535	0.537	0.541	0.547	0.549	0.554	0.557	0.557	0.561	0.570	0.561	0.578	0.583	0.591	0.597	0.601	0.604	0.615	0.617	0.618	0.621	0.635
May	0.516	0.523	0.530	0.531	0.535	0.541	0.543	0.549	0.552	0.551	0.555	0.565	0.555	0.572	0.578	0.585	0.592	0.595	0.599	0.609	0.612	0.613	0.616	0.629
June	0.513	0.520	0.526	0.528	0.532	0.538	0.539	0.545	0.548	0.548	0.552	0.561	0.552	0.569	0.574	0.582	0.588	0.591	0.595	0.605	0.608	0.609	0.612	0.625
July	0.518	0.525	0.531	0.533	0.537	0.543	0.545	0.551	0.554	0.553	0.557	0.567	0.557	0.574	0.579	0.587	0.594	0.597	0.601	0.611	0.613	0.615	0.618	0.631
Aug	0.518	0.525	0.531	0.533	0.537	0.543	0.545	0.551	0.554	0.553	0.557	0.567	0.557	0.574	0.579	0.587	0.594	0.597	0.601	0.611	0.613	0.615	0.618	0.631
Sept	0.507	0.514	0.521	0.522	0.526	0.532	0.534	0.540	0.543	0.542	0.546	0.556	0.546	0.563	0.568	0.576	0.582	0.586	0.589	0.600	0.602	0.603	0.606	0.620
Oct	0.508	0.515	0.522	0.523	0.527	0.533	0.535	0.541	0.544	0.543	0.547	0.557	0.547	0.564	0.569	0.577	0.583	0.587	0.590	0.601	0.603	0.604	0.607	0.621
Nov	0.504	0.511	0.517	0.519	0523	0.529	0.531	0.536	0.539	0.539	0.543	0.552	0.543	0.560	0.565	0.572	0.579	0.582	0.586	0.596	0.598	0.600	0.603	0.616
Dec	0.503	0.510	0.516	0.518	0522	0.528	0.530	0.535	0.538	0.538	0.542	0.551	0.542	0.559	0.564	0.571	0.578	0.581	0.585	0.595	0.598	0.599	0.602	0.615
2001																								
Jan	0.513	0.520	0.526	0.528	0.532	0.538	0.539	0.545	0.548	0.548	0.552	0.561	0.552	0.569	0.574	0.582	0.588	0.591	0.595	0.605	0.608	0.609	0.612	0.625
Feb	0.505	0.512	0.518	0.520	0.524	0.530	0.531	0.537	0.540	0.540	0.544	0.553	0.544	0.560	0.566	0.573	0.580	0.583	0.587	0.597	0.599	0.601	0.603	0.617
Mar	0.503	0.510	0.516	0.518	0.522	0.528	0530	0.535	0.538	0.538	0.542	0.551	0.542	0.559	0.564	0.571	0.578	0.581	0.585	0.595	0.598	0.599	0.602	0.615
Apr	0.495	0.502	0.508	0.510	0.514	0.520	0.522	0.527	0.530	0.530	0.534	0.543	0.534	0.551	0.556	0.563	0.570	0.573	0.577	0.587	0.589	0.590	0.593	0.607
May	0.486	0.493	0.499	0.501	0.505	0.510	0.512	0.518	0.521	0.520	0.524	0.533	0.524	0.541	0.546	0.553	0.560	0.563	0.567	0.577	0.579	0.580	0.583	0.596
June	0.484	0.491	0.497	0.499	0.503	0.509	0.510	0.516	0.519	0.518	0.522	0.532	0.522	0.539	0.544	0.552	0.558	0.561	0.565	0.575	0.577	0.579	0.581	0.595
July	0.493	0.500	0.507	0.508	0.512	0.518	0.520	0.526	0.529	0.528	0.532	0.541	0.532	0.549	0.554	0.561	0.568	0.571	0.575	0.585	0.587	0.589	0.591	0.605
Aug	0.487	0.494	0.501	0.502	0.506	0.512	0.514	0.520	0.522	0.522	0.526	0.535	0.526	0.543	0.548	0.555	0.561	0.565	0.568	0.579	0.581	0.582	0.585	0.598
Sept	0.482	0.489	0.495	0.497	0.501	0.507	0.509	0.514	0.517	0.517	0.521	0.530	0.521	0.537	0.542	0.550	0.556	0.560	0.563	0.573	0.576	0.577	0.580	0.593
Oct	0.485	0.492	0.498	0.500	0.504	0.509	0.511	0.517	0.520	0.519	0.523	0.532	0.523	0.540	0.545	0.552	0.559	0.562	0.566	0.576	0.578	0.579	0.582	0.596
Nov	0.491	0.498	0.504	0.506	0.510	0.516	0.517	0.523	0.526	0.525	0.529	0.539	0.529	0.546	0.551	0.559	0.565	0.569	0.572	0.582	0.585	0.586	0.589	0.602
Dec	0.493	0.499	0.506	0.507	0.512	0.517	0.519	0.525	0.528	0.527	0.531	0.540	0.531	0.548	0.553	0.561	0.567	0.570	0.574	0.584	0.587	0.588	0.591	0.604
2002																								
Jan	0.493	0.500	0.507	0.508	0.512	0.518	0.520	0526	0.529	0.528	0.532	0.541	0.532	0.549	0.554	0.561	0.568	0.571	0.575	0.585	0.587	0.589	0.591	0.605
Feb	0.489	0.496	0.502	0.504	0.508	0.514	0.516	0.521	0.524	0.524	0.528	0.537	0.528	0.544	0.549	0.557	0.563	0.567	0.570	0.581	0.583	0.584	0.587	0.600
Mar	0.483	0.490	0.496	0.498	0.502	0.508	0.509	0.515	0.518	0.517	0.521	0.531	0.521	0.538	0.543	0.551	0.557	0.560	0.564	0.574	0.577	0.578	0.581	0.594
Apr	0.473	0.480	0.486	0.488	0.492	0.497	0.499	0.505	0.508	0.507	0.511	0.520	0.511	0.528	0.533	0.540	0.546	0.550	0.553	0.563	0.566	0.567	0.570	0.583
May	0.469	0.476	0.482	0.484	0.488	0.493	0.495	0.501	0.503	0.503	0.507	0.516	0.507	0.523	0.528	0.536	0.542	0.545	0.549	0.559	0.561	0.562	0.565	0.578
June	0.469	0.476	0.482	0.484	0.488	0.493	0.495	0.501	0.503	0.503	0.507	0.516	0.507	0.523	0.528	0.536	0.542	0.545	0.549	0.559	0.561	0.562	0.565	0.578
July	0.471	0.478	0.484	0.486	0.490	0.496	0.497	0.503	0.506	0.505	0.509	0.518	0.509	0.526	0.531	0.538	0.545	0.548	0.551	0.562	0.564	0.565	0.568	0.581
Aug	0.467	0.474	0.480	0.482	0.486	0.491	0.493	0.499	0.502	0.501	0.505	0.514	0.505	0.522	0.527	0.534	0.540	0.544	0.547	0.557	0.560	0.561	0.563	0.577
Sept	0.457	0.464	0.470	0.472	0.476	0.481	0.483	0.489	0.492	0.491	0.495	0.504	0.495	0.511	0.516	0.524	0.530	0.533	0.537	0.547	0.549	0.550	0.553	0.566
Oct	0.455	0.461	0.468	0.469	0.473	0.479	0.481	0.486	0.489	0.488	0.492	0.501	0.492	0.509	0.514	0.521	0.527	0.531	0.534	0.544	0.546	0.547	0.550	0.563
Nov	0.452	0.459	0.465	0.467	0.471	0.476	0.478	0.484	0.487	0.486	0.490	0.499	0.490	0.506	0.511	0.519	0.525	0.528	0.531	0.542	0.544	0.545	0.548	0.561
Dec	0.450	0.457	0.463	0.464	0.468	0.474	0.476	0.481	0.484	0.483	0.487	0.496	0.487	0.504	0.509	0.516	0.522	0.525	0.529	0.539	0.541	0.542	0.545	0.558

Capital gains indexation allowances for companies (January 2016 – December 2017)

Month of acquisition	2016 Jan	Feb	Mar	Apr	May	June	July	Aug	Sept	Oct	Nov	Dec	2017 Jan	Feb	Mar	Apr	May	June	July	Aug	Sept	Oct	Nov	Dec
2003																								
Jan	0.451	0.457	0.464	0.465	0.469	0.475	0.476	0.482	0.485	0.484	0.488	0.497	0.488	0.504	0.510	0.517	0.523	0.526	0.530	0.540	0.542	0.543	0.546	0.559
Feb	0.443	0.450	0.456	0.458	0.462	0.467	0.469	0.475	0.477	0.477	0.481	0.490	0.481	0.497	0.502	0.509	0.515	0.519	0.522	0.532	0.534	0.535	0.538	0.551
Mar	0.439	0.445	0.451	0.453	0.457	0.462	0.464	0.470	0.472	0.472	0.476	0.485	0.476	0.492	0.497	0.504	0.510	0.514	0.517	0.527	0.529	0.530	0.533	0.546
Apr	0.428	0.435	0.441	0.443	0.446	0.452	0.454	0.459	0.462	0.461	0.465	0.474	0.465	0.481	0.486	0.493	0.499	0.503	0.506	0.516	0.518	0.519	0.522	0.535
May	0.426	0.433	0.439	0.440	0.444	0.450	0.451	0.457	0.460	0.459	0.463	0.472	0.463	0.479	0.484	0.491	0.497	0.500	0.504	0.513	0.516	0.517	0.520	0.532
June	0.427	0.434	0.440	0.442	0.446	0.451	0.453	0.458	0.461	0.461	0.464	0.473	0.464	0.480	0.485	0.493	0.499	0.502	0.505	0.515	0.517	0.518	0.521	0.534
July	0.427	0.434	0.440	0.442	0.446	0.451	0.453	0.458	0.461	0.461	0.464	0.473	0.464	0.480	0.485	0.493	0.499	0.502	0.505	0.515	0.517	0.518	0.521	0.534
Aug	0.425	0.432	0.438	0.439	0.443	0.449	0.450	0.456	0.459	0.458	0.462	0.471	0.462	0.478	0.483	0.490	0.496	0.499	0.503	0.513	0.515	0.516	0.519	0.531
Sept	0.418	0.425	0.431	0.432	0.436	0.442	0.443	0.449	0.452	0.451	0.455	0.464	0.455	0.471	0.476	0.483	0.489	0.492	0.495	0.505	0.507	0.508	0.511	0.524
Oct	0.417	0.424	0.430	0.432	0.435	0.441	0.442	0.448	0.451	0.450	0.454	0.463	0.454	0.470	0.475	0.482	0.488	0.491	0.495	0.504	0.507	0.508	0.510	0.523
Nov	0.417	0.423	0.429	0.431	0.435	0.440	0.442	0.447	0.450	0.449	0.453	0.462	0.453	0.469	0.474	0.481	0.487	0.490	0.494	0.504	0.506	0.507	0.510	0.522
Dec	0.410	0.417	0.423	0.425	0.428	0.434	0.435	0.441	0.444	0.443	0.447	0.456	0.447	0.463	0.468	0.475	0.481	0.484	0.487	0.497	0.499	0.500	0.503	0.516
2004																								
Jan	0.413	0.420	0.426	0.428	0.431	0.437	0.439	0.444	0.447	0.446	0.450	0.459	0.450	0.466	0.471	0.478	0.484	0.487	0.490	0.500	0.502	0.504	0.506	0.519
Feb	0.408	0.415	0.421	0.422	0.426	0.431	0.433	0.439	0.441	0.441	0.445	0.453	0.445	0.460	0.465	0.472	0.478	0.482	0.485	0.495	0.497	0.498	0.501	0.513
Mar	0.402	0.408	0.414	0.416	0.420	0.425	0.427	0.432	0.435	0.434	0.438	0.447	0.438	0.454	0.459	0.466	0.472	0.475	0.478	0.488	0.490	0.491	0.494	0.507
Apr	0.394	0.400	0.406	0.408	0.411	0.417	0.418	0.424	0.426	0.426	0.430	0.438	0.430	0.445	0.450	0.457	0.463	0.466	0.470	0.479	0.481	0.482	0.485	0.498
May	0.388	0.394	0.400	0.402	0.405	0.411	0.412	0.418	0.420	0.420	0.424	0.432	0.424	0.439	0.444	0.451	0.457.	0.460	0.463	0.473	0.475	0.476	0.479	0.491
June	0.385	0.392	0.398	0.399	0.403	0.408	0.410	0.415	0.418	0.418	0.421	0.430	0.421	0.437	0.442	0.449	0.454	0.458	0.461	0.471	0.473	0.474	0.476	0.489
July	0.385	0.392	0.398	0.399	0.403	0.408	0.410	0.415	0.418	0.418	0.421	0.430	0.421	0.437	0.442	0.449	0.454	0.458	0.461	0.471	0.473	0.474	0.476	0.489
Aug	0.381	0.387	0.393	0.395	0.399	0.404	0.406	0.411	0.414	0.413	0.417	0.425	0.417	0.432	0.437	0.444	0.450	0.453	0.456	0.466	0.468	0.469	0.472	0.484
Sept	0.376	0.382	0.388	0.390	0.393	0.399	0.400	0.406	0.408	0.408	0.411	0.420	0.411	0.427	0.432	0.439	0.444	0.448	0.451	0.460	0.463	0.464	0.466	0.478
Oct	0.372	0.379	0.384	0.386	0.390	0.395	0.397	0.402	0.405	0.404	0.408	0.416	0.408	0.423	0.428	0.435	0.441	0.444	0.447	0.457	0.459	0.460	0.462	0.475
Nov	0.369	0.376	0.381	0.383	0.387	0.392	0.394	0.399	0.402	0.401	0.405	0.413	0.405	0.420	0.425	0.432	0.438	0.441	0.444	0.453	0.456	0.457	0.459	0.471
Dec	0.363	0.369	0.375	0.377	0.380	0.385	0.387	0.392	0.395	0.394	0.398	0.407	0.398	0.413	0.418	0.425	0.431	0.434	0.437	0.447	0.449	0.450	0.452	0.464
2005																								
Jan	0.370	0.376	0.382	0.384	0.388	0.393	0.394	0.400	0.402	0.402	0.406	0.414	0.406	0.421	0.426	0.433	0.438	0.442	0.445	0.454	0.456	0.457	0.460	0.472
Feb	0.365	0.371	0.377	0.379	0.382	0.388	0.389	0.395	0.397	0.397	0.400	0.409	0.400	0.416	0.420	0.427	0.433	0.436	0.439	0.449	0.451	0.452	0.455	0.467
Mar	0.359	0.365	0.371	0.372	0.376	0.381	0.383	0.388	0.391	0.390	0.394	0.402	0.394	0.409	0.414	0.420	0.426	0.429	0.433	0.442	0.444	0.445	0.448	0.460
Apr	0.351	0.357	0.363	0.364	0.368	0.373	0.375	0.380	0.383	0.382	0.386	0.394	0.386	0.401	0.406	0.412	0.418	0.421	0.424	0.434	0.436	0.437	0.439	0.451
May	0.348	0.354	0.360	0.361	0.365	0.370	0.372	0.377	0.380	0.379	0.383	0.391	0.383	0.398	0.403	0.409	0.415	0.418	0.421	0.431	0.433	0.434	0.436	0.448
June	0.347	0.353	0.358	0.360	0.364	0.369	0.370	0.376	0.378	0.378	0.381	0.390	0.381	0.396	0.401	0.408	0.414	0.417	0.420	0.429	0.431	0.432	0.435	0.447
July	0.347	0.353	0.358	0.360	0.364	0.369	0.370	0.376	0.378	0.378	0.381	0.390	0.381	0.396	0.401	0.408	0.414	0.417	0.420	0.429	0.431	0.432	0.435	0.447
Aug	0.344	0.350	0.356	0.357	0.361	0.366	0.368	0.373	0.375	0.375	0.379	0.387	0.379	0.394	0.398	0.405	0.411	0.414	0.417	0.426	0.428	0.429	0.432	0.444
Sept	0.340	0.346	0.352	0.354	0.357	0.363	0.364	0.369	0.372	0.371	0.375	0.383	0.375	0.390	0.395	0.401	0.407	0.410	0.413	0.423	0.425	0.426	0.428	0.440
Oct	0.339	0.345	0.351	0.352	0.356	0.361	0.363	0.368	0.370	0.370	0.374	0.382	0.374	0.389	0.393	0.400	0.406	0.409	0.412	0.421	0.423	0.424	0.427	0.439
Nov	0.337	0.343	0.349	0.350	0.354	0.359	0.361	0.366	0.368	0.368	0.371	0.380	0.371	0.386	0.391	0.398	0.403	0.407	0.410	0.419	0.421	0.422	0.425	0.436
Dec	0.333	0.340	0.345	0.347	0.350	0.355	0.357	0.362	0.365	0.364	0.368	0.376	0.368	0.383	0.387	0.394	0.400	0.403	0.406	0.415	0.417	0.418	0.421	0.433

Capital gains indexation allowances for companies (January 2016 – December 2017)

Month of acquisition	2016 Jan	Feb	Mar	Apr	May	June	July	Aug	Sept	Oct	Nov	Dec	2017 Jan	Feb	Mar	Apr	May	June	July	Aug	Sept	Oct	Nov	Dec
2006																								
Jan	0.338	0.344	0.350	0.352	0.355	0.360	0.362	0.367	0.370	0.369	0.373	0.381	0.373	0.388	0.392	0.399	0.405	0.408	0.411	0.420	0.422	0.423	0.426	0.438
Feb	0.333	0.339	0.344	0.346	0.350	0.355	0.356	0.361	0.364	0.364	0.367	0.375	0.367	0.382	0.387	0.393	0.399	0.402	0.405	0.415	0.417	0.418	0.420	0.432
Mar	0.327	0.333	0.339	0.341	0.344	0.349	0.351	0.356	0.358	0.358	0.362	0.370	0.362	0.376	0.381	0.388	0.393	0.396	0.399	0.409	0.411	0.412	0.414	0.426
Apr	0.317	0.323	0.329	0.330	0.334	0.339	0.340	0.346	0.348	0.348	0.351	0.359	0.351	0.366	0.370	0.377	0.383	0.386	0.389	0.398	0.400	0.401	0.404	0.415
May	0.309	0.315	0.321	0.322	0.326	0.331	0.332	0.337	0.340	0.339	0.343	0.351	0.343	0.358	0.362	0.369	0.374	0.377	0.380	0.389	0.392	0.393	0.395	0.407
June	0.304	0.310	0.315	0.317	0.320	0.325	0.327	0.332	0.335	0.334	0.338	0.346	0.338	0.352	0.357	0.363	0.369	0.372	0.375	0.384	0.386	0.387	0.389	0.401
July	0.304	0.310	0.315	0.317	0.320	0.325	0.327	0.332	0.335	0.334	0.338	0.346	0.338	0.352	0.357	0.363	0.369	0.372	0.375	0.384	0.386	0.387	0.389	0.401
Aug	0.299	0.305	0.311	0.312	0.316	0.321	0.322	0.327	0.330	0.329	0.333	0.341	0.333	0.347	0.352	0.358	0.364	0.367	0.370	0.379	0.381	0.382	0.385	0.396
Sept	0.293	0.299	0.305	0.306	0.310	0.315	0.316	0.321	0.324	0.323	0.327	0.335	0.327	0.341	0.346	0.352	0.358	0.361	0.364	0.373	0.375	0.376	0.378	0.390
Oct	0.291	0.297	0.303	0.304	0.308	0.313	0.314	0.319	0.322	0.321	0.325	0.333	0.325	0.339	0.344	0.350	0.356	0.359	0.362	0.371	0.373	0.374	0.376	0.388
Nov	0.287	0.293	0.298	0.300	0.303	0.308	0.310	0.315	0.317	0.317	0.320	0.328	0.320	0.335	0.339	0.346	0.351	0.354	0.357	0.366	0.368	0.369	0.371	0.383
Dec	0.277	0.283	0.288	0.290	0.293	0.298	0.299	0.304	0.307	0.306	0.310	0.318	0.310	0.324	0.329	0.335	0.340	0.343	0.346	0.355	0.357	0.358	0.361	0.372
2007																								
Jan	0.284	0.290	0.295	0.297	0.300	0.305	0.307	0.312	0.314	0.313	0.317	0.325	0.317	0.331	0.336	0.342	0.348	0.351	0.354	0.363	0.365	0.366	0.368	0.379
Feb	0.274	0.280	0.286	0.287	0.290	0.295	0.297	0.302	0.304	0.304	0.307	0.315	0.307	0.322	0.326	0.332	0.338	0.341	0.344	0.353	0.355	0.355	0.358	0.369
Mar	0.266	0.272	0.277	0.279	0.282	0.287	0.289	0.294	0.296	0.295	0.299	0.307	0.299	0.313	0.318	0.324	0.329	0.332	0.335	0.344	0.346	0.347	0.349	0.361
Apr	0.260	0.266	0.271	0.273	0.276	0.281	0.282	0.287	0.290	0.289	0.293	0.300	0.293	0.307	0.311	0.317	0.323	0.326	0.329	0.337	0.339	0.340	0.343	0.354
May	0.255	0.261	0.266	0.268	0.271	0.276	0.277	0.282	0.285	0.284	0.288	0.295	0.288	0.302	0.306	0.312	0.318	0.321	0.323	0.332	0.334	0.335	0.338	0.349
June	0.248	0.254	0.260	0.261	0.264	0.269	0.271	0.275	0.278	0.277	0.281	0.288	0.281	0.295	0.299	0.305	0.311	0.314	0.316	0.325	0.327	0.328	0.330	0.342
July	0.256	0.262	0.267	0.268	0.272	0.277	0.278	0.283	0.285	0.285	0.288	0.296	0.288	0.302	0.307	0.313	0.318	0.321	0.324	0.333	0.335	0.336	0.338	0.349
Aug	0.248	0.254	0.260	0.261	0.264	0.269	0.271	0.275	0.278	0.277	0.281	0.288	0.281	0.295	0.299	0.305	0.311	0.314	0.316	0.325	0.327	0.328	0.330	0.342
Sept	0.244	0.250	0.255	0.257	0.260	0.265	0.266	0.271	0.274	0.273	0.276	0.284	0.276	0.290	0.295	0.301	0.306	0.309	0.312	0.321	0.323	0.324	0.326	0.337
Oct	0.239	0.245	0.250	0.251	0.255	0.259	0.261	0.266	0.268	0.268	0.271	0.279	0.271	0.285	0.289	0.295	0.301	0.303	0.306	0.315	0.317	0.318	0.320	0.331
Nov	0.234	0.240	0.245	0.247	0.250	0.255	0.256	0.261	0.263	0.263	0.266	0.274	0.266	0.280	0.284	0.290	0.296	0.299	0.301	0.310	0.312	0.313	0.315	0.326
Dec	0.227	0.233	0.238	0.239	0.243	0.248	0.249	0.254	0.256	0.256	0.259	0.266	0.259	0.273	0.277	0.283	0.288	0.291	0.294	0.303	0.304	0.305	0.308	0.319
2008																								
Jan	0.234	0.239	0.245	0.246	0.249	0.254	0.255	0.260	0.263	0.262	0.265	0.273	0.265	0.279	0.284	0.290	0.295	0.298	0.301	0.309	0.311	0.312	0.315	0.326
Feb	0.224	0.230	0.235	0.237	0.240	0.245	0.246	0.251	0.253	0.253	0.256	0.263	0.256	0.270	0.274	0.280	0.285	0.288	0.291	0.299	0.301	0.302	0.305	0.316
Mar	0.220	0.226	0.231	0.232	0.236	0.240	0.242	0.247	0.249	0.248	0.252	0.259	0.252	0.265	0.270	0.276	0.281	0.284	0.287	0.295	0.297	0.298	0.300	0.311
Apr	0.209	0.215	0.220	0.221	0.225	0.229	0.231	0.236	0.238	0.237	0.241	0.248	0.241	0.254	0.258	0.264	0.270	0.272	0.275	0.284	0.286	0.286	0.289	0.300
May	0.203	0.209	0.214	0.215	0.219	0.223	0.225	0.229	0.232	0.231	0.234	0.242	0.234	0.248	0.252	0.258	0.263	0.266	0.269	0.277	0.279	0.280	0.282	0.293
June	0.194	0.199	0.204	0.206	0.209	0.214	0.215	0.220	0.222	0.221	0.225	0.232	0.225	0.238	0.242	0.248	0.253	0.256	0.259	0.267	0.269	0.270	0.272	0.283
July	0.195	0.201	0.206	0.207	0.211	0.215	0.217	0.221	0.224	0.223	0.226	0.234	0.226	0.240	0.244	0.250	0.255	0.258	0.261	0.269	0.271	0.272	0.274	0.285
Aug	0.192	0.197	0.202	0.203	0.207	0.211	0.213	0.217	0.220	0.219	0.222	0.230	0.222	0.236	0.240	0.246	0.251	0.254	0.256	0.265	0.267	0.267	0.270	0.280
Sept	0.185	0.190	0.196	0.197	0.200	0.205	0.206	0.211	0.213	0.212	0.216	0.223	0.216	0.229	0.233	0.239	0.244	0.247	0.250	0.258	0.260	0.261	0.263	0.273
Oct	0.189	0.194	0.199	0.201	0.204	0.209	0.210	0.215	0.217	0.216	0.220	0.227	0.220	0.233	0.237	0.243	0.248	0.251	0.254	0.262	0.264	0.265	0.267	0.277
Nov	0.198	0.204	0.209	0.210	0.213	0.218	0.219	0.224	0.226	0.226	0.229	0.237	0.229	0.243	0.247	0.253	0.258	0.261	0.263	0.272	0.274	0.275	0.277	0.288
Dec	0.216	0.221	0.226	0.228	0.231	0.236	0.237	0.242	0.244	0.244	0.247	0.255	0.247	0.261	0.265	0.271	0.276	0.279	0.282	0.290	0.292	0.293	0.295	0.306

Capital gains indexation allowances for companies (January 2016 – December 2017)

Month of acquisition	2016 Jan	Feb	Mar	Apr	May	June	July	Aug	Sept	Oct	Nov	Dec	2017 Jan	Feb	Mar	Apr	May	June	July	Aug	Sept	Oct	Nov	Dec
2009																								
Jan	0.232	0.238	0.243	0.244	0.248	0.252	0.254	0.258	0.261	0.260	0.264	0.271	0.264	0.277	0.282	0.288	0.293	0.296	0.299	0.307	0.309	0.310	0.313	0.324
Feb	0.224	0.230	0.235	0.237	0.240	0.245	0.246	0.251	0.253	0.253	0.256	0.263	0.256	0.270	0.274	0.280	0.285	0.288	0.291	0.299	0.301	0.302	0.305	0.316
Mar	0.225	0.230	0.236	0.237	0.240	0.245	0.247	0.251	0.252	0.253	0.257	0.264	0.257	0.270	0.274	0.281	0.286	0.289	0.292	0.300	0.302	0.303	0.305	0.316
Apr	0.224	0.229	0.235	0.236	0.239	0.244	0.245	0.250	0.252	0.252	0.255	0.263	0.255	0.269	0.273	0.279	0.285	0.287	0.290	0.299	0.301	0.302	0.304	0.315
May	0.216	0.222	0.227	0.228	0.232	0.236	0.238	0.242	0.245	0.244	0.248	0.255	0.248	0.261	0.266	0.272	0.277	0.280	0.282	0.291	0.293	0.294	0.296	0.307
June	0.213	0.218	0.224	0.225	0.228	0.233	0.234	0.239	0.241	0.241	0.244	0.252	0.244	0.258	0.262	0.268	0.273	0.276	0.279	0.287	0.289	0.290	0.292	0.303
July	0.213	0.218	0.224	0.225	0.228	0.233	0.234	0.239	0.241	0.241	0.244	0.252	0.244	0.258	0.262	0.268	0.273	0.276	0.279	0.287	0.289	0.290	0.292	0.303
Aug	0.207	0.213	0.218	0.219	0.222	0.227	0.229	0.233	0.236	0.235	0.238	0.246	0.238	0.252	0.256	0.262	0.267	0.270	0.273	0.281	0.283	0.284	0.286	0.297
Sept	0.202	0.208	0.213	0.214	0.217	0.222	0.223	0.228	0.230	0.230	0.233	0.241	0.233	0.247	0.251	0.257	0.262	0.265	0.268	0.276	0.278	0.279	0.281	0.292
Oct	0.198	0.204	0.209	0.210	0.213	0.218	0.219	0.224	0.226	0.226	0.229	0.237	0.229	0.243	0.247	0.253	0.258	0.261	0.263	0.272	0.274	0.275	0.277	0.288
Nov	0.195	0.200	0.205	0.207	0.210	0.215	0.216	0.221	0.223	0.223	0.226	0.233	0.226	0.239	0.243	0.249	0.254	0.257	0.260	0.268	0.270	0.271	0.273	0.284
Dec	0.187	0.193	0.198	0.199	0.202	0.207	0.208	0.213	0.215	0.215	0.218	0.225	0.218	0.231	0.235	0.241	0.246	0.249	0.252	0.260	0.262	0.263	0.265	0.276
2010																								
Jan	0.188	0.193	0.198	0.200	0.203	0.207	0.209	0.213	0.216	0.215	0.218	0.226	0.218	0.232	0.236	0.242	0.247	0.250	0.252	0.261	0.263	0.263	0.266	0.276
Feb	0.181	0.186	0.191	0.193	0.196	0.200	0.202	0.206	0.208	0.208	0.211	0.219	0.211	0.224	0.229	0.234	0.240	0.242	0.245	0.253	0.255	0.256	0.258	0.269
Mar	0.173	0.178	0.183	0.184	0.188	0.192	0.193	0.198	0.200	0.200	0.203	0.210	0.203	0.216	0.220	0.226	0.231	0.234	0.237	0.245	0.246	0.247	0.250	0.260
Apr	0.162	0.167	0.172	0.173	0.176	0.181	0.182	0.187	0.189	0.189	0.192	0.199	0.192	0.205	0.209	0.215	0.219	0.222	0.225	0.233	0.235	0.236	0.238	0.248
May	0.157	0.163	0.168	0.169	0.172	0.177	0.178	0.182	0.185	0.184	0.187	0.195	0.187	0.200	0.204	0.210	0.215	0.218	0.220	0.229	0.230	0.231	0.233	0.244
June	0.155	0.160	0.165	0.166	0.170	0.174	0.175	0.180	0.182	0.182	0.185	0.192	0.185	0.198	0.202	0.207	0.212	0.215	0.218	0.226	0.228	0.228	0.231	0.241
July	0.157	0.163	0.168	0.169	0.172	0.177	0.178	0.182	0.185	0.184	0.187	0.195	0.187	0.200	0.204	0.210	0.215	0.218	0.220	0.229	0.230	0.231	0.233	0.244
Aug	0.153	0.158	0.163	0.164	0.167	0.172	0.173	0.178	0.180	0.180	0.183	0.190	0.183	0.196	0.200	0.205	0.210	0.213	0.216	0.224	0.225	0.226	0.229	0.239
Sept	0.149	0.154	0.159	0.160	0.163	0.168	0.169	0.174	0.176	0.175	0.178	0.186	0.178	0.191	0.195	0.201	0.206	0.209	0.211	0.219	0.221	0.222	0.224	0.234
Oct	0.146	0.151	0.156	0.158	0.161	0.165	0.167	0.171	0.173	0.173	0.176	0.183	0.176	0.189	0.193	0.198	0.203	0.206	0.209	0.217	0.218	0.219	0.221	0.232
Nov	0.141	0.146	0.151	0.153	0.156	0.160	0.161	0.166	0.168	0.168	0.171	0.178	0.171	0.183	0.187	0.193	0.198	0.201	0.203	0.211	0.213	0.214	0.216	0.226
Dec	0.133	0.138	0.143	0.144	0.148	0.152	0.153	0.158	0.160	0.159	0.162	0.169	0.162	0.175	0.179	0.185	0.190	0.192	0.195	0.203	0.204	0.205	0.208	0.218
2011																								
Jan	0.130	0.135	0.140	0.141	0.145	0.149	0.150	0.155	0.157	0.156	0.159	0.166	0.159	0.172	0.176	0.182	0.186	0.189	0.192	0.200	0.201	0.202	0.204	0.214
Feb	0.119	0.124	0.129	0.130	0.133	0.137	0.139	0.143	0.145	0.145	0.148	0.155	0.148	0.160	0.164	0.170	0.175	0.177	0.180	0.188	0.189	0.190	0.192	0.202
Mar	0.113	0.118	0.123	0.124	0.127	0.132	0.133	0.137	0.139	0.139	0.142	0.149	0.142	0.154	0.158	0.164	0.169	0.171	0.174	0.182	0.183	0.184	0.186	0.196
Apr	0.104	0.109	0.114	0.115	0.118	0.122	0.124	0.128	0.130	0.130	0.133	0.140	0.133	0.145	0.149	0.154	0.159	0.162	0.164	0.172	0.174	0.174	0.177	0.186
May	0.100	0.105	0.110	0.111	0.114	0.119	0.120	0.124	0.126	0.126	0.129	0.136	0.129	0.141	0.145	0.151	0.155	0.158	0.160	0.168	0.170	0.170	0.173	0.182
June	0.100	0.105	0.110	0.111	0.114	0.119	0.120	0.124	0.126	0.126	0.129	0.136	0.129	0.141	0.145	0.151	0.155	0.158	0.160	0.168	0.170	0.170	0.173	0.182
July	0.103	0.108	0.112	0.114	0.117	0.121	0.122	0.127	0.129	0.128	0.131	0.138	0.131	0.144	0.147	0.153	0.158	0.160	0.163	0.170	0.172	0.173	0.175	0.185
Aug	0.096	0.101	0.106	0.107	0.110	0.114	0.116	0.120	0.122	0.122	0.125	0.131	0.125	0.137	0.141	0.146	0.151	0.153	0.156	0.163	0.165	0.166	0.168	0.178
Sept	0.088	0.093	0.098	0.099	0.102	0.106	0.107	0.111	0.113	0.113	0.116	0.123	0.116	0.128	0.132	0.137	0.142	0.145	0.147	0.155	0.156	0.157	0.159	0.169
Oct	0.087	0.092	0.097	0.098	0.101	0.105	0.107	0.111	0.113	0.113	0.116	0.122	0.116	0.128	0.132	0.137	0.142	0.144	0.147	0.154	0.156	0.157	0.159	0.168
Nov	0.085	0.090	0.095	0.096	0.099	0.103	0.104	0.109	0.111	0.110	0.113	0.120	0.113	0.125	0.129	0.135	0.139	0.142	0.144	0.152	0.153	0.154	0.156	0.166
Dec	0.081	0.086	0.091	0.092	0.095	0.099	0.100	0.104	0.107	0.106	0.109	0.116	0.109	0.121	0.125	0.130	0.135	0.137	0.140	0.147	0.149	0.150	0.152	0.162

Capital gains indexation allowances for companies (January 2016 – December 2017)

Month of acquisition	2016 Jan	Feb	Mar	Apr	May	June	July	Aug	Sept	Oct	Nov	Dec	2017 Jan	Feb	Mar	Apr	May	June	July	Aug	Sept	Oct	Nov	Dec
2012																								
Jan	0.087	0.092	0.097	0.098	0.101	0.105	0.107	0.111	0.113	0.113	0.116	0.122	0.116	0.128	0.132	0.137	0.142	0.144	0.147	0.154	0.156	0.157	0.159	0.168
Feb	0.079	0.084	0.088	0.090	0.093	0.097	0.098	0.102	0.104	0.104	0.107	0.113	0.107	0.119	0.123	0.128	0.133	0.135	0.138	0.145	0.147	0.148	0.150	0.159
Mar	0.075	0.080	0.084	0.086	0.088	0.093	0.094	0.098	0.100	0.100	0.103	0.109	0.103	0.115	0.118	0.124	0.128	0.131	0.133	0.141	0.142	0.143	0.145	0.155
Apr	0.067	0.072	0.077	0.078	0.081	0.085	0.086	0.090	0.092	0.092	0.095	0.101	0.095	0.107	0.111	0.116	0.120	0.123	0.125	0.133	0.134	0.135	0.137	0.147
May	0.068	0.073	0.077	0.078	0.081	0.085	0.087	0.091	0.093	0.092	0.095	0.102	0.095	0.107	0.111	0.116	0.121	0.123	0.126	0.133	0.135	0.136	0.138	0.147
June	0.070	0.075	0.080	0.081	0.084	0.088	0.089	0.093	0.096	0.095	0.098	0.105	0.098	0.110	0.114	0.119	0.124	0.126	0.129	0.136	0.138	0.139	0.141	0.150
July	0.069	0.074	0.078	0.080	0.083	0.087	0.088	0.092	0.094	0.094	0.097	0.103	0.097	0.109	0.112	0.118	0.122	0.125	0.127	0.135	0.136	0.137	0.139	0.149
Aug	0.065	0.070	0.074	0.076	0.079	0.083	0.084	0.088	0.090	0.090	0.093	0.099	0.093	0.105	0.108	0.114	0.118	0.121	0.123	0.130	0.132	0.133	0.135	0.144
Sept	0.060	0.065	0.069	0.070	0.073	0.077	0.079	0.083	0.085	0.084	0.087	0.094	0.087	0.099	0.103	0.108	0.113	0.115	0.118	0.125	0.127	0.127	0.129	0.139
Oct	0.054	0.059	0.063	0.064	0.067	0.071	0.072	0.077	0.079	0.078	0.081	0.088	0.081	0.093	0.096	0.102	0.106	0.109	0.111	0.118	0.120	0.121	0.123	0.132
Nov	0.054	0.059	0.063	0.064	0.067	0.071	0.072	0.077	0.079	0.078	0.081	0.088	0.081	0.093	0.096	0.102	0.106	0.109	0.111	0.118	0.120	0.121	0.123	0.132
Dec	0.049	0.053	0.058	0.059	0.062	0.066	0.067	0.071	0.073	0.073	0.076	0.082	0.076	0.088	0.091	0.096	0.101	0.103	0.106	0.113	0.115	0.115	0.118	0.127
2013																								
Jan	0.053	0.058	0.062	0.063	0.066	0.070	0.072	0.076	0.078	0.077	0.080	0.087	0.080	0.092	0.096	0.101	0.105	0.108	0.110	0.118	0.119	0.120	0.122	0.131
Feb	0.045	0.050	0.055	0.056	0.059	0.063	0.064	0.068	0.070	0.069	0.072	0.079	0.072	0.084	0.088	0.093	0.097	0.100	0.102	0.109	0.111	0.112	0.114	0.123
Mar	0.041	0.045	0.050	0.051	0.054	0.058	0.059	0.063	0.065	0.065	0.068	0.074	0.068	0.079	0.083	0.088	0.092	0.095	0.097	0.105	0.106	0.107	0.109	0.118
Apr	0.037	0.042	0.046	0.048	0.051	0.055	0.056	0.060	0.062	0.061	0.064	0.071	0.064	0.076	0.079	0.085	0.089	0.091	0.094	0.101	0.103	0.103	0.105	0.115
May	0.035	0.040	0.044	0.046	0.048	0.052	0.054	0.058	0.060	0.059	0.062	0.068	0.062	0.074	0.077	0.082	0.087	0.089	0.092	0.099	0.100	0.101	0.103	0.112
June	0.036	0.041	0.046	0.047	0.050	0.054	0.055	0.059	0.061	0.060	0.063	0.070	0.063	0.075	0.078	0.084	0.088	0.091	0.093	0.100	0.102	0.103	0.105	0.114
July	0.036	0.041	0.046	0.047	0.050	0.054	0.055	0.059	0.061	0.060	0.063	0.070	0.063	0.075	0.078	0.084	0.088	0.091	0.093	0.100	0.102	0.103	0.105	0.114
Aug	0.031	0.036	0.040	0.041	0.044	0.048	0.049	0.053	0.055	0.055	0.058	0.064	0.058	0.069	0.073	0.078	0.082	0.085	0.087	0.094	0.096	0.097	0.099	0.108
Sept	0.027	0.032	0.037	0.038	0.040	0.044	0.046	0.050	0.052	0.051	0.054	0.060	0.054	0.066	0.069	0.074	0.079	0.081	0.083	0.091	0.092	0.093	0.095	0.104
Oct	0.027	0.032	0.037	0.038	0.040	0.044	0.046	0.050	0.052	0.051	0.054	0.060	0.054	0.066	0.069	0.074	0.079	0.081	0.083	0.091	0.092	0.093	0.095	0.104
Nov	0.027	0.031	0.036	0.037	0.040	0.044	0.045	0.049	0.051	0.050	0.053	0.060	0.053	0.065	0.068	0.073	0.078	0.080	0.083	0.090	0.091	0.092	0.094	0.103
Dec	0.025	0.029	0.034	0.035	0.038	0.042	0.043	0.047	0.049	0.048	0.051	0.057	0.051	0.063	0.066	0.071	0.076	0.078	0.080	0.087	0.089	0.090	0.092	0.101
2014																								
Jan	0.025	0.029	0.034	0.035	0.038	0.042	0.043	0.047	0.049	0.048	0.051	0.057	0.051	0.063	0.066	0.071	0.076	0.078	0.080	0.087	0.089	0.090	0.092	0.101
Feb	0.018	0.023	0.027	0.028	0.031	0.035	0.036	0.040	0.042	0.042	0.044	0.051	0.044	0.056	0.059	0.065	0.069	0.071	0.074	0.081	0.082	0.083	0.085	0.094
Mar	0.016	0.020	0.025	0.026	0.029	0.033	0.034	0.038	0.040	0.039	0.042	0.048	0.042	0.053	0.057	0.062	0.066	0.069	0.071	0.078	0.080	0.080	0.082	0.091
Apr	0.012	0.017	0.021	0.022	0.025	0.029	0.030	0.034	0.036	0.036	0.038	0.045	0.038	0.050	0.053	0.058	0.063	0.065	0.067	0.074	0.076	0.077	0.079	0.088
May	0.011	0.016	0.020	0.021	0.024	0.028	0.029	0.033	0.035	0.035	0.038	0.044	0.038	0.049	0.052	0.057	0.062	0.064	0.066	0.073	0.075	0.076	0.078	0.087
June	0.010	0.014	0.019	0.020	0.023	0.027	0.028	0.032	0.034	0.033	0.036	0.042	0.036	0.047	0.051	0.056	0.060	0.062	0.065	0.072	0.073	0.074	0.076	0.085
July	0.011	0.016	0.020	0.021	0.024	0.028	0.029	0.033	0.035	0.034	0.037	0.043	0.037	0.048	0.052	0.057	0.061	0.064	0.066	0.073	0.075	0.075	0.077	0.086
Aug	0.007	0.012	0.016	0.017	0.020	0.024	0.025	0.029	0.031	0.030	0.033	0.039	0.033	0.044	0.048	0.053	0.057	0.060	0.062	0.069	0.070	0.071	0.073	0.082
Sept	0.005	0.009	0.014	0.015	0.017	0.021	0.023	0.026	0.028	0.028	0.031	0.037	0.031	0.042	0.045	0.050	0.055	0.057	0.059	0.066	0.068	0.069	0.071	0.080
Oct	0.004	0.009	0.013	0.014	0.017	0.021	0.022	0.026	0.028	0.028	0.030	0.036	0.030	0.042	0.045	0.050	0.054	0.057	0.059	0.066	0.068	0.068	0.070	0.079
Nov	0.007	0.011	0.016	0.017	0.019	0.023	0.025	0.028	0.030	0.030	0.033	0.039	0.033	0.044	0.047	0.053	0.057	0.059	0.061	0.068	0.070	0.071	0.073	0.082
Dec	0.005	0.010	0.014	0.015	0.018	0.022	0.023	0.027	0.029	0.028	0.031	0.037	0.031	0.042	0.046	0.051	0.055	0.057	0.060	0.067	0.068	0.069	0.071	0.080

Capital gains indexation allowances for companies (January 2016 – December 2017)

Month of acquisition	2016 Jan	Feb	Mar	Apr	May	June	July	Aug	Sept	Oct	Nov	Dec	2017 Jan	Feb	Mar	Apr	May	June	July	Aug	Sept	Oct	Nov	Dec
2015																								
Jan	0.013	0.018	0.022	0.023	0.026	0.030	0.031	0.035	0.037	0.037	0.040	0.046	0.040	0.051	0.054	0.060	0.064	0.066	0.069	0.076	0.077	0.078	0.080	0.089
Feb	0.008	0.013	0.017	0.018	0.021	0.025	0.026	0.030	0.032	0.032	0.034	0.041	0.034	0.046	0.049	0.054	0.058	0.061	0.063	0.070	0.072	0.072	0.074	0.083
Mar	0.007	0.011	0.016	0.017	0.019	0.023	0.025	0.028	0.030	0.030	0.033	0.039	0.033	0.044	0.047	0.053	0.057	0.059	0.061	0.068	0.070	0.071	0.073	0.082
Apr	0.003	0.008	0.012	0.013	0.016	0.020	0.021	0.025	0.027	0.026	0.029	0.035	0.029	0.040	0.044	0.049	0.053	0.055	0.058	0.065	0.066	0.067	0.069	0.078
May	0.001	0.006	0.010	0.011	0.014	0.018	0.019	0.023	0.025	0.024	0.027	0.033	0.027	0.038	0.042	0.047	0.051	0.053	0.056	0.063	0.064	0.065	0.067	0.076
June	0.000	0.004	0.008	0.010	0.012	0.016	0.017	0.021	0.023	0.023	0.025	0.032	0.025	0.037	0.040	0.045	0.049	0.052	0.054	0.061	0.063	0.063	0.065	0.074
July	0.001	0.005	0.010	0.011	0.014	0.017	0.019	0.022	0.024	0.024	0.027	0.033	0.027	0.038	0.041	0.046	0.051	0.053	0.055	0.062	0.064	0.065	0.067	0.075
Aug	0.000	0.001	0.005	0.006	0.009	0.013	0.014	0.018	0.020	0.019	0.022	0.028	0.022	0.033	0.037	0.042	0.046	0.048	0.050	0.057	0.059	0.060	0.062	0.070
Sept	0.000	0.002	0.006	0.007	0.010	0.013	0.015	0.018	0.020	0.020	0.023	0.029	0.023	0.034	0.037	0.042	0.047	0.049	0.051	0.058	0.060	0.060	0.062	0.071
Oct	0.000	0.002	0.006	0.007	0.010	0.014	0.015	0.019	0.021	0.020	0.023	0.029	0.023	0.034	0.038	0.043	0.047	0.049	0.052	0.059	0.060	0.061	0.063	0.072
Nov	0.000	0.001	0.005	0.006	0.009	0.013	0.014	0.018	0.020	0.019	0.022	0.028	0.022	0.033	0.037	0.042	0.046	0.048	0.050	0.057	0.059	0.060	0.062	0.070
Dec	0.000	0.000	0.002	0.003	0.006	0.010	0.011	0.015	0.017	0.016	0.019	0.025	0.019	0.030	0.033	0.038	0.043	0.045	0.047	0.054	0.056	0.056	0.058	0.067
2016																								
Jan	—	0.005	0.009	0.010	0.013	0.017	0.018	0.022	0.024	0.023	0.026	0.032	0.026	0.037	0.041	0.046	0.050	0.052	0.054	0.061	0.063	0.064	0.066	0.075
Feb	—	—	0.004	0.005	0.008	0.012	0.013	0.017	0.019	0.018	0.021	0.027	0.021	0.032	0.036	0.041	0.045	0.047	0.050	0.057	0.058	0.059	0.061	0.070
Mar	—	—	—	0.001	0.004	0.008	0.009	0.013	0.015	0.014	0.017	0.023	0.017	0.028	0.031	0.036	0.041	0.043	0.045	0.052	0.054	0.054	0.056	0.065
Apr	—	—	—	—	0.003	0.007	0.008	0.011	0.013	0.013	0.016	0.022	0.016	0.027	0.030	0.035	0.039	0.042	0.044	0.051	0.052	0.053	0.055	0.064
May	—	—	—	—	—	0.004	0.005	0.009	0.011	0.010	0.013	0.019	0.013	0.024	0.027	0.032	0.037	0.039	0.041	0.048	0.050	0.050	0.052	0.061
June	—	—	—	—	—	—	0.001	0.005	0.007	0.006	0.009	0.015	0.009	0.020	0.024	0.029	0.033	0.035	0.037	0.044	0.046	0.046	0.048	0.057
July	—	—	—	—	—	—	—	0.004	0.006	0.005	0.008	0.014	0.008	0.019	0.022	0.027	0.032	0.034	0.036	0.043	0.044	0.045	0.047	0.056
Aug	—	—	—	—	—	—	—	—	0.002	0.002	0.004	0.010	0.004	0.015	0.019	0.023	0.028	0.030	0.032	0.039	0.040	0.041	0.043	0.052
Sept	—	—	—	—	—	—	—	—	—	0.000	0.002	0.008	0.002	0.013	0.017	0.022	0.026	0.028	0.030	0.037	0.039	0.039	0.041	0.050
Oct	—	—	—	—	—	—	—	—	—	—	0.003	0.009	0.003	0.014	0.017	0.022	0.026	0.028	0.031	0.037	0.039	0.040	0.042	0.050
Nov	—	—	—	—	—	—	—	—	—	—	—	0.006	0.000	0.011	0.014	0.019	0.023	0.026	0.028	0.035	0.036	0.037	0.039	0.047
Dec	—	—	—	—	—	—	—	—	—	—	—	—	0.000	0.005	0.008	0.013	0.017	0.019	0.022	0.028	0.030	0.031	0.033	0.041
2017																								
Jan	—	—	—	—	—	—	—	—	—	—	—	—	—	0.011	0.014	0.019	0.023	0.026	0.028	0.035	0.036	0.037	0.039	0.047
Feb	—	—	—	—	—	—	—	—	—	—	—	—	—	—	0.003	0.008	0.012	0.015	0.017	0.023	0.025	0.026	0.028	0.036
Mar	—	—	—	—	—	—	—	—	—	—	—	—	—	—	—	0.005	0.009	0.011	0.013	0.020	0.022	0.022	0.024	0.033
Apr	—	—	—	—	—	—	—	—	—	—	—	—	—	—	—	—	0.004	0.006	0.008	0.015	0.017	0.017	0.019	0.028
May	—	—	—	—	—	—	—	—	—	—	—	—	—	—	—	—	—	0.002	0.004	0.011	0.013	0.013	0.015	0.024
June	—	—	—	—	—	—	—	—	—	—	—	—	—	—	—	—	—	—	0.002	0.009	0.010	0.011	0.013	0.021
July	—	—	—	—	—	—	—	—	—	—	—	—	—	—	—	—	—	—	—	0.007	0.008	0.009	0.011	0.019
Aug	—	—	—	—	—	—	—	—	—	—	—	—	—	—	—	—	—	—	—	—	0.001	0.002	0.004	0.012
Sept	—	—	—	—	—	—	—	—	—	—	—	—	—	—	—	—	—	—	—	—	—	0.001	0.003	0.011
Oct	—	—	—	—	—	—	—	—	—	—	—	—	—	—	—	—	—	—	—	—	—	—	0.002	0.010
Nov	—	—	—	—	—	—	—	—	—	—	—	—	—	—	—	—	—	—	—	—	—	—	—	0.008
Dec	—	—	—	—	—	—	—	—	—	—	—	—	—	—	—	—	—	—	—	—	—	—	—	—

Certificates of tax deposit

Rates of interest

Deposits of less than £100,000

Date	A	B
9 February — 5 April 2001	2¼%	1¼%
6 April — 2 August	2%	1%
3 August — 18 September	1½%	¾%
19 September — 4 October	1¼%	¾%
5 October — 8 November	1%	½%
9 November — 6 February 2003	½%	¼%
7 February — 10 July	¼%	Nil
11 July — 6 November	Nil	Nil
7 November — 5 February 2004	¼%	Nil
6 February — 6 May	½%	¼%
7 May — 10 June	¾%	¼%
11 June — 5 August	1%	½%
6 August — 4 August 2005	1¼%	½%
5 August — 3 August 2006	1%	½%
4 August — 9 November	1¾%	¾%
10 November — 10 May 2007	1½%	¾%
11 May — 5 July	2%	1%
6 July — 6 December	2¼%	1 1/10%
7 December — 7 February 2008	3%	1½%
8 February — 10 April	2%	1%
11 April — 8 October	2%	1%
9 October — 6 November	2½%	1¼%
7 November — 4 December	1¾%	¾%
5 December —	0%	0%

Deposits of £100,000 or more

Date	A and held for Under 1 mth	1–3 mths	3–6 mths	6–9 mths	9–12 mths	B and held for under 1 mth	1–3 mths	3–6 mths	6–9 mths	9–12 mths
9 February — 5 April 2001	2¼%	4¾%	4¼%	4¼%	4%	1¼%	2½%	2¼%	2¼%	2%
6 April — 10 May	2%	4¼%	4%	3¾%	3½%	1%	2¼%	2%	2%	1¾%
11 May — 2 August	2%	4%	4%	3¾%	3¾%	1%	2%	2%	2%	2%
3 August — 18 September	1½%	4%	3¾%	3¾%	3¾%	¾%	2%	1⅞%	1⅞%	1⅞%
19 September — 4 October	1¼%	3½%	3¼%	3¼%	3%	¾%	1¾%	1¾%	1¾%	1½%
5 October — 8 November	1%	3¼%	3%	3%	3%	½%	1¾%	1½%	1½%	1½%
9 November — 6 February 2003	½%	2¾%	2½%	2¼%	2¼%	¼%	1½%	1¼%	1¼%	1¼%
7 February — 10 July	¼%	2¾%	2¼%	2¼%	2%	Nil	1¼%	1%	1%	1%
11 July — 6 November	Nil	2½%	2¼%	2%	2%	Nil	1¼%	1%	1%	1%
7 November — 5 February 2004	¼%	3%	3%	3%	3%	Nil	1½%	1½%	1½%	1½%
6 February — 6 May	½%	3%	3%	3%	3%	¼%	1½%	1½%	1½%	1½%
7 May — 10 June	¾%	3¼%	3¼%	3¼%	3¼%	¼%	1½%	1½%	1½%	1½%
11 June — 5 August	1%	3¾%	3½%	3¾%	3¾%	½%	1¾%	1¾%	1¾%	1¾%
6 August — 4 August 2005	1¼%	3¾%	3¾%	3¾%	3¾%	½%	1¾%	1¾%	1¾%	1¾%
5 August — 3 August 2006	1%	3½%	3¼%	3%	3%	½%	1¾%	1½%	1½%	1½%
4 August — 9 November	1¾%	4¼%	4¼%	4%	4%	¾%	2%	2%	2%	2%
10 November — 11 January 2007	1½%	4%	4%	3¾%	3¾%	¾%	2%	2%	1¾%	1¾%
12 January — 10 May	1½%	4¼%	4%	4%	4%	¾%	2%	2%	2%	2%
11 May — 5 July	2%	4¾%	4½%	4½%	4½%	1%	2¼%	2¼%	2¼%	2¼%
6 July — 6 December	2¼%	5%	4¾%	4¾%	4¾%	1 1/10%	2½%	2¼%	2¼%	2¼%
7 December — 7 February 2008	3%	5½%	5%	4¾%	4½%	1½%	2¾%	2½%	2¼%	2¼%
8 February — 10 April	2%	4½%	4¼%	4%	3¾%	1%	2¼%	2%	2%	1½%
11 April — 8 October	2%	4¾%	4½%	4¼%	4¼%	1%	2¼%	2¼%	2%	2%
9 October — 6 November	2½%	5¼%	5%	5%	4¾%	1¼%	2½%	2½%	2½%	2¼%
7 November — 4 December	1¾%	4½%	4¼%	4¼%	4%	¾%	2¼%	2%	2%	2%
5 December — 8 January 2009	0%	2½%	2½%	2½%	2¼%	0%	1¼%	1¼%	1¼%	1%
9 January — 5 February	0%	1½ %	1¼%	1¼%	1¼%	0%	¾%	½	½%	½%
6 February — 5 March	0%	1%	1%	1%	¾%	0%	½%	½%	½%	¼%
6 March —	0%	¾%	¾%	¾%	¾%	0%	¼%	¼%	¼%	¼%

A = used to pay tax
B = withdrawn for cash

Notes

(a) From 23 November 2017 the scheme is closed for new purchases, but existing certificates will be honoured until 23 November 2023. Any certificates remaining after this date should be submitted to HMRC for refund. HMRC will seek to repay the balance of any certificate remaining unpaid and unclaimed. If they are unable to contact the current certificate holder after reasonable effort the balance will be forfeited.

(b) Certificates may be used by taxpayers generally – that is to say companies, individuals, partnerships, personal representatives, trustees etc. for payment of tax but not corporation tax, PAYE, tax deducted from payments to construction subcontractors, capital gains tax payable by companies on disposals of high value dwellings (see page 19) or VAT.

(c) Interest accrues daily (without compounding) for a maximum of six years from the date of deposit to (i) the deemed due date for tax paid with deposits; or (ii) the day on which the deposit is withdrawn for cash. It is payable gross but taxable.

(d) Rates of interest on certificates are, for the first year, those applying on the date of deposit, and thereafter rates are realigned with current rates on each anniversary.

Corporation tax

Rates

Financial year	2023	2022	2021	2020	2019	2018	2017	2016
Full rate	25%	19%	19%	19%	19%	19%	19%	20%
Small profits rate	19%	—	—	—	—	—	—	—
Upper profit limit	£50,000	—	—	—	—	—	—	—
Marginal relief — upper profit limit	£250,000	—	—	—	—	—	—	—
Marginal relief fraction	3/200	—	—	—	—	—	—	—
Effective marginal rate	26.5%	—	—	—	—	—	—	—
Close company loans/benefits to participators (note (i))	33.75%	33.75%	32.5%	32.5%	32.5%	32.5%	32.5%	32.5%
Restitution payments rate (note (j))	45%	45%	45%	45%	45%	45%	45%	45%
Chargeable gains	(a) The whole of the chargeable gains (less allowable losses) is included in the taxable total profits. The rate of corporation tax applicable will be either the full rate, or the small profits rate (with marginal relief as appropriate). For disposals before 6 April 2019, gains and losses within the charge to capital gains tax in respect of high value disposals of dwellings (see page 19) and of non-resident disposals of residential property interests (see page 19) are excluded from the taxable total profits. (b) For authorised unit and investment trusts, gains are not chargeable. Gains on disposals of investment properties by UK real estate investment trusts are not chargeable.							

Notes

(a) **For the financial year 2023 and subsequent years,** where 'profits' of an accounting period exceed the upper profit limit for the small profits rate, but are less than the appropriate marginal relief upper profit limit, corporation tax is reduced by:

$$F(U - \text{augmented profits}) \times \frac{\text{taxable total profits}}{\text{augmented profits}}$$

where F is the marginal relief fraction and U is the marginal relief upper profit limit.

(b) 'Augmented profits' are total taxable profits plus exempt qualifying distribution income (other than from UK companies within the same group or owned by a consortium of which the recipient is a member).

(c) The upper profit limits and the marginal relief upper profit limits for the small profits rate are proportionately reduced for accounting periods of less than 12 months.

(d) Where a company has associated companies, the upper profit limits and the marginal relief upper profit limits for the small profits rate are divided by one plus the number of associated companies in the accounting period, including those associated for part only of the period but ignoring companies which have not traded at any time in the period.

(e) For financial year 2022 and earlier years, the corporation tax rates applicable to North Sea oil and gas ring fence activities are as follows: main rate 30%; small profits rate 19%; upper profit limit £300,000; marginal relief upper profit limit £1,500,000; marginal relief fraction 11/400. For financial year 2023, the rates remain the same but the upper profit limit is £50,000, the marginal upper profit limit is £250,000 and the marginal relief fraction is 11/400.

Rules similar to those at notes (a) to (d) above apply. For financial year 2022 and earlier years, the references in note (d) above to 'associated companies' should be read as a reference to 'related 51% group companies' and the reference in note (b) above to 'exempt qualifying distribution income' should be read as a reference to 'exempt ABGH distributions'.

(f) A corporation tax surcharge of 8% is chargeable on the taxable profits of banks and building societies. The rate will be reduced to 3% with effect from 1 April 2023. [FA 2022, s 6]

(g) The increase in the rate to 33.75% applies for loans made or benefits conferred on or after 6 April 2022.

(h) The charge to corporation tax on restitution interest (i.e. interest paid by HMRC in respect of a claim to restitution for tax paid to HMRC under a mistake of law or collected by HMRC unlawfully) applies to interest arising as a result of a judgment or an agreement between the parties which becomes final on or after 21 October 2015.

Corporation tax

Payment of tax

Corporation tax	Without assessment, no later than nine months and one day after the end of the accounting period (the 'due date').	*CTA 2009, s 8*
	Instalments. Subject to the exceptions below, a 'large company' (i.e. one whose augmented profits exceed £1.5m a year (but from 1 April 2019, do not exceed £20m, see below), both thresholds being divided by one plus the number of active related 51% group companies (for accounting periods ending on or after 1 April 2023, active associated companies), if any), must pay its CT in four quarterly instalments on the basis of anticipated liabilities for the accounting period. For a company with a 12 month accounting period, the first two instalments are due on the 14th day of months 7 and 10 in the accounting period, the third is due 14 days after the end of the accounting period and the final instalment is due 3 months and 14 days after the end of the period.	*TMA 1970, s 59* *F(No 2)A 2015, s 39* *SI 1998 No 3175* *SI 2014 No 2409*
	For accounting periods beginning on or after 1 April 2019, a 'very large company' (i.e. one whose augmented profits exceed £20m a year divided by one plus the number of active related 51% group companies) will have to pay instalments in the third, sixth, ninth and twelfth months of the accounting periods.	*SI 2017 No 1072*
	Any company which pays the bank levy is also a large company unless, from 1 April 2019, it exceeds the £20m threshold resulting in it being a very large company.	
	Exceptions. (i) A company which would otherwise be large or very large is not treated as such for an accounting period if its CT liability for that period does not exceed £10,000. (ii) A company is not large for an accounting period if it was not large (or from 1 April 2019, very large) in the 12 months preceding the accounting period and its profits for the accounting period do not exceed £10m, divided by one plus the number of related 51% group companies (or active associated companies) as at the end of the preceding accounting period. This 'grace period' does not apply to very large companies.	
	The limits of £20m, £10m, £1.5m and £10,000 are proportionately reduced for accounting periods of less than 12 months.	
	Groups can enter into group payment arrangements provided the paying company enters into a standard contract at least two months prior to the first instalment payment due date.	
Income tax	Within 14 days of end of return period during which the income tax was deducted. Return periods end on 31 March, 30 June, 30 September, 31 December, at the end of each of the company's accounting periods.	*ITA 2007, ss 947–950*
Tax returns	Filing date is normally the later of (i) twelve months after the end of the return period; and (ii) three months after the receipt of Notice. Special rules apply where accounts are prepared for periods exceeding twelve months. Returns may not be amended more than twelve months after the filing date unless otherwise provided.	*TMA 1970, s 12ZB; FA 1998, Sch 18 paras 14, 15*
Interest on tax	See page 77.	
Research and development	*Deduction scheme.* An 'SME' incurring R & D expenditure can claim to deduct 230% of the expenditure when computing its trading profit or loss. A company not in profit, or which has not started to trade, can claim relief up front as a cash payment of 14.5% of 'surrenderable loss' (an 'R & D tax credit') subject to a cap for accounting periods beginning on or after 1 April 2021. The capped amount a company can claim in any one year from April 2021 is £20,000 plus three times the company's total PAYE and NIC for the period and, broadly, three times the relevant PAYE and NIC of certain connected companies. These reliefs are limited to €7.5m per project.	*CTA 2009, ss 104A–104Y, 1039–1142; FA 2021, s 19* *FA 2011, s 43*
	An SME can also claim relief for expenditure on R & D contracted out to it by a large company or by any other person not carrying on a trade etc. and for R & D expenditure which is subsidised or to which the project limit above applies. The relief provides for a deduction equal to 130% of the expenditure.	*FA 2012, s 20, Sch 3* *FA 2013, Sch 15* *FA 2014, s 31* *FA 2015, s 27*
	An 'SME' is a company with fewer than 500 employees and either or both of annual turnover not exceeding €100m and annual balance sheet total not exceeding €86m.	*F(No 2)A 2015, s 31*
	Large companies (i.e. companies which are not SMEs) can claim a relief similar to that for SMEs above, including tax credits, for expenditure incurred before 1 April 2017 on certain vaccine research. The rate of relief is 140%. See also page 10.	*FA 2016, ss 47, 48*
	Large companies incurring R & D expenditure before 1 April 2016 could generally claim to deduct 130% of the expenditure from trading profits. The relief is abolished for expenditure incurred on or after 1 April 2016 but companies can instead claim an above the line credit (see below).	*FA 2018, s 19* *FA 2020, s 28*
	R&D expenditure credit (RDEC) scheme. For R & D expenditure incurred on or after 1 April 2013, large companies (and certain SMEs with subcontracted or subsidised R & D, or R & D subject to the project limit) can claim R & D expenditure credit (RDEC) to the value of 13% of the qualifying expenditure (12% for expenditure before 1 April 2020; 11% for expenditure before 1 January 2018 and after 31 March 2015; 49% for ring fence trades). The RDEC is a taxable receipt and is paid net of tax to companies with no corporation tax liability. Higher education institutions and charities are excluded.	

Corporation tax

Community investment tax credit	Tax relief worth up to 25% of qualifying investments. See page 64.	*CTA 2010, ss 218–269*
Charitable giving		
Gift aid scheme	Relief is available for qualifying donations to charity or to a community amateur sports club. Relief is given by deducting the amount of the donation from the company's total profits for the accounting period in which the payment is made. The donation is not taxable in the hands of the charity or club if applied to charitable purposes only.	*CTA 2010, ss 189–202*
Gifts in kind	Relief is available for gifts by companies to charities, community amateur sports clubs or educational establishments of goods produced or sold or of plant and machinery used in the donor's trade, etc.	*CTA 2009, ss 105–108* *CAA 2001, s 63(2)*
Gifts of land, shares and securities etc.	Relief is available where a company disposes of a freehold or leasehold interest in land, listed shares or securities, units in an authorised unit trust, etc. to a charity by way of gift or sale at an undervalue. The market value of the land, shares etc. on the date of disposal (plus, in the case of a gift, incidental disposal costs) less any consideration or value of benefits received by the donor or a connected person is deducted from the total profits of the company for the accounting period in which the disposal is made.	*CTA 2010, ss 189, 190, 203–216*
Gifts of pre-eminent objects to the nation	Under the cultural gifts scheme, companies which donate pre-eminent objects, or collections of objects, to the nation may qualify for a tax reduction of 20% of the value of the objects.	*FA 2012, s 49*
Groups of companies		
Group relief	A company which is a member of a group of companies can surrender certain losses, etc. to be claimed by another member of the group against its own corporation tax liability. Companies are members of a group of companies for this purpose broadly if one is the 75% subsidiary of the other or both are 75% subsidiaries of a third company. Post–1 April 2017 losses which are carried forward can be surrendered, though restrictions apply where the group's profit is more than £5m. The following are eligible for surrender as group relief: trading losses, non-trading loan relationship deficits, certain excess capital allowances on plant or machinery used for special leasing, management expenses, qualifying charitable donations, property business losses, non-trading losses on intangible fixed assets, qualifying overseas losses of non-resident companies, and from 1 April 2017, excess contributions on grassroots sport.	*CTA 2010, ss 97–188FD* *FA 2013, s 30*
Chargeable gains	Disposals of capital assets by one member of a group to another member are treated as if made at a 'no gain/no loss' disposal value. A 'group' for this purpose consists of a principal company, its 75% subsidiaries and those subsidiaries' 75% subsidiaries (and so on), but excluding any subsidiary which is not an effective 51% subsidiary of the principal company. Two members of a group can elect to transfer a gain or loss between them. A de-grouping charge will apply where a company leaves a group and owns a capital asset which has been transferred to it by another group member within the preceding six years.	*TCGA 1992, ss 170–171B, 179*
Patent box	For profits arising on or after 1 April 2013, a company can make an election under which its trading profits from patents and certain other intellectual property are effectively charged to corporation tax at 10%. The lower rate is given effect by way of a deduction in computing the trading profits of the company. The relief was phased in, so that for financial year 2013 only 60% of the relevant profits qualify. The percentage was increased by 10 percentage points in each subsequent financial year until 100% of the profits qualify from financial year 2017 onwards.	*CTA 2010, ss 357A–357GE; FA 2012, s 19, Sch 2*

Corporation tax

Diverted profits tax	A diverted profits tax of 25% applies to counter the use of aggressive tax planning techniques by multinational enterprises to divert profits from the UK. Two basic rules apply. The first counter-acts arrangements by which foreign companies exploit the permanent establishment rules, and comes into effect if a person is carrying on activity in the UK in connection with supplies of goods and services by a non-UK resident company to customers in the UK, provided that the detailed conditions are met. The second applies to certain arrangements which lack economic substance involving entities with an existing UK taxable presence. **The rate of tax will increase to 31% for accounting periods beginning on or after 1 April 2023.**	*FA 2015, ss 77–116; FA 2021, s 8*
Digital services tax	From April 2020 a digital services tax (DST) of 2% applies to revenues which are attributable to UK users and are from digital services activities that fall into three categories: a social media service; an internet search engine; or an online marketplace. There is an annual threshold of £500m digital services revenues and £25m UK digital services revenues below which the DST will not apply, and businesses with low margins or losses can make a safe-harbour election which allows a calculation of DST based on operating margins.	*FA 2020, ss 39–72, Schs 8–10*
Residential property developer tax	From 1 April 2022 a residential property developer tax of 4% applies to profits of companies arising from UK residential property development. The charge will only apply to profits exceeding an annual allowance of £25 million. Groups of companies are entitled only to one £25 million allowance, but this can be allocated between group companies.	*FA 2022, ss 32–52, Schs 7–9*
Cultural sector tax credits	A company which is treated as carrying on a separate trade under one of the creative sector tax regimes can claim a tax credit equal to a percentage of its 'surrenderable loss' (as defined) for an accounting period. The percentages are as indicated in the following table.	*CTA 2009, ss 1180–1218Z; FA 2022, ss 16–22*

		% of surrenderable loss	
		Before 27.10.21	**27.10.21–31.3.23**
Museums and Galleries Exhibition tax relief			
	Touring	20%	45%
	Non-touring	25%	50%
Theatre tax relief			
	Touring	20%	45%
	Non-touring	25%	50%
Orchestra tax relief		25%	50%
Film tax relief		25%	25%
High-end TV tax relief		25%	25%
Video Games tax relief		25%	25%

Where applicable, the increased rates for 27.10.21 onwards apply where production activities commence on or after that date.

Museums and galleries exhibition tax credits are subject to a maximum credit of £100,000 for a touring exhibition and £80,000 for a non-touring exhibition. Under State Aid rules, orchestra tax credits and theatre tax credits are capped at Euro 5 million per undertaking per year, and museums and galleries exhibition tax credits at Euro 75 million.

Double taxation treaties

Agreements covering taxes on income and capital gains

Country	SI or SR & O Number
Albania	**2013 No 3145**
Algeria	**2015 No 1888**
Antigua and Barbuda	**1947 No 2865**
	1968 No 1096
Argentina	**1997 No 1777**
Armenia	**2011 No 2722**
Australia	**2003 No 3199**
Austria	**2019 No 255**
Azerbaijan	**1995 No 762**
Bahrain	**2012 No 3075**
Bangladesh	**1980 No 708**
Barbados	**2012 No 3076**
Belarus	**2018 No 778**
Belgium	**1987 No 2053**
	2010 No 2979
Belize	**1947 No 2866**
	1968 No 573
	1973 No 2097
Bolivia	**1995 No 2707**
Bosnia-Herzegovina (see note (c))	**1981 No 1815**
Botswana	**2006 No 1925**
British Virgin Islands	**2009 No 3013**
Brunei	**1950 No 1977**
	1968 No 306
	1973 No 2098
	2013 No 3146
Bulgaria	**2015 No 1890**
Canada	**1980 No 709**
	1980 No 1528
	1985 No 1996
	2003 No 2619
	2014 No 3274
	2015 No 2011
Cayman Islands	**2010 No 2973**
Chile	**2003 No 3200**
China	**2011 No 2724**
	2013 No 3142
Colombia	**2018 No 377**
Croatia	**2015 No 1889**
Cyprus	**2018 No 839**
	2019 No 1113
Czech Republic (see note (b))	**1991 No 2876**
Denmark	**1980 No 1960**
	1991 No 2877
	1996 No 3165
Egypt	**1980 No 1091**
Estonia	**1994 No 3207**
Ethiopia	**2011 No 2725**
Falkland Islands	**1997 No 2985**
Faroes	**2007 No 3469**
Fiji	**1976 No 1342**
Finland	**1970 No 153**
	1980 No 710
	1985 No 1997
	1991 No 2878
	1996 No 3166
France	**2009 No 226**
Gambia	**1980 No 1963**
Georgia	**2004 No 3325**
	2010 No 2972
Germany	**2010 No 2975**
	2014 No 1874
	2021 No 634
Gibraltar	**2020 No 275**
Ghana	**1993 No 1800**
Greece	**1954 No 142**
Grenada	**1949 No 361**
	1968 No 1867
Guernsey	**2018 No 1345**
Guyana	**1992 No 3207**
Hong Kong	**2010 No 2974**
Hungary	**2011 No 2726**
Iceland	**2014 No 1879**
India	**1993 No 1801**
	2013 No 3147
Indonesia	**1994 No 769**
Irish Republic	**1976 No 2151**
	1976 No 2152
	1995 No 764
	1998 No 3151
Isle of Man	**2018 No 1347**
Israel	**1963 No 616**
	1971 No 391
	2019 No 1111
Italy	**1990 No 2590**
Ivory Coast	**1987 No 169**
Jamaica	**1973 No 1329**
Japan	**2006 No 1924**
	2014 No 1881
Jersey	**2018 No 1348**
Jordan	**2001 No 3924**
Kazakhstan	**1994 No 3211**
	1998 No 2567
Kenya	**1977 No 1299**
Kiribati (and Tuvalu)	**1950 No 750**
	1968 No 309
	1974 No 1271
Korea (South)	**1996 No 3168**
Kosovo	**2015 No 2007**
Kuwait	**1999 No 2036**
Kyrgyzstan	**2018 No 525**
Latvia	**1996 No 3167**
Lesotho (see note (d))	**1997 No 2986**
	2018 No 376
Libya	**2010 No 243**
Liechtenstein	**2012 No 3077**
Lithuania	**2001 No 3925**
	2002 No 2847
Luxembourg	**1968 No 1100**
	1980 No 567
	1984 No 364
	2010 No 237
Macedonia	**2007 No 2127**
Malawi	**1956 No 619**
	1964 No 1401
	1968 No 1101
	1979 No 302
Malaysia	**1997 No 2987**
	2010 No 2971
Malta	**1995 No 763**
Mauritius	**1981 No 1121**
	1987 No 467
	2003 No 2620

Double taxation treaties

Country	SI or SR & O Number
	2011 No 2442
	2018 No 840
Mexico	**1994 No 3212**
	2010 No 2686
Moldova	**2008 No 1795**
Mongolia	**1996 No 2598**
Montenegro (see note (c))	**1981 No 1815**
Montserrat	**1947 No 2869**
	1968 No 576
	2011 No 1083
Morocco	**1991 No 2881**
Myanmar	**1952 No 751**
Namibia	**1962 No 2352**
	1962 No 2788
	1967 No 1489
	1967 No 1490
Netherlands	**2009 No 227**
	2013 No 3143
New Zealand	**1984 No 365**
	2004 No 1274
	2008 No 1793
Nigeria	**1987 No 2057**
Norway	**2013 No 3144**
Oman	**1998 No 2568**
	2010 No 2687
Pakistan	**1987 No 2058**
Panama	**2013 No 3149**
Papua New Guinea	**1991 No 2882**
Philippines	**1978 No 184**
Poland	**2006 No 3323**
Portugal	**1969 No 599**
Qatar	**2010 No 241**
	2011 No 1684
Romania	**1977 No 57**
Russian Federation	**1994 No 3213**
St. Kitts and Nevis	**1947 No 2872**
Saudi Arabia	**2008 No 1770**
Senegal	**2015 No 1892**
Serbia (see note (c))	**1981 No 1815**
Sierra Leone	**1947 No 2873**
	1968 No 1104
Singapore	**1997 No 2988**
	2010 No 2685
	2012 No 3078
Slovak Republic (see note (b))	**1991 No 2876**
Slovenia	**2008 No 1796**
Solomon Islands	**1950 No 748**
	1968 No 574
	1974 No 1270
South Africa	**2002 No 3138**
	2011 No 2441
Spain	**2013 No 3152**
Sri Lanka	**1980 No 713**
Sudan	**1977 No 1719**
Swaziland	**1969 No 380**
Sweden	**2015 No 1891**
	2021 No 633
Switzerland	**1978 No 1408**
	1982 No 714
	1994 No 3215
	2007 No 3465
	2010 No 2689
	2012 No 3079
	2018 No 627
Taiwan	**2002 No 3137**
	2021 No 1447
Tajikistan	**2014 No 3275**
Thailand	**1981 No 1546**
Trinidad & Tobago	**1983 No 1903**
Tunisia	**1984 No 133**
Turkey	**1988 No 932**
Turkmenistan	**2016 No 1217**
Tuvalu (and Kiribati)	**1950 No 750**
	1968 No 309
	1974 No 1271
Uganda	**1993 No 1802**
Ukraine	**1993 No 1803**
	2018 No 779
USA	**2002 No 2848**
United Arab Emirates	**2016 No 754**
Uruguay	**2016 No 753**
Uzbekistan	**1994 No 770**
	2018 No 628
Venezuela	**1996 No 2599**
Vietnam	**1994 No 3216**
Yugoslavia (see note (c))	**1981 No 1815**
Zambia	**2014 No 1876**
Zimbabwe	**1982 No 1842**

Notes

(a) Entries in bold are for main agreements. Entries in Roman are for amending protocols.

(b) The convention published as *SI 1991 No 2876* is treated as remaining in force between the UK and, respectively, the Czech Republic and the Slovak Republic. (HMRC SP 5/93).

(c) The Agreement published as *SI 1981 No 1815* between the UK and Yugoslavia is regarded as in force between the UK and Bosnia-Herzegovina and Serbia and Montenegro. (HMRC SP 3/07).

(d) The 2018 treaty replaces 1997 No 2986 but where, immediately before the entry into force on 18 September 2018, an individual is entitled to the benefits of the 1997 agreement and was in receipt of pensions or other similar remuneration, or pensions paid and other payments made under a public scheme which is part of the social security system of a Contracting State, a political subdivision or a local authority thereof, the provisions of the 1997 agreement will continue to apply to such pensions and payments.

Double taxation treaties

Tax information exchange agreements

Country	SI Number
Agreements in force	
Anguilla (note (a))	2010 No 2677
Antigua and Barbuda	2011 No 1075
Aruba	2011 No 2435
Bahamas	2010 No 2684
Belize	2011 No 1685
Bermuda	2018 No 518
British Virgin Islands (note (a))	2009 No 3013
Curaçao, Sint Maarten and BES Islands	2011 No 2433
Dominica	2011 No 1686
Gibraltar (note (a))	2010 No 2680
Grenada	2011 No 1687
Guernsey (note (a))	2009 No 3011
Isle of Man	2009 No 228
Jersey (note (a))	2009 No 3012
Liberia	2011 No 2434
Liechtenstein	2010 No 2678
Macao	2015 No 801
Marshall Islands	2013 No 3153
Monaco	2015 No 804
San Marino	2011 No 1688
St Christopher and Nevis	2011 No 1077
St Lucia	2011 No 1076
St Vincent and the Grenadines	2011 No 1078
Turks and Caicos Islands (note (a))	2010 No 2679
Uruguay	2014 No 1358
Agreements signed but not in force	
Brazil	2015 No 1887
Tax compliance agreements	
Isle of Man, Guernsey, Jersey, Gibraltar	2014 No 520
USA	2015 No 878

Agreements covering taxes on capital

Country	SI/ SR& O Number
Estate duty agreements	
France	1963 No 1319
India	1956 No 998
Italy	1968 No 304
Pakistan	1957 No 1522
Capital transfer and inheritance tax agreements	
Irish Republic	1978 No 1107
Netherlands	1980 No 706
	1996 No 730
South Africa	1979 No 576
Sweden	1981 No 840
	1989 No 986
Switzerland	1994 No 3214
USA	1979 No 1454

Shipping and air transport only

Country	SI or SR & O Number
Brazil	1968 No 572
—aircraft crew only	2011 No 2723
Cameroon (air transport only)	1982 No 1841
China (air transport only)	1981 No 1119
Congo Democratic Republic	1977 No 1298
Iran (air transport only)	1960 No 2419
Lebanon	1964 No 278
Saudi Arabia	1994 No 767

Reciprocal agreements on social security

(see notes (b) and (c))

Country	SI Number
Barbados	1992 No 812
Bermuda	1969 No 1686
Bosnia-Herzegovinia	1958 No 1263
Canada	1995 No 2699
	1998 No 263
Chile	2015 No 828
Iceland (note (c))	1985 No 1202
	1992 No 3211
Isle of Man	1977 No 2150
	1989 No 483
	1989 No 2001
Israel	1957 No 1879
	1984 No 354
Jamaica	1997 No 871
Japan	2000 No 3063
Jersey and Guernsey	1994 No 2802
Korea (Republic of)	2000 No 1823
Kosovo	1958 No 1263
Macedonia	1958 No 1263
Mauritius	1981 No 1542
Montenegro	1958 No 1263
New Zealand	1964 No 495
	1983 No 1894
Norway (note (c))	1991 No 767
	1992 No 3212
Philippines	1989 No 2002
Serbia	1958 No 1263
Switzerland (note (c))	1969 No 384
Turkey	1961 No 584
USA	1984 No 1817
	1997 No 1778

Notes

(a) The 2013 and 2014 exchanges of letters amending the agreements are not yet in force.

(b) Agreements with countries containing articles specifically relating to contribution (as distinct from benefit) matters are listed.

(c) Agreements with other EC member states have been superseded for most purposes by *EC Council Regulations 883/2004* and *987/2009* and are not listed. The *Regulations* are applied also to Switzerland and, from 1 June 2012, to Iceland, Liechtenstein and Norway. Following Brexit, under the EU–UK Trade and Cooperation Agreement, the effects of the *Regulations* broadly continue to apply. For social security purposes, the UK includes Gibraltar but excludes the Isle of Man and the Channel Islands.

Foreign exchange rates averages for tax year

Country	Method of quoting	Currency per £1			
		2021/22	2020/21	2019/20	2018/19
Albania	Lek	143.280958	137.970833	140.6141667	142.6475
Algeria	Dinar	186.727808	166.886667	152.9641667	155.033333
Angola	Readj Kwanza	840.224358	785.983333	504.7191667	358.4575
Antigua	E Caribbean Dollar	3.702267	3.492542	3.454033333	3.5637
Argentina	Peso	134.622542	97.953417	65.96833333	41.434542
Armenia	Dram	679.396625	642.707500	612.795	637.659167
Aruba	Florin	2.454475	2.315417	2.2899	2.362617
Australia	Dollar	1.8529	1.836092	1.850933333	1.795092
Azerbaijan	New Manat	2.32985	2.196692	2.170275	2.24215
Bahamas	Dollar	1.371217	1.293542	1.279266667	1.319892
Bahrain	Dinar	0.51695	0.487058	0.482275	0.4978
Bangladesh	Taka	116.877292	109.718333	108.225	110.600833
Barbados	Dollar	2.742417	2.587067	2.55855	2.639783
Belarus	Rouble	3.474067	3.232717	2.670708333	2.721175
Belize	Dollar	2.742417	2.587067	2.558416667	2.638142
Benin	CFA Franc	770.204875	731.237500	754.9858333	743.184167
Bermuda	Dollar (US)	1.371217	1.293542	1.279266667	1.319892
Bhutan	Ngultrum	101.97445	96.196700	90.24666667	91.846667
Bolivia	Boliviano	9.475058	8.938317	8.839783333	9.120467
Bosnia-Herzegovina	Marka	2.296483	2.180308	2.23615	2.215933
Botswana	Pula	15.346392	14.796667	13.785	13.646925
Brazil	Real	7.383258	6.942050	5.143041667	4.944692
Brunei	Dollar	1.849633	1.773183	1.746025	1.789833
Bulgaria	Lev	2.296692	2.180367	2.243708333	2.215967
Burkina Faso	CFA Franc	770.204875	731.237500	754.9858333	743.184167
Burundi	Franc	2,720.572308	2,495.950000	2,372.325	2,367.751667

Foreign exchange rates averages for tax year

Country	Method of quoting	Currency per £1			
		2021/22	2020/21	2019/20	2018/19
Cambodia	Riel	5,377.713067	5,272.730000	5,191.7775	5,336.055833
Cameroon Republic	CFA Franc	770.204875	731.237500	754.9858333	743.184167
Canada	Dollar	1.718633	1.723967	1.693958333	1.728133
Cape Verde Islands	Escudo	129.912975	138.523333	126.7458333	125.289167
Cayman Islands	Dollar	1.124392	1.060692	1.049	1.082308
Central African Republic	CFA Franc	770.204875	731.237500	754.9858333	743.184167
Chad	CFA Franc	770.204875	731.237500	754.9858333	743.184167
Chile	Peso	1,061.542942	1,007.135000	923.7366667	863.108333
China	Renminbi Yuan	8.822225	8.789867	8.87015	8.808783
Colombia	Peso	5,246.333825	4,833.270000	4,219.970833	3,958.056667
Comoros	Franc	577.653042	548.425833	564.3633333	557.3875
Congo (Brazzaville)	CFA Franc	770.204875	731.237500	754.9858333	743.184167
Congo Dem Rep	Cong Franc	2,724.914992	2,463.205000	7,956.9025	2,138.955833
Costa Rica	Colon	856.750483	765.158333	740.8725	766.96
Cote d'Ivoire	CFA Franc	770.204875	731.237500	754.9858333	743.184167
Croatia	Kuna	8.832933	8.423958	8.515383333	8.403867
Cuba	Peso	1.371208	1.293542	1.279266667	1.319892
Czech Republic	Koruna	29.749125	29.739167	29.315	29.111667
Denmark	Krone	8.733058	8.303700	8.5666	8.449217
Djibouti	Franc	243.687983	229.883333	227.3475	234.565833
Dominica	E Caribbean Dollar	3.702267	3.492542	3.454033333	3.5637
Dominican Republic	Peso	77.971208	74.263333	66.345	65.701667
Ecuador	Dollar	1.371217	1.293542	1.279266667	1.319892
Egypt	Egyptian pound	21.528508	20.430833	21.15166667	23.5325
El Salvador	Colon	11.997025	11.317500	11.18833333	11.545833
Equatorial Guinea	CFA Franc	770.204875	731.237500	754.9858333	743.184167
Eritrea	Nakfa	20.5646	19.398333	19.18416667	19.793333
Ethiopia	Birr	62.526067	47.111667	38.07	36.584167
Eurozone	Euro (note (b))	1.174183	1.114767	1.147166667	1.132983
Fiji	Dollar	2.862567	2.767367	2.765566667	2.765633
French Polynesia	CFP franc	140.11265	133.023333	136.88	135.195833

Foreign exchange rates averages for tax year

Country	Method of quoting	Currency per £1			
		2021/22	2020/21	2019/20	2018/19
Gabon	CFA Franc	770.204875	731.237500	754.9858333	743.184167
Gambia	Dalasi	71.145883	66.932317	64.65	64.351667
Georgia	Lari	4.356567	4.127825	3.6389	3.380358
Ghana	Cedi	8.246033	7.486900	6.912391667	6.324283
Grenada/Windward Isles	E. Caribbean dollar	3.702267	3.492542	3.454033333	3.5637
Guatemala	Quetzal	10.588517	10.001933	9.837058333	10.07415
Guinea Bissau	CFA Franc	770.204875	731.237500	754.9858333	743.184167
Guinea Republic	Franc	13,226.28354	12,628.364167	11,896.815	11,955.29083
Guyana	Dollar	286.946792	270.505833	267.1966667	275.079167
Haiti	Gourde	128.812592	114.690000	114.7375	93.466067
Honduras	Lempira	33.058825	31.647500	31.405	31.7275
Hong Kong	Dollar	10.665842	10.026542	10.00035833	10.349583
Hungary	Forint	420.910308	396.121667	375.9525	362.254167
Iceland	Krona	173.975733	175.959167	157.9741667	147.640833
India	Rupee	101.973617	96.196700	90.24666667	91.846667
Indonesia	Rupiah	19,666.16168	18,809.988333	17,981.0175	18,905.83083
Iraq	Dinar	2,002.72125	1,602.635833	1,522.913333	1,501.203333
Israel	Shekel	4.40695	4.415492	4.532491667	4.783058
Jamaica	Dollar	208.703925	186.800000	171.3341667	171.441667
Japan	Yen	152.927892	136.731667	140.1766667	145.915
Jordan	Dinar	0.972192	0.917108	0.907083333	0.936617
Kazakhstan	Tenge	588.500883	546.324167	488.3433333	466.338333
Kenya	Kenyan shilling	151.35675	140.160000	130.45	133.354167
Korea (South)	Won	1,593.502258	1,506.367500	1,492.601667	1,465.995
Kuwait	Dinar	0.413583	0.396475	0.389016667	0.399475
Kyrgyz Republic	Som	116.155558	103.279167	89.25	91.198333
Laos	Kip	13,844.41001	11,834.261667	11,192.2025	11,175.88417
Lebanon	Lebanese pound	2,077.124725	1,958.484167	1,931.20	1,995.086667
Lesotho	Loti	20.347292	21.266667	18.52666667	17.850833
Liberia	Dollar	1.371217	1.293542	1.279266667	1.319892
Libya	Libyan dinar	6.211958	2.497567	1.793108333	1.8114

Foreign exchange rates averages for tax year

Country	Method of quoting	Currency per £1			
		2021/22	2020/21	2019/20	2018/19
Macao	Pataca	10.984792	10.327725	10.297525	10.659167
Macedonia	Denar	72.294242	68.645833	70.59	69.740833
Madagascar	Malagasy Ariary	5,335.710233	4,948.669167	4,680.174167	4,488.0575
Malawi	Kwacha	1,107.938783	972.155000	947.33	960.068333
Malaysia	Ringgit	5.731425	5.417408	5.302833333	5.368717
Maldive Islands	Rufiyaa	21.182592	19.932500	19.75166667	20.386667
Mali Republic	CFA Franc	770.204875	731.237500	754.9858333	743.184167
Mauritania	Ouguiya	49.851075	47.439167	352.52	470.811667
Mauritius	Rupee	57.922183	51.450000	46.05416667	45.18
Mexico	Peso	27.867567	28.140833	24.49083333	25.420833
Moldova	Leu	24.403783	22.356667	22.165	22.28
Mongolia	Tugrik	3,910.600783	3,663.994167	3,433.8275	3,311.475833
Montserrat	E Caribbean Dollar	3.702267	3.492542	3.454033333	3.5637
Morocco	Dirham	12.425783	12.065000	12.29583333	12.4575
Mozambique	Metical	86.85835	92.478333	80.17666667	80.041667
Myanmar	Kyat	2,310.2158	1,771.008333	1,940.684167	1,949.66
Nepal	Rupee	163.158283	153.920000	144.3975	146.9575
New Caledonia	CFP Franc	140.11265	133.023333	136.88	135.195833
New Zealand	Dollar	1.967325	1.959167	1.949025	1.925333
Nicaragua	Gold Cordoba	48.278775	44.655000	42.62666667	41.9925
Niger Republic	CFA Franc	770.204875	731.237500	754.9858333	743.184167
Nigeria	Naira	565.677667	501.564167	463.2416667	477.175
Norway	Krone	11.878892	12.086667	11.34583333	10.894167
Oman (Sultanate of)	Rial	0.528292	0.498067	0.492541667	0.508133
Pakistan	Rupee	227.258283	209.940833	194.5241667	167.225833
Panama	Balboa	1.371208	1.293542	1.279266667	1.319892
Papua New Guinea	Kina	4.814617	4.505708	4.341941667	4.374908
Paraguay	Guarani	9,317.166592	8,832.770833	8,049.758333	7,676.394167
Peru	New sol	5.371342	4.581367	4.268375	4.354525
Philippines	Peso	68.433592	63.600833	65.9925	69.8275
Poland	Zloty	5.370367	5.007900	4.915541667	4.855567
Qatar	Riyal	4.992908	4.709917	4.657791667	4.805792
Romania	Leu	5.792775	5.415200	5.447533333	5.2947
Russia	Rouble	107.382983	96.965000	81.9125	84.786667
Rwanda	Rwanda franc	1,375.6681	1,244.740000	1,176.019167	1,162.525

Foreign exchange rates averages for tax year

Country	Method of quoting	Currency per £1			
		2021/22	2020/21	2019/20	2018/19
São Tomé & Principe	Dobra	29,136.46667	27,681.016667	28,188.20833	27,778.32167
Saudi Arabia	Riyal	5.143233	4.852992	4.798216667	4.950583
Senegal	CFA Franc	770.204875	731.237500	754.9858333	743.184167
Serbia	Dinar	138.033525	131.072500	135.0566667	133.96
Seychelles	Seychelles rupee	21.394775	24.449167	17.81083333	18.2525
Sierra Leone	Leone	14,576.45433	12,957.001667	11,925.09167	10,797.69667
Singapore	Dollar	1.849633	1.773183	1.746025	1.788167
Solomon Islands	Dollar	11.026867	10.553000	10.33748333	10.396667
Somali Republic	Shilling	802.327075	754.263333	743.9033333	764.484167
South Africa	Rand	20.347292	21.268750	18.52666667	17.850833
Sri Lanka	Rupee	273.656017	243.107500	229.2983333	220.923333
St Christopher & Anguilla	E Caribbean Dollar	3.702267	3.492542	3.454033333	3.5637
St Lucia	E Caribbean Dollar	3.702267	3.492542	3.454033333	3.5637
St Vincent	E Caribbean Dollar	3.702267	3.492542	3.454033333	3.5637
Sudan Republic	Pound	549.858583	71.515000	59.365	39.674167
Surinam	Dollar	26.606775	14.131467	9.540825	9.847992
Swaziland	Lilangeni	20.347292	21.266667	18.52666667	17.850833
Sweden	Krona	11.977483	11.605000	12.11666667	11.714167
Switzerland	Franc	1.261917	1.195758	1.26615	1.302
Taiwan	New Taiwan Dollar	38.315242	37.559167	39.2825	40.125833
Tanzania	Tanzanian shilling	3,173.298867	2,997.416667	2,950.009167	3,023.423333
Thailand	Baht	44.561967	40.240000	39.64416667	42.57
Togo Republic	CFA Franc	770.204875	731.237500	754.9858333	743.184167
Tonga Islands	Pa anga	1.812217	1.836092	1.813441667	1.88715
Trinidad &Tobago	Dollar	9.26325	8.735967	8.637966667	8.906358
Tunisia	Dinar	3.85635	3.597400	3.706508333	3.612325
Turkey	Turkish Lira	13.726917	9.361358	7.334416667	6.743333
Turkmenistan	New Manat	4.80555	4.533900	4.484966667	4.625608
Uganda	New shilling	4,887.814	4,806.030000	4,722.220833	4,927.553333
Ukraine	Hryvnia	37.438425	35.803333	32.53	35.79
United Arab Emirates	Dirham	5.036608	4.751333	4.6984	4.848117
Uruguay	Peso uruguayo	60.047917	55.613333	46.00083333	41.600833
USA	Dollar	1.371217	1.293542	1.279266667	1.319892
Uzbekistan	Sum	14,632.27089	13,272.061667	11,547.23667	10,703.90167

Foreign exchange rates averages for tax year

Country	Method of quoting	Currency per £1			
		2021/22	2020/21	2019/20	2018/19
Vanuatu	Vatu	153.041225	148.303333	148.8058333	147.9225
Venezuela	Bolivar Fuerte	337,689.5808	310,877.333333	317,237.2425	225,552.1842
Vietnam	Dong	31,393.55474	29,998.280833	29,699.93667	30,484.0975
Wallis & Futuna Islands	CFP Franc	140.11265	133.023333	136.88	135.195833
Western Samoa	Tala	3.527625	3.395500	3.3766	3.393825
Yemen (Rep of)	Rial	344.221367	323.984167	319.9191667	330.29
Zambia	Kwacha	26.643017	25.295833	16.96333333	14.2625
Zimbabwe	Dollar	496.236267	468.124167	462.9641667	477.663333

Notes

(a) The material on pp 43–55 is reproduced from information provided by HMRC and is Crown copyright. The averages for 2021/22 are correct as at 5 May 2022.
(b) The following countries use the Euro: Austria, Belgium, Cyprus, Estonia, Finland, France, Germany, Greece, Ireland, Italy, Latvia, Lithuania, Luxembourg, Malta, The Netherlands, Portugal, Slovakia, Slovenia, Spain.

Foreign exchange rates averages for calendar year

For general use Country	Method of quoting	Currency per £1 2021	2020	2019	2018
Albania	Lek	142.095833	139.310833	139.573333	145.201667
Algeria	Dinar	185.1375	160.590833	152.099167	156.345000
Angola	Readj Kwanza	880.195	719.303333	447.933333	325.015833
Antigua	E Caribbean Dollar	3.719283	3.447167	3.445167	3.627567
Argentina	Peso	129.08	88.141750	58.739542	35.519167
Armenia	Dram	696.846667	619.242500	613.691667	647.473333
Aruba	Florin	2.46575	2.285333	2.284033	2.404958
Australia	Dollar	1.826717	1.873142	1.821708	1.784817
Azerbaijan	New Manat	2.34055	2.167325	2.164708	2.279708
Bahamas	Dollar	1.377525	1.276733	1.275983	1.343550
Bahrain	Dinar	0.519342	0.480725	0.481017	0.506725
Bangladesh	Taka	117.01	108.395833	107.621667	112.336667
Barbados	Dollar	2.755017	2.553458	2.551983	2.687092
Belarus	Rouble	3.489917	3.055558	2.664100	2.710508
Belize	Dollar	2.755017	2.553458	2.551450	2.685417
Benin	CFA Franc	760.395833	740.530833	746.490833	743.493333
Bermuda	Dollar	1.377525	1.276733	1.275983	1.343550
Bhutan	Ngultrum	101.6892	94.385833	89.925833	91.165833
Bolivia	Boliviano	9.5186	8.822192	8.817100	9.283917
Bosnia-Herzegovina	Marka	2.267242	2.200517	2.218333	2.216842
Botswana	Pula	15.165833	14.591667	13.675000	13.584425
Brazil	Real	7.369158	6.491583	4.997225	4.843425
Brunei	Dollar	1.848725	1.764075	1.741092	1.808050
Bulgaria	Lev	2.267458	2.208083	2.218375	2.216892
Burkina Faso	CFA Franc	760.395833	740.530833	746.490833	743.493333
Burundi	Franc	2,715.426667	2,440.217500	2,346.036667	2,389.508333

Foreign exchange rates averages for calendar year

For general use Country	Method of quoting	Currency per £1 2021	2020	2019	2018
Cambodia	Riel	5,605.188333	5,207.861667	5,161.497500	5,433.167500
Cameroon Republic	CFA Franc	760.395833	740.530833	746.490833	743.493333
Canada	Dollar	1.725308	1.718633	1.694733	1.735442
Cape Verde Islands	Escudo	128.2375	140.077500	125.342500	125.360000
Cayman Islands	Dollar	1.12955	1.046908	1.046317	1.101700
Central African Republic	CFA Franc	760.395833	740.530833	746.490833	743.493333
Chad	CFA Franc	760.395833	740.530833	746.490833	743.493333
Chile	Peso	1,033.0825	1,011.877500	887.849167	856.401667
China	Renminbi/Yuan	8.908242	8.836050	8.794575	8.842617
Colombia	Peso	5,105.273333	4,728.159167	4,146.051667	3,935.857500
Comoros	Franc	570.295	555.396667	557.992500	557.619167
Congo (Brazzaville)	CFA Franc	760.395833	740.530833	746.490833	743.493333
Congo Dem Rep	Cong Franc	2,729.225833	2,337.635000	7,931.699167	2,167.139167
Costa Rica	Colon	850.896667	741.578333	750.643333	769.060833
Cote d'Ivoire	CFA Franc	760.395833	740.530833	746.490833	743.493333
Croatia	Kuna	8.729233	8.498333	8.412700	8.421225
Cuba	Peso	1.377517	1.276733	1.275983	1.343550
Czech Republic	Koruna	29.786375	29.850000	29.131667	29.055000
Denmark	Krone	8.621517	8.418783	8.468158	8.447250
Djibouti	Franc	244.806667	226.896667	226.764167	238.769167
Dominica	E Caribbean Dollar	3.719283	3.447167	3.445167	3.627567
Dominican Republic	Peso	78.701667	71.733333	65.210000	66.312500
Ecuador	Dollar	1.377525	1.276733	1.275983	1.343550
Egypt	Egyptian pound	21.621667	20.204167	21.734167	23.943333
El Salvador	Colon	12.050833	11.170000	11.160833	11.752500
Equatorial Guinea	CFA Franc	760.395833	740.530833	746.490833	743.493333
Eritrea	Nakfa	20.6575	19.146667	19.135000	20.147500
Ethiopia	Birr	59.2825	44.015833	36.790833	36.927500
Eurozone	Euro (note (b))	1.159233	1.128925	1.134225	1.133458
Fiji	Dollar	2.841058	2.780583	2.741392	2.779633
French Polynesia	CFP franc	138.3275	134.714167	135.334167	135.252500

Foreign exchange rates averages for calendar year

For general use

Country	Method of quoting	Currency per £1			
		2021	2020	2019	2018
Gabon	CFA Franc	760.395833	740.530833	746.490833	743.493333
Gambia	Dalasi	70.8975	66.004817	63.955833	64.870000
Georgia	Lari	4.455608	3.935558	3.560042	3.390500
Ghana	Cedi	8.115208	7.308000	6.725642	6.255850
Grenada/Windward Isles	E. Caribbean dollar	3.719283	3.447167	3.445167	3.627567
Guatemala	Quetzal	10.658333	9.838883	9.897775	10.059158
Guinea Bissau	CFA Franc	760.395833	740.530833	746.490833	743.493333
Guinea Republic	Franc	13,592.07	12,279.964167	11,730.221667	12,140.861667
Guyana	Dollar	288.2525	266.823333	266.640000	279.440833
Haiti	Gourde	119.556667	120.159167	110.145000	90.108567
Honduras	Lempira	33.073333	31.422500	31.225000	32.034167
Hong Kong	Dollar	10.698183	9.904692	9.995125	10.527500
Hungary	Forint	414.65	394.454167	367.214167	360.226667
Iceland	Krona	174.98	172.778333	156.032500	144.255000
India	Rupee	101.688367	94.385833	89.925833	91.165833
Indonesia	Rupiah	19,678.37667	18,468.680833	18,081.008333	18,993.146667
Iraq	Dinar	1,981.900833	1,520.055000	1,519.003333	1,526.995000
Israel	Shekel	4.463075	4.426167	4.590842	4.796125
Jamaica	Dollar	206.474167	181.420000	168.676667	172.675000
Japan	Yen	150.054167	136.966667	140.052500	148.226667
Jordan	Dinar	0.97665	0.905200	0.904850	0.953292
Kazakhstan	Tenge	585.908333	526.415000	486.048333	457.677500
Kenya	Kenyan shilling	151.085833	135.229167	130.166667	136.114167
Korea (South)	Won	1,570.145833	1,511.498333	1,472.813333	1,475.541667
Kuwait	Dinar	0.415833	0.391633	0.387808	0.405575
Kyrgyz Republic	Som	116.456667	97.189167	89.015000	92.521667
Laos	Kip	13,250.84083	11,536.412500	11,057.975000	11,289.119167
Lebanon	Pound	2,088.468333	1,930.905000	1,924.861667	2,032.495000
Lesotho	Loti	20.205	20.923333	18.305000	17.507500
Liberia	Dollar	1.377525	1.276733	1.275983	1.343550
Libya	Libyan Dinar	5.846542	1.775383	1.784458	1.827208

Foreign exchange rates averages for calendar year

For general use Country	Method of quoting	Currency per £1 2021	2020	2019	2018
Macao	Pataca	11.018333	10.201058	10.293358	10.843333
Macedonia	Denar	71.3725	69.519167	69.791667	69.770000
Madagascar	Malagasy Ariary	5,286.916667	4,863.433333	4,618.100000	4,454.696667
Malawi	Kwacha	1,097.516667	947.640000	942.931667	975.765833
Malaysia	Ringgit	5.7043	5.374058	5.291067	5.409158
Maldive Islands	Rufiyaa	21.259167	19.687500	19.715833	20.729167
Mali Republic	CFA Franc	760.395833	740.530833	746.490833	743.493333
Mauritania	Ouguiya	50.075	47.225000	455.907500	478.062500
Mauritius	Rupee	56.763333	49.938333	45.067500	45.548333
Mexico	Peso	27.799167	27.360000	24.652500	25.654167
Moldova	Leu	24.3325	22.127500	22.281667	22.589167
Mongolia	Tugrik	3,924.9125	3,580.108333	3,389.214167	3,296.170833
Montserrat	E Caribbean Dollar	3.719283	3.447167	3.445167	3.627567
Morocco	Dirham	12.355	12.150833	12.225833	12.585833
Mozambique	Metical	91.033333	87.615000	79.435000	80.731667
Myanmar	Kyat	2,180.525	1,782.799167	1,959.816667	1,915.314167
Nepal	Rupee	162.703333	151.020833	143.885000	145.868333
New Caledonia	CFP Franc	138.3275	134.714167	135.334167	135.252500
New Zealand	Dollar	1.943825	1.982358	1.921167	1.931267
Nicaragua	Gold Cordoba	48.303333	43.752500	42.040833	42.225000
Niger Republic	CFA Franc	760.395833	740.530833	746.490833	743.493333
Nigeria	Naira	562.569167	483.495000	461.618333	484.997500
Norway	Krone	11.81	12.116667	11.161667	10.879167
Oman (Sultanate of)	Rial	0.530308	0.491600	0.491283	0.517233
Pakistan	Rupee	222.594167	205.564167	188.920000	160.697500
Panama	Balboa	1.377517	1.276733	1.275983	1.343550
Papua New Guinea	Kina	4.839467	4.410667	4.317808	4.406750
Paraguay	Guarani	9,333.338333	8,614.231667	7,872.609167	7,674.501667
Peru	New sol	5.291608	4.430742	4.253775	4.402258
Philippines	Peso	67.805542	63.585833	66.444167	70.557500
Poland	Zloty	5.286592	5.003908	4.871825	4.819975
Qatar	Riyal	5.015858	4.648642	4.645950	4.891900
Romania	Leu	5.698425	5.455892	5.370883	5.275600
Russia	Rouble	102.370833	91.295000	82.883333	83.146667
Rwanda	Rwanda franc	1,369.264167	1,213.141667	1,159.481667	1,169.408333

Foreign exchange rates averages for calendar year

For general use Country	Method of quoting	Currency per £1 2021	2020	2019	2018
São Tome & Principé	Dobra	28,749.33333	27,989.925000	27,830.600000	27,773.471667
Saudi Arabia	Riyal	5.166683	4.789858	4.785925	5.039008
Senegal	CFA Franc	760.395833	740.530833	746.490833	743.493333
Serbia	Dinar	136.270833	132.730000	133.750000	134.122500
Seychelles	Seychelles rupee	23.761667	21.707500	17.756667	18.529167
Sierra Leone	Leone	14,245.12833	12,664.014167	11,477.059167	10,709.942500
Singapore	Dollar	1.848725	1.764075	1.739425	1.808050
Solomon Islands	Dollar	11.051667	10.488000	10.222483	10.510833
Somali Republic	Shilling	805.554167	743.965833	741.514167	780.475833
South Africa	Rand	20.205	20.925417	18.305000	17.507500
Sri Lanka	Rupee	271.3975	236.467500	228.442500	215.935833
St Chrisopher & Anguilla	E Caribbean Dollar	3.719283	3.447167	3.445167	3.627567
St Lucia	E Caribbean Dollar	3.719283	3.447167	3.445167	3.627567
St Vincent	E Caribbean Dollar	3.719283	3.447167	3.445167	3.627567
Sudan Republic	Pound	420.705	68.125000	59.182500	27.970775
Surinam	Dollar	24.3425	11.709608	9.516350	10.025850
Swaziland	Lilangeni	20.205	20.923333	18.305000	17.507500
Sweden	Krona	11.7425	11.870833	11.943333	11.581667
Switzerland	Franc	1.257175	1.209258	1.268692	1.311442
Taiwan	New Taiwan Dollar	38.569167	37.768333	39.425833	40.379167
Tanzania	Tanzanian shilling	3,191.265833	2,953.545000	2,946.275833	3,055.229167
Thailand	Baht	43.768017	39.922500	39.945833	43.361667
Togo Republic	CFA Franc	760.395833	740.530833	746.490833	743.493333
Tonga Islands	Pa anga	1.786033	1.873142	1.876275	1.784817
Trinidad &Tobago	Dollar	9.310583	8.620492	8.615733	9.067208
Tunisia	Dinar	3.814233	3.599142	3.751750	3.478283
Turkey	Turkish Lira	11.579225	8.765433	7.095000	6.343417
Turkmenistan	New Manat	4.828742	4.476125	4.474533	4.707442
Uganda	New shilling	4,955.909167	4,744.462500	4,715.306667	4,996.244167
Ukraine	Hryvnia	37.650833	34.065000	33.555000	36.569167
United Arab Emirates	Dirham	5.059783	4.689050	4.686892	4.934967
Uruguay	Peso uruguayo	59.855833	53.310000	44.200000	40.993333
USA	Dollar	1.377525	1.276733	1.275983	1.343550
Uzbekistan	Sum	14,588.7475	12,779.250833	11,137.847500	10,827.040000

Foreign exchange rates averages for calendar year

For general use

Country	Method of quoting	Currency per £1			
		2021	2020	2019	2018
Vanuatu	Vatu	152.045	149.078333	147.373333	148.480000
Venezuela	Bolivar Fuerte	333,147.7217	312,878.370833	315,942.907500	148,482.375833
Vietnam	Dong	31,620.9925	29,649.391667	29,637.330000	30,853.250833
Wallis & Futuna Islands	CFP Franc	138.3275	134.714167	135.334167	135.252500
Western Samoa	Tala	3.507625	3.397967	3.346683	3.419792
Yemen (Rep of)	Rial	346.2125	319.280833	319.185833	336.214167
Zambia	Kwacha	28.196667	22.721667	16.060833	13.795833
Zimbabwe	Dollar	498.515	462.043333	461.775833	486.223333

Notes

(a) The material on pp 43–55 is reproduced from information provided by HMRC and is Crown copyright. The averages for 2021/22 are correct as at 5 May 2022.
(b) The following countries use the Euro: Austria, Belgium, Cyprus, Estonia, Finland, France, Germany, Greece, Ireland, Italy, Latvia, Lithuania, Luxembourg, Malta, The Netherlands, Portugal, Slovakia, Slovenia, Spain.

Foreign exchange rates at specified dates

For general use Country	Method of quoting	Currency per £1							
		31.3.22	31.12.21	31.3.21	31.12.20	31.3.20	31.12.19	31.3.19	31.12.18
Australia	Dollar	1.7506	1.8607	1.8043	1.7709	2.0167	1.8743	1.8458	1.8091
Canada	Dollar	1.6401	1.7259	1.7316	1.7363	1.7582	1.7122	1.7535	1.7395
Denmark	Krone	8.7765	8.8575	8.6959	8.2306	8.4041	8.7442	8.7452	8.314
Eurozone	Euro (note (b))	1.18	1.1911	1.1692	1.1064	1.1254	1.1705	1.1715	1.1141
Hong Kong	Dollar	10.3114	10.5279	10.6597	10.5506	9.6246	10.2117	10.3185	9.9714
Japan	Yen	160.7428	155.4195	151.2457	140.5114	134.16	142.9100	146.1715	139.7323
Norway	Krone	11.2926	11.8857	11.7222	11.6191	13.1533	11.5128	11.2768	11.0282
South Africa	Rand	19.0397	21.5793	20.4492	19.8767	22.30	18.4622	18.6034	18.3206
Sweden	Krona	12.188	12.2103	11.9964	11.14	12.47	12.2205	12.1817	11.2915
Switzerland	Franc	1.215	1.2332	1.2932	1.2016	1.1914	1.2709	1.3112	1.2555
USA	Dollar	1.3174	1.3497	1.3712	1.361	1.2412	1.3114	1.3145	1.2736

Notes

(a) The material on pp 43–55 is reproduced from information provided by HMRC and is Crown copyright. The spot rates for 31.3.22 are correct as at 5 May 2022.
(b) The following countries use the Euro: Austria, Belgium, Cyprus, Estonia, Finland, France, Germany, Greece, Ireland, Italy, Latvia, Lithuania, Luxembourg, Malta, The Netherlands, Portugal, Slovakia, Slovenia, Spain.

Government securities

Security		Interest dates
Treasury Gilt/Stock Index Linked		
0⅛%	2024	22 Mar/Sept
0⅛%	2026	22 Mar/Sept
0⅛%	2028	10 Feb/Aug
0⅛%	2029	22 Mar/Sept
0⅛%	2031	10 Feb/Aug
0⅛%	2036	22 May/Nov
0⅛%	2039	22 Mar/Sep
0⅛%	2041	10 Feb/Aug
0⅛%	2044	22 Mar/Sept
0⅛%	2046	22 Mar/Sept
0⅛%	2048	10 Feb/Aug
0⅛%	2051	22 Mar/Sept
0⅛%	2056	22 May/Nov
0⅛%	2058	22 Mar/Sept
0⅛%	2065	22 May/Nov
0⅛%	2068	22 Mar/Sept
0⅛%	2073	22 Mar/Sept
0¼%	2052	22 Mar/Sept
0⅜%	2062	22 Mar/Sept
0½%	2050	22 Mar/Sept
0⅝%	2040	22 Mar/Sept
0⅝%	2042	22 May/Nov
0¾%	2034	22 Mar/Sept
0¾%	2047	22 May/Nov
1⅛%	2037	22 May/Nov
1⅛%	2039	31 Jan/Jul
1¼%	2027	22 May/Nov
1¼%	2032	22 May/Nov
1¼%	2055	22 May/Nov
1⅞%	2022	22 May/Nov
2%	2035	26 Jan/Jul
2½%	2024	17 Jan/Jul
4⅛%	2030	22 Jan/Jul
Treasury Gilt/Stock		
0¼%	2025	31 Jan/Jul
0¼%	2031	31 Jan/Jul
0½%	2022	22 Jan/Jul
0½%	2029	31 Jan/Jul
0½%	2061	22 Apr/Oct
0⅛%	2023	31 Jan/Jul
0⅛%	2024	31 Jan/Jul
0⅛%	2026	30 Jan/Jul
0⅛%	2028	31 Jan/Jul
0⅜%	2026	22 Apr/Oct
0⅜%	2030	22 Apr/Oct
0⅝%	2025	7 Jun/Dec
0⅝%	2035	31 Jan/Jul
0⅝%	2050	22 Apr/Oct
0⅞%	2029	22 Apr/Oct
0⅞%	2033	31 Jan/Jul
0⅞%	2046	31 Jan/Jul
0¾%	2023	22 Jan/Jul
1%	2024	22 Apr/Oct
1%	2032	31 Jan/Jul
1⅛%	2073	22 Apr/Oct
1¼%	2027	22 Jan/Jul
1¼%	2041	22 Apr/Oct
1¼%	2051	31 Jan/Jul
1½%	2026	22 Jan/Jul
1½%	2053	31 Jan/Jul
1½%	2047	22 Jan/Jul
1⅝%	2028	22 Apr/Oct
1⅝%	2054	22 Apr/Oct
1⅝%	2071	22 Apr/Oct
1¾%	2022	7 Mar/Sept
1¾%	2037	7 Mar/Sept
1¾%	2049	22 Jan/Jul
1¾%	2057	22 Jan/Jul
2%	2025	7 Mar/Sept
2¼%	2023	7 Mar/Sept
2½%	2065	22 Jan/Jul
2¾%	2024	7 Mar/Sept
3¼%	2044	22 Jan/Jul
3½%	2045	22 Jan/Jul
3½%	2068	22 Jan/Jul
3¾%	2052	22 Jan/Jul
4%	2060	22 Jan/Jul
4¼%	2027	7 Jun/Dec
4¼%	2032	7 Jun/Dec
4¼%	2036	7 Mar/Sept
4¼%	2039	7 Mar/Sept
4¼%	2040	7 Jun/Dec
4¼%	2046	7 Jun/Dec
4¼%	2049	7 Jun/Dec
4¼%	2055	7 Jun/Dec
4½%	2034	7 Mar/Sept
4½%	2042	7 Jun/Dec
4¾%	2030	7 Jun/Dec
4¾%	2038	7 Jun/Dec
5%	2025	7 Mar/Sept
6%	2028	7 Jun/Dec

Notes

(a) The government securities listed above are those in issue on 11 April 2022.

(b) Interest on all government securities is exempt from income tax if beneficially owned by persons who are not resident (for securities issued before 6 April 2013, not ordinarily resident) in the UK. [*FA 1998, s 161*; *ITTOIA 2005, ss 713, 714*].
The securities are also excluded property for inheritance tax purposes if beneficially owned by persons who are not resident (ordinarily resident) in the UK. [*IHTA 1984, s 6(2)*].

Income tax rates

Starting, basic, higher and additional rates

	Taxable income	Rate	Tax	Cumulative tax
2022/23	£		£	£
Basic rate (notes (f), (g))	0–37,700	20%	7,540	7,540
Higher rate	37,701–150,000	40%	44,920	52,460
Additional rate	Over 150,000	45%		
2021/22	£		£	£
Basic rate (notes (f), (g))	0–37,700	20%	7,540	7,540
Higher rate	37,701–150,000	40%	44,920	52,460
Additional rate	Over 150,000	45%		
2020/21	£		£	£
Basic rate (notes (f), (g))	0–37,500	20%	7,500	7,500
Higher rate	37,501–150,000	40%	45,000	52,500
Additional rate	Over 150,000	45%		
2019/20	£		£	£
Basic rate (notes (f), (g))	0–37,500	20%	7,500	7,500
Higher rate	37,501–150,000	40%	45,000	52,500
Additional rate	Over 150,000	45%		
2018/19	£		£	£
Basic rate (note (f))	0–34,500	20%	6,900	6,900
Higher rate	34,501–150,000	40%	46,200	53,100
Additional rate	Over 150,000	45%		
2017/18	£		£	£
Basic rate (note (f))	0–33,500	20%	6,700	6,700
Higher rate	33,501–150,000	40%	46,600	53,300
Additional rate	Over 150,000	45%		
2016/17	£		£	£
Basic rate (note (f))	0–32,000	20%	6,400	6,400
Higher rate	32,001–150,000	40%	47,200	53,600
Additional rate	Over 150,000	45%		

Notes

(a) A starting rate for savings band of **£5,000** for individuals applies. Where an individual's non-savings income is less than the starting rate limit for savings, the savings income is taxable at the 0% starting rate for savings up to the limit. Where taxable non-savings income exceeds the limit, the starting rate for savings does not apply. Income taxable at the starting rate for savings does not fall within the savings allowance (see page 60).

(b) **Dividend income.** A 0% rate applies to the extent that dividend income falls within the dividend allowance (see page 60). Where dividend income falls within the basic rate band (treating dividend income as the top slice of taxable income), the rate of income tax is 8.75%(7.5% for 2021/22 and earlier years). Dividend income within the higher rate band is taxable at the rate of 33.75% (32.5% for 2021/22 and earlier years) and such income within the additional rate band is taxable at the rate of 39.35% (38.1% for 2021/22 and earlier years). Discretionary and accumulation trusts pay tax on dividends at the rate of 39.35% (38.1% for 2021/22 and earlier years). No tax credits are applied.

(c) **Interest income.** Interest income (i.e. bank and building society interest, interest distributions from authorised unit trusts, interest on gilts and other securities including qualifying corporate bonds and purchased life annuities) is treated as the second top slice of taxable income behind dividends. A 0% rate applies to the extent that such income falls within the savings allowance (see page 60). Where the income falls within the basic rate band, it is chargeable at 20% and to the extent that it falls within the higher rate band it is taxed at 40%. Interest income within the additional rate band is taxed at the rate of 45% for 2016/17 to 2022/23. See note (a) above where the income falls within the starting rate for savings band.
Tax is not deducted from bank and building society interest. For 2017/18 onwards tax is not deducted from interest distributions from open-ended investment companies, authorised unit trusts and investment trust companies, and from interest on peer-to-peer loans.

(d) **Personal representatives etc.** The starting, higher and additional rates do not apply to persons other than individuals (e.g. personal representatives). Tax is chargeable at the ordinary dividend rate for dividends (covered by the tax credit where applicable) and at the basic rate for other income.

(e) Trusts for vulnerable beneficiaries can be taxed (on election) as if the income arising were that of the beneficiary, taking into account personal allowances and the starting, basic, higher and additional rate bands.
Where any trust income consists of or includes income otherwise chargeable at the dividend trust rate or the trust rate ('special trust tax rate income'), so much of that income as does not exceed £1,000 is chargeable to income tax at the basic rate, savings rate or the ordinary dividend rate, depending on the nature of the income.

Income tax rates

Scottish rate of income tax (note (f))

	Taxable income	Rate	Tax	Cumulative tax
2022/23	£		£	£
Starter rate	0–2,162	19%	410	410
Basic rate	2,163–13,118	20%	2,191	2,601
Intermediate rate	13,119–31,092	21%	3,774	6,375
Higher rate	31,093–150,000	41%	48,752	55,127
Top rate	Over 150,000	46%	–	–
2021/22	£		£	£
Starter rate	0–2,097	19%	398	398
Basic rate	2,098–12,726	20%	2,125	2,523
Intermediate rate	12,727–31,092	21%	3,856	6,379
Higher rate	31,093–150,000	41%	48,752	55,131
Top rate	Over 150,000	46%	–	–
2020/21	£		£	£
Starter rate	0–2,085	19%	396	396
Basic rate	2,086–12,658	20%	2,114	2,510
Intermediate rate	12,659–30,930	21%	3,837	6,347
Higher rate	30,931–150,000	41%	48,818	55,165
Top rate	Over 150,000	46%	–	–
2019/20	£		£	£
Starter rate	0–2,049	19%	389	389
Basic rate	2,050–12,444	20%	2,079	2,468
Intermediate rate	12,445–30,930	21%	3,882	6,350
Higher rate	30,931–150,000	41%	48,818	55,168
Top rate	Over 150,000	46%		
2018/19	£		£	£
Starter rate	0–2,000	19%	380	380
Basic rate	2,001–12,150	20%	2,030	2,410
Intermediate rate	12,151–31,580	21%	4,080	6,490
Higher rate	31,581–150,000	41%	48,552	55,042
Top rate	Over 150,000	46%		
2017/18	£		£	£
Basic rate	0–31,500	20%	6,300	6,300
Higher rate	31,501–150,000	40%	47,400	53,700
Additional rate	Over 150,000	45%		
2016/17				
Basic rate	0–32,000	20%	6,400	6,400
Higher rate	32,001–150,000	40%	47,200	53,600
Additional rate	Over 150,000	45%		

Welsh rate of income tax (note (g))

	Taxable income	Rate	Tax	Cumulative tax
2022/23	£		£	£
Basic rate	0–37,700	20%	7,540	7,540
Higher rate	37,701–150,000	40%	44,920	52,460
Additional rate	Over 150,000	45%		
2021/22	£		£	£
Basic rate	0–37,700	20%	7,540	7,540
Higher rate	37,701–150,000	40%	44,920	52,460
Additional rate	Over 150,000	45%		
2020/21	£		£	£
Basic rate	0–37,500	20%	7,500	7,500
Higher rate	37,501–150,000	40%	45,000	52,500
Additional rate	Over 150,000	45%		
2019/20	£		£	£
Basic rate	0–37,500	20%	7,500	7,500
Higher rate	37,501–150,000	40%	45,000	52,500
Additional rate	Over 150,000	45%		

Trust rate (note (f))

	Rate
2016/17–2022/23	45%

Construction industry sub-contractors' rates

	Rate
Registered rate	20%
Unregistered rate	30%

Notes

(f) **Scottish rate of income tax.** From 6 April 2016 a Scottish rate of income tax applies to Scottish taxpayers' non-dividend, non-savings income. [*Scotland Act 2016*]. From 2017/18 the Scottish Parliament has been able to set its own Scottish income tax rates and bands and did so from 2018/19 onwards when the higher rate and additional rate were increased by 1% over UK rates, and the basic rate band was split into three, giving a total of five tax bands. The UK basic rate band still applies to Scottish taxpayers' dividend and savings income. [*Scotland Act 1998*].

(g) **Welsh rate of income tax.** From 6 April 2019 a Welsh rate of income tax applies to Welsh taxpayers' non-dividend, non-savings income. [*Government of Wales Act 2006; Wales Act 2014*]. The Welsh basic, higher and additional rates are calculated by reducing each of the UK basic, higher and additional rates by ten percentage points and then adding the Welsh rate. This means for 2019/20 to 2022/23 the rates of income tax paid by Welsh taxpayers stay the same as for England and Northern Ireland.

Income tax allowances

	2022/23	2021/22	2020/21	2019/20	2018/19	2017/18	2016/17
	£	£	£	£	£	£	£
Personal allowance	12,570	12,570	12,500	12,500	11,850	11,500	11,000
Transferable marriage allowance (note (a))	1,260	1,260	1,250	1,250	1,190	1,150	1,100
Income limit (allowance reduced by ½ excess)	100,000	100,000	100,000	100,000	100,000	100,000	100,000
Married couple's allowance — either partner born before 6.4.1935 and over 75 (note (b))	9,415	9,125	9,075	8,915	8,695	8,445	8,355
Income limit (allowance reduced by ½ excess, after reduction of personal allowance)	31,400	30,400	30,200	29,600	28,900	28,000	27,700
— reduced to minimum if income exceeds	42,950	41,590	41,330	40,530	39,570	38,370	37,970
— Minimum where income exceeds limit	3,640	3,530	3,510	3,450	3,360	3,260	3,220
Savings allowance (note (c))							
— Basic rate taxpayer	1,000	1,000	1,000	1,000	1,000	1,000	1,000
— Higher rate taxpayer	500	500	500	500	500	500	500
Dividend allowance (note (d))	2,000	2,000	2,000	2,000	2,000	5,000	5,000
Trading allowance (note (e))	1,000	1,000	1,000	1,000	1,000	1,000	—
Property allowance (note (e))	1,000	1,000	1,000	1,000	1,000	1,000	—
Blind person's allowance	2,600	2,520	2,500	2,450	2,390	2,320	2,290

Notes

(a) A spouse or civil partner may elect to transfer part of their personal allowance to their spouse or civil partner. The relief is only available where neither spouse or civil partner is a higher or additional rate (or from 2018/19 a Scottish higher or top rate) taxpayer. It is not available if either spouse or partner makes a claim to the married couple's allowance. With effect from 29 November 2017, regardless of when death occurred, transfers can be made on behalf of a deceased spouse or partner or from a surviving spouse / partner to a deceased spouse / partner.

(b) The married couple's allowance is available only where at least one of the spouses or civil partners reached the age of 65 before 6 April 2000.

For marriages entered into before 5 December 2005, the allowance is given initially to the husband and the amount is determined by the level of his income. For marriages and civil partnerships entered into on or after that date, the allowance is initially given to whichever of the two individuals has the higher total income for the tax year and the amount is determined by the level of that individual's income. (If their total incomes are exactly the same, the partners may make a joint election to determine which of them receives the allowance.) A couple who married before 5 December 2005 may make a joint election for the rules for marriages on or after that date to apply.

The partner not initially entitled can elect in advance to be entitled to claim one-half of the minimum allowance. A couple may jointly elect for the full amount of the minimum allowance to be transferred between them (although the partner initially entitled can subsequently elect to be able to transfer back one-half of the basic allowance).

The allowance is given as a reduction in income tax liability restricted to the lower of 10% of the amount of the allowance and the claimant's total income tax liability.

(c) The savings allowance is not available to additional rate taxpayers. An individual is an additional rate taxpayer for this purpose if any income falls within the additional rate band. An individual is a higher rate taxpayer if any income falls within the higher rate band but no income falls within the additional rate band. Income, for this purpose, includes income which falls (or would otherwise fall) within the savings allowance and income falling within the dividend allowance. See page 58 for the effect of the allowance.

(d) See page 58 for the effect of the allowance.

(e) From 2017/18 onwards a trading allowance and a property allowance of £1,000 each per year are available to certain individuals. They are not available on income of partners or close company participators, or where rent-a-room relief could be claimed. Where total receipts are no more than £1,000, the allowance is given automatically, no tax is payable and the income need not be declared. A election can be made for relief not to apply at all, or for partial relief to apply where receipts exceed £1,000 so that the allowance rather than expenses is deducted from gross receipts.

	2008/09 onwards
	£
Agriculture — all workers	100
Aluminium (Note (b))	
Continual casting and process operators, de-dimplers, driers, drill punchers, dross unloaders, firemen, furnace operators and their helpers, leaders, mouldmen, pourers, remelt department labourers, roll flatteners	140
Cable hands, case-makers, labourers, mates, truck drivers and measurers, storekeepers	80
Apprentices	60
All other workers	120
Banks and building societies — uniformed doormen and messengers	60
Brass and copper — all workers	120
Building	
Joiners and carpenters	140
Cement workers and roofing felt and asphalt labourers	80
Labourers and navvies	60
All other workers	120
Building materials	
Stone masons	120
Tile makers and labourers	60
All other workers	80
Clothing	
Lacemakers, hosiery bleachers, dyers, scourers and knitters, and knitwear bleachers and dyers	60
All other workers	60
Constructional engineering (Note (b))	
Blacksmiths and their strikers, burners, caulkers, chippers, drillers, erectors, fitters, holders up, markers off, platers, riggers, riveters, rivet heaters, scaffolders, sheeters, template workers, turners and welders	140
Banksmen labourers, shophelpers, slewers and straighteners	80
Apprentices and storekeepers	60
All other workers	100
Docks and inland waterways	
Dockers, dredger drivers and hopper steerers	80
All other workers	60
Electrical and electricity supply	
Those workers incurring laundry costs only	60
All other workers	120
Engineering (trades ancillary to)	

	2008/09 onwards
	£
Pattern makers	140
Labourers, supervisory and unskilled workers	80
Apprentices and storekeepers	60
Motor mechanics in garage repair shops	120
All other workers	120
Fire service	
Uniformed fire fighters and fire officers	80
Food — all workers	60
Forestry — all workers	100
Glass — all workers	80
Healthcare (staff in the NHS, private hospitals and nursing homes)	
Ambulance staff on active service	185
Nurses, midwives, chiropodists, dental nurses, occupational, speech and other therapists, healthcare assistants, phlebotomists, physiotherapists, radiographers. See note (d) below for shoes and stockings/tights/socks allowances	125
Plaster room orderlies, hospital porters, ward clerks, sterile supply workers, hospital domestics, hospital catering staff	125
Laboratory staff, pharmacists, pharmacy assistants	80
Uniformed ancillary staff, maintenance workers, grounds staff, drivers, parking attendants and security guards, receptionists and other uniformed staff	80
Heating	
Pipe fitters and plumbers	120
Coverers, laggers, domestic glaziers, heating engineers and their mates	120
All gas workers and all other workers	100
Iron and steel	
Day labourers, general labourers, stockmen, timekeepers, warehouse staff and weighmen	80
Apprentices	60
All other workers	140
Iron mining	
Fillers, miners and underground workers	120
All other workers	100
Leather	
Curriers (wet workers), fellmongering workers and tanning operatives (wet)	80
All other workers	60
Particular engineering (Note (b))	
Pattern makers	140

	2008/09 onwards £
All chainmakers—cleaners, galvanisers, tinners and wire drawers in the wire drawing industry—toolmakers in the lockmaking industry	120
Apprentices and storekeepers	60
All other workers	80
Police force	
Uniformed police officers (ranks up to and including Chief Inspector) and community support officers	140
Precious metals—all workers	100
Printing	
Letterpress section—electrical engineers (rotary presses), electrotypers, ink and roller markers, machine minders (rotary), maintenance engineers (rotary presses) and stereotypers	140
Bench hands (periodical and bookbinding section), compositors and readers (letterpress section), telecommunication and electronic section wireroom operators, warehousemen (paper box making section)	60
All other workers	100
Prisons	
Uniformed prison officers	80
Public transport	
Garage hands (including cleaners)	80
Conductors and drivers	60
Quarrying — all workers	100
Railways	
All workers except craftsmen	100
For craftsmen see the appropriate category (eg engineers)	

	2008/09 onwards £
Seamen	
Carpenters (passenger liners)	165
Carpenters (cargo vessels, tankers, coasters and ferries)	140
Shipyards	
Blacksmiths and their strikers, boilermakers, burners, carpenters, caulkers, drillers, furnacemen (platers), holders up, fitters, platers, plumbers, riveters, sheet iron workers, shipwrights, tubers and welders	140
Labourers	80
Apprentices and storekeepers	60
All other workers	100
Textiles and textile printing	
Carders, carding engineers, overlookers and technicians in spinning mills	120
All other workers	80
Vehicles	
Builders, railway vehicle repairers, and railway wagon lifters	140
Railway vehicle painters, letterers and builders' and repairers' assistants	80
All other workers	60
Wood and furniture	
Carpenters, cabinet makers, joiners, wood carvers and woodcutting machinists	140
Artificial limb makers (other than in wood), organ builders and packing-case makers	120
Coopers not providing own tools, labourers, polishers and upholsterers	60
All other workers	100

Notes

(a) The table above is reproduced from the HMRC Employment Income Manual, EIM 32712 and sets out the flat rate expenses agreed under *ITEPA 2003, s 367*. An employee may instead request a deduction under *ITEPA 2003, s 336* for the actual expenses incurred but should then retain evidence to demonstrate the expenditure.

(b) In the table above: (i) in the entry relating to aluminium, 'firemen' means persons engaged to light and maintain furnaces; (ii) 'constructional engineering' means engineering undertaken on a construction site, including buildings, shipyards, bridges, roads and other similar operations; and (iii) 'particular engineering' means engineering undertaken on a commercial basis in a factory or workshop for the purposes of producing components such as wire, springs, nails and locks.

(c) For flat rate expenses for uniformed airline pilots, co-pilots and other flight deck crew see HMRC Employment Income Manual EIM 50050 and for cabin crew see EIM 50070. For flat rate laundry expenses allowances for armed forces personnel (other than officers) see EIM 50125.

(d) For flat rate expenses for nurses, midwives, auxiliaries, students, dental nurses, nursing assistants and healthcare assistants or workers see HMRC Employment Income Manual EIM 67200 where the wearing of a prescribed style or colour for stockings/tights/socks (style only for shoes) is obligatory.

(e) Correct as at 11 April 2022.

Business use of own vehicle

Vehicle	Rate per business mile
Car or goods vehicle	45p for the first 10,000 miles
	25p after that
Motor cycle	24p

Notes

(a) If, in computing the profits of a trade, profession or vocation carried on by an individual or partnership of individuals, a deduction would otherwise by allowable for qualifying expenditure in relation to a car, goods vehicle or motor cycle, a fixed rate deduction can be made in respect of the expenditure. This applies also where the expenditure would be allowable but for the fact that it is capital expenditure. If a fixed rate deduction is made no other deduction is allowed for the expenditure for that or any other period. No capital allowances (or no further capital allowances) can be claimed on a vehicle once a fixed rate deduction is made. From 2017/18 deductions for vehicle expenditure are available to those carrying on a property business.

(b) Qualifying expenditure is expenditure incurred in respect of the acquisition, ownership, hire, leasing or other use of a vehicle, other than incidental expenses incurred in connection with a particular journey.

(c) The 10,000 mile band for which 45p per mile is available is shared between all the vehicles used for the trade etc. and in relation to which a fixed rate deduction is made for the period.

[*ITTOIA 2005, ss 94B–94G; FA 2018, s 36*]

Business use of home

Number of hours worked per month	Applicable amount per month
	£
25 or more	10
51 or more	18
101 or more	26

Notes

(a) Where, in computing the profits of a trade, profession or vocation for a period, a deduction would otherwise be allowable for the use of the trader's home for the purposes of the trade etc., a fixed rated deduction can be made instead. The amount of the deduction for a period is the sum of the applicable amounts for each month, or part of a month, falling in the period.

(b) The fixed rate deduction can be used by individuals and partnerships of individuals.

[*ITTOIA 2005, s 94H*]

Private use of business premises

Number of occupants	Disallowable amount per month
	£
1	350
2	500
3 or more	650

Notes

(a) Where a person carries on a trade, profession or vocation at a premises and the premises are used mainly for the purposes of the trade etc. but are also used by the person as a home, a fixed rate adjustment can be used in calculating taxable profits for expenses incurred in relation to the premises mainly for the purposes of the trade etc. The amount of the deduction in respect of the expenses is the amount of expenses incurred less an amount representing non-business use. The restriction for non-business use is the sum of the disallowable amounts for each month, or part of a month, falling in the period concerned. 'Occupants' are individuals who at any time in the month under review either occupy the premises as a home or stay at the premises otherwise than in the case of the trade etc.

(b) The fixed rate disallowance can be used by individuals and partnerships of individuals.

[*ITTOIA 2005, s 94I*]

Bonus payments to employees *[ITEPA 2003, ss 312A–312I]*

An exemption from income tax applies to qualifying bonus payments made to employees by a company which is owned directly or indirectly by an employee-ownership trust. The bonus must be paid to all employees on equal terms, although they can be paid by reference to a percentage of salary, length of service or hours worked, and are subject to a cap of £3,600 per employee for each tax year.

Cap on tax reliefs *[ITA 2007, s 24A]*

A limit applies to the aggregate amount of certain income tax reliefs that may be claimed against general income by an individual in a tax year. The limit is the greater of £50,000 and 25% of the individual's adjusted total income for the tax year. The cap applies to:

- trade loss relief against general income (*ITA 2007, s 64*);
- early trade losses relief (*ITA 2007, s 72*);
- post-cessation trade relief (*ITA 2007, s 96*);
- property loss relief against general income (*ITA 2007, s 120*);
- post-cessation property relief (*ITA 2007, s 125*);
- employment loss relief against general income (*ITA 2007, s 128*);
- former employees deduction for liabilities (*ITEPA 2003, s 555*);
- share loss relief on non-enterprise investment scheme/seed enterprise investment scheme shares (*ITA 2007, Pt 4 Ch 6*);
- losses on deeply discounted securities (*ITTOIA 2005, ss 446, 454*); and
- qualifying loan interest (*ITA 2007, Pt 8 Ch 1*).

Charitable giving

Gift Aid scheme *[ITA 2007, ss 413–430]*

Relief is available for qualifying donations to charity. The charity claims basic rate relief on the grossed up amount of the donation and the donor claims higher rate relief on the grossed up amount against income tax and capital gains tax by extension of the basic rate band. The donor may elect to treat any donation as made in the preceding tax year for higher rate relief purposes. The basic rate tax deemed to have been deducted by the donor at source is clawed back if they have insufficient liability (to income tax and capital gains tax) to match it. The scheme also applies to gifts to Community Amateur Sports Clubs.

Gifts in kind *[CAA 2001, s 63(2)–(4); ITTOIA 2005, ss 107–109; CTA 2009, ss 105–108]*

Relief is available for gifts by traders, etc. to charities, community amateur sports clubs or educational establishments of goods produced or sold or of plant and machinery used in the donor's trade, etc.

Gifts of land, shares and securities etc. *[ITA 2007, ss 431–446; CTA 2010, ss 203–217]*

Relief is available where a person disposes of listed shares and securities, unit trust units, AIM shares etc. or of freehold or leasehold interests in land to a charity by way of gift or sale at an undervalue. The amount deductible in calculating net income is the market value of the shares etc. on the date of disposal plus incidental disposal costs less any consideration or value of benefits received by the donor or a connected person.

Payroll giving scheme *[ITEPA 2003, ss 713–715]*

An employee may make charitable donations of any amount by tax allowable deduction from earnings subject to PAYE.

Gifts of pre-eminent objects to the nation *[FA 2012, s 49, Sch 14]*

Under the cultural gifts scheme, individuals who donate pre-eminent objects, or collections of objects, to the nation may qualify for an income tax reduction of 30% of the value of the objects. The taxpayer can spread the reduction forward across up to five years starting with the tax year in which the object is offered.

Child trust funds *[SI 2004 No 1450, Regs 24–38; SI 2019 No 381]*

The child trust fund scheme operates to provide savings funds for eligible children born after 31 August 2002 and before 3 January 2011. HMRC made an initial contribution in the form of a voucher, worth £250 (£500 for children in lower income families) for children born before 3 August 2010, and £50 (£100) for children born on or after that date but before 3 January 2011. The voucher is then used to open an account. Anyone may then pay money into the account up to a yearly limit of £9,000 from 6 April 2020 (£4,368 before 6 April 2020; £4,260 before 6 April 2019; £4,128 before 6 April 2018; £4,080 before 6 April 2017) and HMRC also make further contributions in certain cases. The account provider invests the funds in a limited range of qualifying investments. Normally no withdrawals are permitted before the fund matures when the child reaches 18. No tax is chargeable in respect of interest, dividends, distributions, alternative financial arrangement return or building society bonus on account investments. Income from account investments is not regarded as income for any income tax purposes. From 6 April 2015 the savings in a fund can be transferred to a Junior ISA. Child trust funds have matured for the first time in September 2020. If, at maturity, no instructions are received from the account holder on the future of the investments in the fund, the investments will be held in a 'protected account' pending instruction. Funds in the 'protected account' will retain their tax advantaged status, and the terms and conditions which applied before maturity. See also page 19.

Community investment tax credit *[ITA 2007, ss 333–382; FA 2002, s 57, Sch 16; FA 2013, s 74, Sch 27]*

A tax relief worth up to 25% is available for qualifying investments in disadvantaged communities by individuals and companies via accredited intermediaries (Community Development Finance Institutions). The investment may be a loan or a subscription for shares or securities. The relief is given by way of tax reductions over a five-year period, the relief for each year being 5% of the invested amount (i.e. the average capital balance outstanding) but restricted, if necessary, to the amount which reduces the investor's tax liability to nil. Any tax reduction so restricted is carried forward to increase the tax reduction for subsequent years (but not beyond the five-year period).

Employee share schemes

Share incentive plans [*ITEPA 2003, ss 488–515, Sch 2; ITA 2007, ss 488–490*]

Under a share incentive plan ('SIP') (open to all employees)

- a company may give an employee shares worth up to £3,600 per tax year for which performance targets may be set) ('free shares');
- an employee may purchase shares worth up to £1,800 per tax year or 10% of annual salary if lower by deductions from salary ('partnership shares'), these being allowable deductions for income tax and NICs; and
- the company may give an employee up to two free shares ('matching shares') for each partnership share purchased.

Shares are free of tax and NICs if held in the plan for five years. With some exceptions (e.g. on death, disability, retirement, redundancy or certain cash takeovers), if shares are withdrawn within between three and five years, liability arises on the lower of their value on entering the plan and their value on leaving it. With similar exceptions, if shares are withdrawn within three years, liability is on their value on leaving the plan. Dividends which are reinvested in shares are tax-free. No capital gains tax is payable on withdrawal of shares from the plan at any time; the shares withdrawn are treated as acquired by the employee at their market value at that time.

Employee shareholder shares [*ITEPA 2003, ss 226A–226D*]

A special employment status, known as 'employee shareholder' status, was introduced by *Growth and Infrastructure Act 2013, s 31*, but tax relief is abolished for employee shareholder agreements entered into on or after 1 December 2016 (or 2 December 2016 in cases where the potential employee shareholder receives professional advice in relation to the share offer on 23 November 2016 before 1.30pm). Employee shareholders are issued or allotted at least £2,000 worth of shares in consideration of an employee shareholder agreement. For shares received from 1 September 2013, where arrangements were entered into before the abolition date and subject to meeting certain conditions, no income tax (and NIC) is chargeable on the first £2,000 of share value received when an individual becomes an employee shareholder. Relief is given by deeming that the individual had paid £2,000 for the shares. See also pages 5, 19.

Enterprise management incentives [*ITEPA 2003, ss 527–541, Sch 5*]

Certain independent trading companies with gross assets not exceeding £30 million and with fewer than 250 full-time equivalent employees may grant options over shares then worth up to £250,000 to an eligible employee without income tax or NIC consequences (except to the extent that the option is to acquire shares at less than their then market value). The total value of shares in respect of which unexercised qualifying options exist must not exceed £3 million. Any gain on sale of the shares is chargeable to capital gains tax (but, for disposals on or after 6 April 2013, may qualify for business asset disposal relief (formerly known as entrepreneurs' relief); see page 19).

SAYE option schemes [*ITEPA 2003, ss 516–520, Sch 3*]

No income tax charge arises on the receipt of the options or any increase in value of the shares between the date of grant of the option and its exercise provided certain conditions are met. Employees are able to take a pause of up to 12 months from saving into their SAYE scheme. HMRC will allow contributions to be postponed for a longer period where the additional months are missed due to coronavirus (COVID-19).

Maximum monthly contribution	£500
Minimum monthly contribution	£5
Maximum discount	20% of market value at time of grant

Savings arrangement bonus rates

Date contract started	Monthly payment multiple 3-year contract	5-year contract
27.12.14–	0	0
28.7.14–26.12.14	0	0.6
1.8.12–27.7.14	0	0

Savings arrangement effective interest rates

Date contract started	3-year contract	5-year contract	Early withdrawal rate
27.12.14–	0%	0%	0%
28.7.14–26.12.14	0%	0.39%	0%
1.8.12–27.7.14	0%	0%	0%

CSOP (company share option plan) schemes [*ITEPA 2003, ss 521–526, Sch 4*]

No income tax charge arises

(a) when option granted provided the exercise price is not manifestly less than the market value of the shares at the date of the grant (i.e. not at a discount);

(b) when option exercised between 3 and 10 years after grant.

Options exercised within three years of the grant by reason of injury, disability, redundancy or retirement or where there are certain cash takeovers of constituent companies do not lose their tax-exempt status.

Maximum value (at time of grant) of shares subject to options is £30,000.

Enterprise investment scheme *[ITA 2007, ss 156–257; SI 2018 No 931]*

The EIS applies to investments in qualifying unquoted companies trading in the UK. Eligible shares must be held for 3 years from issue date or commencement of trade if later. Subject to this and other conditions relief is given by way of a tax reduction equal to 30% of the amount invested. All or part of an investment may be treated as having been made in the preceding tax year (subject to the annual maximum for that year).

Maximum investment: if amount over £1,000,000 invested in Knowledge Intensive Companies	2018/19 onwards – £2,000,000
Maximum investment: otherwise	2012/13 onwards – £1,000,000
Minimum investment	2012/13 onwards – no minimum

Any loss on a disposal of EIS shares (net of income tax relief) may be relieved against income or capital gains. See also page 19.

Foster carers and shared lives carers *[ITTOIA 2005, ss 803–828]*

In general, to the extent that local authority payments made to a foster carer or shared lives carer do no more than meet the actual costs of caring, the payments are not taxable. In other cases, if gross receipts from foster care or shared lives care do not exceed an 'individual limit' the carer is treated as having a nil profit and nil loss for the tax year concerned. Where gross receipts exceed the individual limit, the carer can choose to be either taxed on the excess or compute profit or loss using the normal business rules. In addition, from 2017/18 the relief is extended to include shared lives schemes that are self-funded by the person receiving care. The 'individual limit' is made up of a fixed amount of £10,000 per residence for a full tax year and an additional amount per placement per week, or part week, that the individual provides care. The amounts are £200 per week for a child under 11 and £250 per week for a child of 11 or over or an adult. Relief for shared lives care is not available if more than three adults are placed with the carer at any time.

Individual savings accounts ('ISAs') *[ITTOIA 2005, ss 694–701; SI 1998 No 1870; SI 2020 No 261]*

Savers can subscribe to an ISA up to the following limits per tax year

	Overall limit	Cash limit	Junior ISA limit
2022/23	£20,000	£20,000	£9,000
2021/22	£20,000	£20,000	£9,000
2020/21	£20,000	£20,000	£9,000
2019/20	£20,000	£20,000	£4,368
2018/19	£20,000	£20,000	£4,260
2017/18	£20,000	£20,000	£4,128
2016/17	£15,240	£15,240	£4,080

Savings are exempt from income tax and capital gains tax. Withdrawals may be made at any time without loss of tax relief. From 6 April 2018 and subject to certain time limits, investments retained in an ISA during the administration period of a deceased saver's estate will retain their tax-advantaged status. Shares acquired under a share incentive plan, profit sharing scheme or SAYE option scheme (see above) may be transferred to an ISA within 90 days without tax consequences. See also page 20.

Help to buy ISAs were available from 1 December 2015 to 30 November 2019. Once opened contributions can continue until 30 November 2029. Provided the balance reaches at least £1,600, the Government provides a 25% top-up on savings of up to £200 per month (plus an initial investment of up to £1,000), subject to a maximum total top up of £3,000. The top-up is paid when the savings are used to make a first-time house purchase. The house must be valued at no more than £450,000 in London and £250,000 elsewhere in the UK. Top-up payments and interest are tax free.

Lifetime ISAs are available from 6 April 2017 for individuals under 40. Contributions can be made up to £4,000 per year and the Government will provide a 25% bonus at the end of each year. Contributions can continue with bonus paid up to age 50. The funds can be withdrawn to buy a first home (value up to £450,000), from age 60, or by the terminally ill without penalty. Other withdrawals are subject to a withdrawal penalty. The bonus from either a lifetime ISA or a help to buy ISA can be used to purchase a first home, but not both. Savings from a help to buy ISA could be transferred to a lifetime ISA in 2017/18.

Insurance benefits in event of sickness etc *[ITTOIA 2005, ss 735–743]*

Certain insurance benefits paid in the event of accident, sickness, disability, infirmity or unemployment are exempt, including benefits payable during convalescence or rehabilitation or to top-up earned income reduced following such disabilities.

Interest received

The following interest is exempt.

(a) On damages for personal injury or death. *[ITTOIA 2005, s 751]*.

(b) On government securities held by persons not resident in the UK. *[ITTOIA 2005, ss 713–716]*. See page 57.

(c) On certain national savings income.

(d) On SAYE certified contractual savings schemes. (Bonuses are also exempt.) *[ITTOIA 2005, ss 702–707]*.

(e) Repayment interest and interest on overpaid tax (including income tax, capital gains tax, VAT and inheritance tax but not interest payable by HMRC in cases of official error under *VATA 1994, s 78*). *[IHTA 1984, s 235; ITTOIA 2005, ss 54, 749, 869]*.

Maintenance payments *[ITA 2007, ss 453–456]*

Payments are made gross and are not subject to tax in the hands of the recipient.

Where either party to the marriage was born before 6 April 1935, the payer obtains relief on qualifying maintenance payments (as defined) by means of a tax reduction on the lesser of the amount paid and the minimum married couple's allowance for the year (see page 60) at the rate of 10%.

Miscellaneous

The following income is exempt from income tax.

(a) **Adoption etc. allowances.** [*ITTOIA 2005, ss 744–747*]. A similar exemption for allowances to special guardians and certain kinship carers applies.
(b) **Awards for bravery.** [*ITEPA 2003, s 638*].
(c) **Compensation for mis-sold pensions.** [*FA 1996, s 148;* HMRC ESC A99].
(d) **Compensation on unclaimed bank accounts of Holocaust victims.** [*ITTOIA 2005, s 756A*].
(e) **Continuity of education allowances.**
(f) **Damages and compensation for personal injury.** [*ITTOIA 2005, ss 731–734*].
(g) **Foreign service allowances.** [*ITEPA 2003, s 299*].
(h) **German and Austrian** pensions and annuities and payments by the Netherlands for victims of Nazi and Japanese persecution. [*ITEPA, s 642*].
(i) **Housing grants.** [*ITTOIA 2005, s 769*].
(j) **Members of Parliament.** Certain accommodation allowances and reimbursed costs paid to MPs and members of devolved assemblies. [*ITEPA 2003, ss 292–295*].
(k) **Miners'** free coal or cash in lieu. [*ITEPA 2003, ss 306, 646*].
(l) **Non-resident competitors in certain sporting events.** Subject to conditions, the income arising to non-resident competitors from certain sporting events. For example, the 2017 World Athletics Championships and the 2020 UEFA Euro Final Tournament. [*FA 2014, s 48; SI 2016 No 771; SI 2021 No 224; SI 2021 No 882*].
(m) **Sandwich courses.** Payments to an employee for periods of attendance provided (i) course lasts at least one academic year with an average of at least 20 weeks per year full-time attendance, and (ii) rate of payment does not exceed greater of £7,000 p.a. and rate of payment receivable in similar circumstances by way of public grant. (HMRC SP 4/86).
(n) **Scholarship** income and bursaries. [*ITTOIA 2005, s 766*]. See also page 7.

See also benefits in kind on pages 4 to 8.

'Rent a room' relief [*ITTOIA 2005, ss 785–802*]

The *gross* rents on letting of rooms in a private residence are exempt up to £7,500. Where gross rents exceed the exempt amount, the taxpayer can elect to pay tax on the excess instead of the profits computed under the normal rules.

Seed enterprise investment scheme [*ITA 2007 ss 257A–257HJ*]

The SEIS applies to investments made in small qualifying companies carrying on or preparing to carry on a new business. Subject to conditions, relief is given by way of a tax reduction equal to 50% of the amount invested, up to a maximum investment of £100,000 per tax year. Relief may be claimed as if all or part of the investment had been made in the preceding tax year (subject to the annual maximum).

Gains on shares within the scope of the SEIS are exempt from capital gains tax. See also page 23.

Social investment relief [*ITA 2007, ss 257J–257TE; FA 2021, s 20*]

Income tax relief is available for investments made on or after 6 April 2014 and before 6 April 2023 in qualifying shares or debentures in a social enterprise. Subject to conditions, relief is given by way of a tax reduction equal to 30% of the amount invested, up to a maximum investment of £1,000,000 per tax year. Relief may be claimed as if all or part of the investment had been made in the preceding tax year (subject to the annual maximum).

Gains on investments to which income tax relief is attributable are exempt from capital gains tax if the investments are held for at least three years. See also page 23.

Social security benefits

Certain social security benefits are not taxable. See page 106.

Termination payments [*ITEPA 2003, ss 401–416*]

Provided payment is not taxable under general employment earnings rules, termination payments (including non-contractual payments in lieu of notice and genuine non-statutory redundancy payments) fall to be taxed under *ITEPA 2003, ss 401–416* subject to the following exemptions.

(a) The first £30,000 of the payments.
(b) Payments where cessation arises from death, injury or disability.
(c) Payments for foreign service broadly before 14 September 2017 where this comprised (i) three-quarters of the whole period of service, or (ii) the last 10 years, or (iii) where employment exceeded 20 years, one half of the whole, including 10 of the last 20 years. (Proportional relief in other cases.) However, foreign service relief is abolished for termination payments and benefits to employees who are UK resident in the tax year in which the employment is terminated. This applies where the date of the termination is on or after 6 April 2018 and the termination payment, or other benefit, is received after 13 September 2017. Foreign service relief continues in termination cases where the employee is non-UK resident in the year of termination, and will continue for UK residents where the payment or benefit is in connection with a change of duties or earnings rather than with termination of the employment. Reductions for foreign service are also retained for seafarers and extended to employees of the Royal Fleet Auxiliary.
(d) Certain benefits under retirement schemes.

Venture capital trusts [*ITA 2007, ss 258–332; ITTOIA 2005, ss 709–712*]

An individual who *subscribes* for ordinary shares in a VCT obtains income tax relief at 30% on an investment limit of £200,000 in any tax year. The shares must be held for at least five years. Any dividends received from a VCT are exempt from income tax to the extent that the shares *acquired* each year do not exceed the investment limit and provided the main purpose of acquiring the shares is not the avoidance of tax; tax credits are not repayable. See also page 23.

Payment of tax

1st interim payment. On or before 31 January in tax year

2nd interim payment. On or before 31 July following tax year

This is subject to relaxations as part of the Government's assistance to taxpayers during the COVID-19 pandemic. The second self-assessment payment on account for the **2019/20** tax year could be deferred from 31 July 2020 to 31 January 2021. No interest was applied for the period between 31 July 2020 and 31 January 2021. In addition, the first late payment penalty of 5% was not charged for any tax due for 2019/20 where it was paid before 2 April 2021, or a time to pay arrangement was set up before that date. There is no deferral of payments on account for **2020/21**. However, as for 2019/20, the first 5% late payment penalty was not charged for any tax due where it was paid before 2 April 2022, or a time to pay arrangement was set up before that date.

Interim payments are normally half the net income tax liability (including Class 4 NIC) of the previous year. Interim payments are not required if either the previous year's liability (net of tax at source) was less than £1,000 or tax at source covered more than 80% of the gross liability. (Tax at source includes PAYE.) The taxpayer may make a claim to reduce (or dispense with) interim payments if the current year liability will be less than that of the previous year (or will be nil).

Final payment. Where necessary, 31 January following tax year (but see above for details of the relaxation of late penalty provisions for 2019/20 and 2020/21) except that

(a) where a person has given notice of chargeability to tax within six months of the tax year but was not given notice to deliver a return until after 31 October following the tax year, the due date is 3 months after the date of notice; and

(b) where a person's self-assessment is amended, the due date is deferred as regards any tax payable by virtue of the amendment until, if later, 30 days after the date of notice of amendment or closure notice following an enquiry (but not so as to defer the date from which interest on overdue tax runs).

The final payment (or repayment) is the total net liability for income tax (including Class 4 NIC and, for 2015/16 onwards, Class 2 NIC) and capital gains tax less any interim payments on account of income tax.

Returns

The deadline for delivering the completed self-assessment return is determined as follows.

- If the return is an electronic return, it must be delivered to HMRC on or before **31 January** following the tax year to which it relates or, if later, within three months beginning with the date of HMRC's notice to deliver the return.
- If the return is a non-electronic return, it must be delivered to HMRC on or before **31 October** following the tax year to which it relates or, if later, within three months beginning with the date of HMRC's notice to deliver the return.

The above is subject to relaxations as part of the Government's assistance to taxpayers during the COVID-19 pandemic. If the 2019/20 return was filed by 28 February 2021 no £100 late filing penalty was issued. Likewise, if the 2020/21 return was filed by 28 February 2022 no £100 late filing penalty was issued.

See page 22 regarding the payment of capital gains tax on certain disposals of UK land within 30 days of completion from April 2019. The payment must be accompanied by a return.

An individual or trustee who has received a notice to make a return may request HMRC to withdraw the notice. If HMRC agree to do so they issue a withdrawal notice and any corresponding penalty for failing to make a return is cancelled. See page 97 for penalties for late filing of returns.

Making tax digital. Self-employed businesses and landlords with annual business or property turnover above £10,000 will need to follow the rules for Making Tax Digital (MTD) for income tax from 6 April 2024. Such taxpayers will be required to keep digital records of business income and expenses which are then sent to HMRC as quarterly updates. At the end of the tax year, the taxpayer will have to finalise their business income and submit an end of period statement. Included in this statement will be any accounting adjustments required such as closing stock amounts, any reliefs and tax adjustment, and also a confirmation statement that the information is correct and complete. The deadline for the end of period statement is 31 January after the end of the tax year, the same as the normal deadline for a self assessment tax return.

Basis of assessment

Property income	All UK property income arising in the current tax year, calculated as for trading profits and using ordinary accounting principles. A restriction on relief for finance costs to the basic rate is being phased in with effect from 2017/18 onwards. See also property allowance page 60
Trading income	*Year 1* — Actual *Year 2* — 12 months ending with accounting date in Year 2 *or* (if period from commencement to accounting date in Year 2 is less than 12 months) the first 12 months *or* (if no accounting date in Year 1 or Year 2) actual *Year 3* — Current year basis (unless Year 3 is the first year in which there is an accounting date falling not less than 12 months after commencement, when assessment based on 12 months ending with the accounting date) *Intermediate years* — Current year basis *Closing year* — Period from end of basis period in the penultimate year to date of cessation (subject to transitional rules covering overlap profits for 1997/98)
	Current year basis normally means that assessment is based on the profits shown by the annual accounts ended within the current tax year
	Future development. For 2024/25 and subsequent years, the profits for a tax year will be the profits arising in that tax year with accounting period profits being apportioned by the number of days or on another reasonable basis. There will be a transitional year, 2023/24, which will bridge the period between the end of the basis period for 2022/23 and the start of the reformed basis period in 2024/25. All overlap relief brought forward must be used in 2023/24 and in subsequent years no further overlap relief can be created. Any additional profits arising for a business under the new rules will be spread over five tax years starting in 2023/24 with an option to elect to accelerate the tax charge.
	See also trading allowance page 59
Savings/investment income	Income arising in the current tax year
Foreign income	As for UK property, trading or savings/investment income above See the table on page 68 for determining whether income is assessed on an arising or remittance basis
Other income	Income arising in the current tax year
Employment income	See the table on page 68 for determining whether earnings are assessed on a receipts or remittance basis
Income taxed at source	Dividends, interest, etc. receivable

Foreign income

The table below shows whether foreign income is assessed on an arising or, where claimed, a remittance basis.

Resident	Domiciled	British subject	Trades, etc.	Pensions	Other income
No	N/A	N/A	Exempt	Exempt	Exempt
Yes	Yes	Yes	Arising	100% (note (f))	Arising
Yes	Yes	Yes	Remittance	Remittance	Remittance
Yes	No	Yes	Remittance	Remittance	Remittance
Yes	Yes	No	Arising	100% (note (f))	Arising
Yes	No	No	Remittance	Remittance	Remittance

Employment income

The table below shows whether employment income is taxed on a receipts or, where claimed, a remittance basis.

Domiciled	Resident	Meeting three-year non-residence requirement (note (b))	UK employer	Foreign employer	Wholly UK income	Wholly overseas income (note (c))	Partly UK/partly overseas duties	
							UK duties	Overseas duties (note (c))
Yes	Yes	N/A	Immaterial	Immaterial	Receipts	Receipts	Receipts	Receipts
Yes	No	N/A	Immaterial	Immaterial	Receipts	Exempt	Receipts	Exempt
No	Yes	No	Yes	N/A	Receipts	Receipts	Receipts	Receipts
No	Yes	No	N/A	Yes	Receipts	Remittances	Receipts	Remittances
No	Yes	Yes	Yes	N/A	Receipts	Remittances	Receipts	Remittances
No	Yes	Yes	N/A	Yes	Receipts	Remittances	Receipts	Remittances
No	No	Yes/No	Yes	N/A	Receipts	Exempt	Receipts	Exempt
No	No	Yes/No	N/A	Yes	Receipts	Exempt	Receipts	Exempt

Notes

(a) For 2013/14 onwards, an individual's residence status is determined by a statutory residence test and the concept of ordinary residence is abolished.

(b) An employee meets the requirement for a three-year period of non-residence for a tax year (X) if he has been non-resident for three consecutive tax years and year X is any of the three tax years immediately following that non-resident period.

(c) Where such duties are performed by seafarers in the course of a qualifying period of 365 days or more, emoluments for those duties receive a 100% deduction. [*ITEPA 2003, s 378*].

(d) An individual who claims to use the remittance basis for a tax year is not entitled to any income tax personal allowances or the capital gains tax annual exemption for that year. This does not apply if the individual's unremitted foreign income and gains for the year are less than £2,000. [*ITA 2007, s 809G*].

(e) Individuals aged over 18 who have been resident in the UK for at least seven years of the past nine years can claim the remittance basis for a tax year only if they pay a £30,000 tax charge in respect of the foreign income and gains they leave outside the UK. The charge is £60,000 for those resident in the UK for at least 12 of the last 14 years. For 2016/17 the charge is £90,000 for those resident in the UK for at least 17 of the last 20 years. From 2017/18 onwards an individual will be deemed UK-domiciled for tax purposes if he has been UK-resident for at least 15 of the last 20 tax years (and therefore ineligible to claim the remittance basis, hence the £90,000 charge will no longer apply). The charge does not apply if the individual's unremitted foreign income and gains for the year are less than £2,000. [*ITA 2007, s 809H*].

(f) 90% arising before 6 April 2017.

Inheritance tax rates

Chargeable lifetime transfers

(a) Tax on gross transfers			Cumulative totals	
Cumulative transfers (gross)	Rate	Tax on band	Taxable transfers	Tax thereon
£	%	£	£	£
6.4.19 onwards				
0–325,000	Nil	Nil	325,000	Nil
Over 325,000	20%			
6.4.18–5.4.19				
0–325,000	Nil	Nil	325,000	Nil
Over 325,000	20%			
6.4.17–5.4.18				
0–325,000	Nil	Nil	325,000	Nil
Over 325,000	20%			
6.4.16–5.4.17				
0–325,000	Nil	Nil	325,000	Nil
Over 325,000	20%			
6.4.15–5.4.16				
0–325,000	Nil	Nil	325,000	Nil
Over 325,000	20%			
6.4.14–5.4.15				
0–325,000	Nil	Nil	325,000	Nil
Over 325,000	20%			
6.4.13–5.4.14				
0–325,000	Nil	Nil	325,000	Nil
Over 325,000	20%			
6.4.12–5.4.13				
0–325,000	Nil	Nil	325,000	Nil
Over 325,000	20%			
6.4.11–5.4.12				
0–325,000	Nil	Nil	325,000	Nil
Over 325,000	20%			
6.4.10–5.4.11				
0–325,000	Nil	Nil	325,000	Nil
Over 325,000	20%			

(b) Grossing-up of net lifetime transfers		Cumulative totals	
Net values	Tax payable thereon	Net values	Gross equivalent
£	%	£	£
6.4.19 onwards			
0–325,000	Nil	325,000	325,000
Over 325,000	Nil+ ¼ for each £1 over £325,000		
6.4.18–5.4.19			
0–325,000	Nil	325,000	325,000
Over 325,000	Nil+ ¼ for each £1 over £325,000		
6.4.17–5.4.18			
0–325,000	Nil	325,000	325,000
Over 325,000	Nil+ ¼ for each £1 over £325,000		
6.4.16–5.4.17			
0–325,000	Nil	325,000	325,000
Over 325,000	Nil+ ¼ for each £1 over £325,000		
6.4.15–5.4.16			
0–325,000	Nil	325,000	325,000
Over 325,000	Nil+ ¼ for each £1 over £325,000		
6.4.14–5.4.15			
0–325,000	Nil	325,000	325,000
Over 325,000	Nil+ ¼ for each £1 over £325,000		
6.4.13–5.4.14			
0–325,000	Nil	325,000	325,000
Over 325,000	Nil+ ¼ for each £1 over £325,000		
6.4.12–5.4.13			
0–325,000	Nil	325,000	325,000
Over 325,000	Nil+ ¼ for each £1 over £325,000		
6.4.11–5.4.12			
0–325,000	Nil	325,000	325,000
Over 325,000	Nil+ ¼ for each £1 over £325,000		
6.4.10–5.4.11			
0–325,000	Nil	325,000	325,000
Over 325,000	Nil+ ¼ for each £1 over £325,000		

Inheritance tax rates

Transfers on death

(a) Tax on transfers			Cumulative totals	
Cumulative transfers (gross) £	Rate %	Tax on band £	Taxable transfers £	Tax thereon £
6.4.19 onwards				
0–325,000 (notes (c), (d))	Nil	Nil	325,000	Nil
Over 325,000	40%			
6.4.18–5.4.19				
0–325,000 (note (d))	Nil	Nil	325,000	Nil
Over 325,000	40%			
6.4.17–5.4.18				
0–325,000 (note (d))	Nil	Nil	325,000	Nil
Over 325,000	40%			
6.4.16–5.4.17				
0–325,000	Nil	Nil	325,000	Nil
Over 325,000	40%			
6.4.15–5.4.16				
0–325,000	Nil	Nil	325,000	Nil
Over 325,000	40%			
6.4.14–5.4.15				
0–325,000	Nil	Nil	325,000	Nil
Over 325,000	40%			
6.4.13–5.4.14				
0–325,000	Nil	Nil	325,000	Nil
Over 325,000	40%			
6.4.12–5.4.13				
0–325,000	Nil	Nil	325,000	Nil
Over 325,000	40%			
6.4.11–5.4.12				
0–325,000	Nil	Nil	325,000	Nil
Over 325,000	40%			
6.4.10–5.4.11				
0–325,000	Nil	Nil	325,000	Nil
Over 325,000	40%			

(b) Grossing-up of net lifetime transfers do not bear their own tax		Cumulative totals	
Net values £	Tax payable thereon %	Net values £	Gross equivalent £
6.4.19 onwards			
0–325,000 (notes (c), (d))	Nil	325,000	325,000
Over 325,000	Nil+ 2/3 for each £1 over £325,000		
6.4.18–5.4.19			
0–325,000 (note (d))	Nil	325,000	325,000
Over 325,000	Nil+ 2/3 for each £1 over £325,000		
6.4.17–5.4.18			
0–325,000 (note (d))	Nil	325,000	325,000
Over 325,000	Nil+ 2/3 for each £1 over £325,000		
6.4.16–5.4.17			
0–325,000	Nil	325,000	325,000
Over 325,000	Nil+ 2/3 for each £1 over £325,000		
6.4.15–5.4.16			
0–325,000	Nil	325,000	325,000
Over 325,000	Nil+ 2/3 for each £1 over £325,000		
6.4.14–5.4.15			
0–325,000	Nil	325,000	325,000
Over 325,000	Nil+ 2/3 for each £1 over £325,000		
6.4.13–5.4.14			
0–325,000	Nil	325,000	325,000
Over 325,000	Nil+ 2/3 for each £1 over £325,000		
6.4.12–5.4.13			
0–325,000	Nil	325,000	325,000
Over 325,000	Nil+ 2/3 for each £1 over £325,000		
6.4.11–5.4.12			
0–325,000	Nil	325,000	325,000
Over 325,000	Nil+ 2/3 for each £1 over £325,000		
6.4.10–5.4.11			
0–325,000	Nil	325,000	325,000
Over 325,000	Nil+ 2/3 for each £1 over £325,000		

Notes

(a) Any nil-rate band which is unused on a person's death can be transferred to their surviving spouse or civil partner for the purposes of the charge to tax on the death of the survivor on or after 9 October 2007. [*IHTA 1984, ss 8A–8C*].

(b) For deaths on or after 6 April 2012, the rate of inheritance tax is 36% where 10% or more of the net estate (after deducting exemptions, reliefs and the nil-rate band) is left to charity. [*IHTA 1984, Sch 1A; FA 2012, s 209, Sch 33*].

(c) The nil rate band will be frozen at £325,000 until 5 April 2026. [*FA 2021, s 86*].

(d) An **additional nil rate band for main residences** is available for deaths on or after 6 April 2017. The band applies where the main residence is passed on to one or more direct descendants or where a person downsizes or ceases to own a home on or after 8 July 2015 and assets of an equivalent value, up to the amount of the band, are passed on death to direct descendants. Initially the band was £100,000; for 2018/19 it is £125,000; for 2019/20 it is £150,000, and **for 2020/21 to 2025/26 it is £175,000.** The band is progressively withdrawn for estates valued at more than £2 million at a rate of £1 for every £2 over the limit. Unused nil-rate band can be transferred to any surviving spouse or civil partner. [*IHTA 1984, ss 8D–8M*].

Inheritance tax accounts and payment of tax

	Delivery of account	Payment of tax	
Chargeable lifetime transfers	Within later of (a) 12 months from the end of the month in which the transfer is made; and (b) 3 months beginning with the date on which the person delivering the account first becomes liable for tax No account need be delivered where: (i) the transfer is of cash or quoted shares or securities and the value of the transfer and other chargeable transfers made in the preceding seven years does not exceed the IHT threshold; or (ii) the value of the transfer and other chargeable transfers made in the preceding seven years does not exceed 80% of the IHT threshold and the value of the transfer does not exceed the net amount of the threshold available to the transferor at the time of the transfer.	6 April–30 September 1 October–5 April	30 April in following year Six months after end of month of transfer
Relevant property settlement charges	Within 6 months from the end of the month in which the chargeable event occurs	6 months after the end of the month in which chargeable event occurs.	
PETs which become chargeable	Within 12 months from the end of the month in which the transferor dies	6 months after the end of the month in which death occurs	
Gifts with reservation chargeable on death	Within 12 months from the end of the month in which death occurs	6 months after the end of the month in which death occurs	
Transfers on death	Within later of (a) 12 months from the end of the month in which death occurs; and (b) 3 months beginning with the date on which the personal representatives first act or the person liable first has reason to believe he is required to deliver an account **Excepted estates** – *Deaths after 31 December 2021.* No account need be delivered where the deceased died domiciled in the UK provided conditions (i)–(iii) below are met. (i) The aggregate of the gross value of the estate, and of any 'specified transfers' or 'specified exempt transfers' does not exceed the 'appropriate IHT threshold' (ii) The gross value of settled property and foreign assets do not exceed £250,000 and £100,000 respectively (iii) There were no chargeable lifetime transfers in the seven years before death other than specified transfers not exceeding £250,000. No account need be delivered where the deceased died domiciled in the UK provided conditions (1)–(4) below are met. (1) The aggregate of the gross value of the estate, and of any 'specified transfers' or 'specified exempt transfers' does not exceed £3,000,000; at least part of the estate passes to the person's spouse, civil partner or to a charity; and after deducting from that aggregate figure any exempt spouse, civil partner and charity transfers and 'total estate liabilities', it does not exceed the 'appropriate IHT threshold'; (2) The gross value of settled property does not exceed £1,000,000, of which not more than £250,000 does not pass to the person's spouse, civil partner or to a charity; (3) The gross value of foreign assets does not exceed £100,000; and (4) There were no chargeable lifetime transfers in the seven years before death other than specified transfers not exceeding £250,000. Where the deceased was never domiciled in the UK, no account need be delivered provided that the value of the estate in the UK is wholly attributable to cash and quoted shares and securities not exceeding £150,000.The deceased must have made no lifetime gifts in the seven years prior to death and must not own overseas property attributable to UK residential property. *Deaths before 1 January 2022.* No account need be delivered where the deceased died domiciled in the UK provided either conditions (a) or (b) below are met, and both conditions (c) and (d) below are met. (a) The aggregate of the gross value of the estate, and of any 'specified transfers' or 'specified exempt transfers' does not exceed the 'appropriate IHT threshold';	6 months after end of the month in which death occurs or on delivery of account by personal representatives if earlier	

	Delivery of account	Payment of tax
	(b) The aggregate of the gross value of the estate, and of any 'specified transfers' or 'specified exempt transfers' does not exceed £1,000,000; at least part of the estate passes to the person's spouse, civil partner or to a charity; and after deducting from that aggregate figure any exempt spouse, civil partner and charity transfers and total estate liabilities, it does not exceed the 'appropriate IHT threshold'; (c) The gross value of settled property and foreign assets do not exceed £150,000 and £100,000 respectively; and (d) There were no chargeable lifetime transfers in the seven years before death other than specified transfers not exceeding £150,000. Where the deceased was never domiciled in the UK, no account need be delivered provided that the value of the estate in the UK is wholly attributable to cash and quoted shares and securities not exceeding £150,000. '*Specified transfers*' are chargeable transfers of cash, personal chattels or corporeal moveable property, quoted shares and securities, and interests in or over land. '*Specified exempt transfers*' are transfers in the seven years before death between spouses or civil partners, gifts to charities, political parties or housing associations, transfers to maintenance funds for historic buildings etc., or to employee trusts. Transfers treated as normal expenditure out of income made within 7 years before death and totalling more than £3,000 in any tax year will be treated as chargeable transfers for these purposes. '*Appropriate IHTT threshold*'. For deaths after 31 December 2021, where the deceased was predeceased by a spouse or civil partner, the IHT threshold for these purposes is increased by the percentage of the spouse or civil partner's IHT threshold which was unused on the first death, provided that a claim has been made for the transfer of the unused nil-rate band and the first deceased met certain other criteria similar to those listed above for excepted estates. For deaths before 1 January 2022, the IHT threshold was increased only if all of the first deceased spouse's or civil partner's nil-rate band was unused (so that the increase was by 100%). '*Total estate liabilities*' do not include those which are not discharged on or after death out of the estate in money or money's worth, or those which are prevented by any other provision in IHTA 1984 from being taken into account, or those attributable to financing the acquisition of, or maintenance or enhancement of the value of, excluded property.	
National heritage property	Within 6 months from the end of the month in which the charge arises on the ending of conditional exemption	6 months after end of the month in which chargeable event occurs

Exempt transfer	Limits and conditions		Reference
Lifetime only			
Potentially exempt transfers	Unless provided to the contrary (e.g. gifts with reservation) (a) transfers by individuals to other individuals; (b) transfers by individuals to certain trusts for the disabled; (c) transfers on or after 22 March 2006 by an individual to a bereaved minor's trust on the coming to an end of an immediate post-death interest; (d) transfers before 22 March 2006 by an individual to an accumulation and maintenance trust; (e) transfers by an individual into interest in possession trusts in which, for transfers on or after 22 March 2006, the beneficiary has a disabled person's interest; and (f) (in restricted circumstances following *FA 2006*) certain transfers on the termination or disposal of an individual's beneficial interest in possession in settled property are potentially exempt transfers. Such transfers made seven years or more before the death of the transferor are exempt transfers		*IHTA 1984, s 3A* *FA 2006, Sch 20 para 9*
Annual gifts	Transfers of value per fiscal year not exceeding Any shortfall in usage can be carried forward to the next year and added to the allowance for that year only	£3,000	*IHTA 1984, s 19*
Gifts in consideration of marriage or civil partnership	Parent of either party to marriage or partnership	£5,000	*IHTA 1984, s 22*
	Grandparent or remoter ancestor of either party to marriage or partnership; or by one party to the other	£2,500	
	Any other person	£1,000	
Normal expenditure out of income	Exempt if (a) transfer made out of post-tax income taking one year with another; and (b) transferor left with sufficient income to maintain usual standard of living		*IHTA 1984, s 21*
Small gifts	All gifts to the same person in the same year not exceeding	£250	*IHTA 1984, s 20*
Lifetime and on death			
Charities	Wholly exempt. Community Amateur Sports Clubs are treated as charities		*IHTA 1984, s 23*
National purposes	Property may be given or bequeathed to any of the bodies listed in the Schedule to the Act (British Museum, National Gallery, local authorities etc.)		*IHTA 1984, s 25, Sch 3*
Political parties	Wholly exempt		*IHTA 1984, s 24*
Shares to an employee trust by individuals	Exempt if trustees hold, within one year of transfer, over 50% of the ordinary shares trust by individuals and have voting control. Beneficiaries must include most of the employees		*IHTA 1984, s 28*
Spouse/civil partner	Wholly exempt unless spouse or civil partner non-UK-domiciled when limit is	£325,000	*IHTA 1984, s 18; FA 2013, s 178*
	For transfers of value before 6 April 2013, the limit was £55,000.		
	For transfers of value made on or after 6 April 2013, individuals who are domiciled outside the UK can elect to be treated as domiciled in the UK for inheritance tax purposes if, at any time on or after 6 April 2013 and during the period of seven years ending with the date on which the election is made, they have a UK-domiciled spouse or civil partner. An election can also be made following the death of a UK-domiciled spouse or civil partner. The election has effect from the date specified in it, which must be on or after 6 April 2013 and within the seven years ending with the date on which the election is made or the spouse or civil partner dies.		*IHTA 1984, ss 267ZA, 267ZB; FA 2013, s 177*
	An election is irrevocable but will cease to have effect if the individual is not resident in the UK for income tax purposes for four successive tax years beginning after the election is made.		
	See also note (a) on page 70.		

Inheritance tax reliefs

Agricultural property relief [*IHTA 1984, ss 115–124B*]

	Rates for disposals After 31.8.95
Vacant possession or right to obtain it within 12 months	100%
Entitled to 50% relief at 9 March 1981 and from that date beneficially entitled to interest but without vacant possession rights	100%
Agricultural land let on tenancy starting after 31 August 1995	100%
Other transfers	50%

The agricultural property must (inter alia) have been (i) *occupied* by the transferor for agricultural purposes throughout the 2 years before the transfer; or (ii) owned by him for the 7 years before the transfer and occupied (by him or another) for agricultural purposes throughout that period. With effect, broadly, from 22 April 2009, relief is extended to agricultural property within the European Economic Area.

Business property relief [*IHTA 1984, ss 103–114*]

	Rates for disposals After 5.4.96
Unincorporated business or interest in	100%
Shares in unquoted company	
— over 25% voting control	100%
— 25% or less	100%
Shares in quoted company giving control	50%
Shares in AIM or USM company	
— controlling interest	100%
— over 25% voting control	100%
— 25% or less	100%
Settled property comprising a life tenant's business or interest in a business	100%
Land, buildings, machinery or plant in a partnership or in a controlled company or in a settlement	50%

The property must (inter alia) (i) have been owned by the transferor for at least the 2 years immediately before the transfer; or (ii) have replaced other qualifying property and the qualifying properties together have been owned by the transferor for at least 2 out of the 5 years immediately before the transfer.

Transfers within seven years of death [*IHTA 1984, s 7, Sch 2 paras 1A, 2*]

Where a transferor dies within seven years of a lifetime transfer, IHT is recomputed at the death rates applying at the time of death but the tax rates (not the value of the lifetime transfer) are, subject to below, tapered as follows.

Years between transfer and death	Percentage of full tax rate
Not more than 3	100%
Over 3 but not more than 4	80%
Over 4 but not more than 5	60%
Over 5 but not more than 6	40%
Over 6 but not more than 7	20%

In the case of a chargeable lifetime transfer, the IHT payable cannot be reduced below that originally chargeable at half death rates.

Quick succession relief [*IHTA 1984, s 141*]

Where there is a later transfer of property within 5 years of an earlier transfer ('the first transfer') which increased the transferor's estate and the later transfer arises on death, the IHT payable on the later transfer is reduced by

$$\text{Percentage} \times \frac{(G - T)}{G} \times T$$

where

G = gross (chargeable) first transfer

T = IHT on first transfer

The percentages are as follow

Years between transfers	Percentage
One year or less	100%
Over 1 but not more than 2	80%
Over 2 but not more than 3	60%
Over 3 but not more than 4	40%
Over 4 but not more than 5	20%

Relief also applies where the later transfer is settled property in which the transferor had an interest in possession and the first transfer was the making of the settlement or was made after that time.

Interest on tax

Harmonised interest regime

FA 2009, ss 101–105, Schs 53–54A created a harmonised interest regime intended to apply eventually to all taxes and duties administered by HMRC. The regime provides for 'late payment interest' and 'repayment interest' at differential rates. Where interest is already accruing immediately before the start date for a particular tax or penalty, it will accrue on and after that date under the new regime. The regime applies to the following taxes and penalties:

(1) (from 31.8.10) bank payroll tax;
(2) (from 6.10.11) penalties relating to construction industry scheme late returns;
(3) (from 31.10.11) income tax and capital gains tax self-assessment amounts;
(4) (from 1.2.13) machine games duty;
(5) (from 1.4.13) penalties relating to dishonest tax agents;
(6) (from 1.10.13) annual tax on enveloped dwellings;
(7) (from 6.5.14) PAYE, Class 1 NICs and construction industry scheme in-year amounts for 2014/15 onwards (including penalties);
(8) (from 1.1.15) stamp duty reserve tax;
(9) (from 1.1.15) remote gambling taxes;
(10) (from 1.4.15) diverted profits tax;
(11) (from 6.4.15) Class 2 NIC;
(12) (from 6.4.19) capital gains tax on disposals of UK land (where not included in a self-assessment);
(13) (from 1.6.19) various DOTAS penalties;
(14) (from 6.9.19) penalties for offshore evasion;
(15) (from 5.10.20) loan charge;
(16) (from 6.4.21) recovery of deemed employer NICs debts; and
(17) (from 1.1.23) VAT.

The regime does not yet apply to corporation tax or inheritance tax but it is expected to be extended to IHT.

Late payment interest

A late payment of tax (or associated penalty) carries interest at the late payment interest rate from the date on which that amount becomes due and payable until the date on which payment is made. A special rule applies to determine the interest start date if:

(i) there is an amendment or correction to an assessment or self-assessment; or
(ii) HMRC make one in place of, or in addition to, an assessment made by a taxpayer; or
(iii) HMRC make an assessment in place of one that a taxpayer ought to have made.

In such a case, the late payment interest start date is what it would have been if:

- the original assessment or self-assessment had been complete and accurate and had been made on the date (if any) by which it was required to be made; and
- accordingly, the amount had been due and payable as a result of that original assessment or self-assessment.

Rates of interest		*Days*
31.10.11 – 22.8.16	3%	1758
23.8.16 – 20.11.17	2.75%	455
21.11.17 – 20.8.18	3%	273
21.8.18 – 29.3.20	3.25%	587
30.3.20 – 6.4.20	2.75%	8
7.4.20 – 6.1.22	2.60%	640
7.1.22 – 20.2.22	2.75%	45
21.2.22 – 4.4.22	3.00%	43
5.4.22 –	3.25%	

Repayment interest

A repayment of tax (or associated penalty) carries interest at the repayment interest rate from the 'repayment interest start date' until the date on which the repayment is made. The '*repayment interest start date*' is arrived at as set out below.

- Where the repayment is of an amount which has been paid to HMRC, the repayment interest start date is the *later* of date A and date B, where:
  date A = the date on which the amount was paid to HMRC; and
  date B = the date on which payment of the amount to HMRC became due and payable to HMRC (where it was paid in connection with a liability to make a payment to HMRC).
- Where the repayment is of an amount which has not been paid to HMRC but is payable by them by virtue of a return having been filed or a claim having been made, the repayment interest start date is the *later* of date C and date D, where:
  date C = the date (if any) on which the return was required to be filed or the claim was required to be made; and
  date D = the date on which the return was in fact filed or the claim was in fact made.
- Where the repayment is the result of a loss relief claim affecting two or more years, the repayment interest start date is 31 January following the *later* year in relation to the claim, i.e. on a claim to carry back a loss, the tax year in which the loss arises.

Rates of interest		*Days*
31.10.11 –	0.5%	

Interest on tax paid by companies

Corporation tax self-assessment

accounting periods ending after 30.6.99

Interest on unpaid tax

Interest on unpaid tax runs from the due date (generally nine months and one day after the end of the accounting period, see page 38) to the actual date of payment. It is deductible from profits.

Rates of interest		*Days*
29.9.09 – 22.8.16	3%	2,520
23.8.16 – 20.11.17	2.75%	455
21.11.17 – 20.8.18	3%	273
21.8.18 – 29.3.20	3.25%	587
30.3.20 – 6.4.20	2.75%	8
7.4.20 – 6.1.22	2.60%	640
7.1.22 – 20.2.22	2.75%	45
21.2.22 – 4.4.22	3.00%	43
5.4.22 –	3.25%	

Interest on overpaid tax

Interest on overpaid tax runs from the later of:

(a) the date on which the tax was paid, and
(b) the due date (generally nine months and one day after the end of the accounting period, see page 38)

to the date the repayment order is issued. The interest is taxable.

Close company loan repayment/release/write-off. Interest runs from the later of the date tax was paid and nine months after the end of the accounting period in which the loan was repaid, released or written off.

Rates of interest		*Days*
29.9.09	0.5%	

Interest on unpaid instalments

Interest on unpaid instalments for 'large companies' and 'very large companies' (see page 38) is paid from the due date to the earlier of

(a) the date of payment, and
(b) nine months after the end of the accounting period

(after which the normal interest rate provisions apply). The interest is deductible from profits.

Rates of interest		*Days*
16.3.09 – 14.8.16	1.5%	2,710
15.8.16 – 12.11.17	1.25%	455
13.11.17 – 12.8.18	1.5%	273
13.8.18 – 22.3.20	1.75%	588
23.3.20 – 29.3.20	1.25%	7
30.3.20 – 26.12.21	1.10%	637
27.12.21 – 13.2.22	1.25%	49
14.2.22 – 27.3.22	1.50%	42
28.3.22	1.75%	

Interest on overpaid instalments and early payments

Interest on overpaid instalments for 'large companies' and 'very large companies' (see page 38), and on early payments by other companies is paid from the date the excess arises (but not earlier than the due date of the first instalment) to the earlier of

(a) the date of repayment, and
(b) nine months after the end of the accounting period

(whereafter the normal interest rate provisions apply). The interest is taxable.

Rates of interest		*Days*
21.9.09 –	0.5%	

Income tax on company payments

Interest on unpaid tax is chargeable on income tax payable by companies from the due date (14 days after the end of the relevant return period) to the actual date of payment.

Interest on tax repaid carries interest from the day after the end of the accounting period in which the payments/franked investment income were received until the repayment order is issued.

Rates of interest		*Days*
Payment due after 13.10.99		
29.9.09 – 22.8.16	3%	2,520
23.8.16 – 20.11.17	2.75%	455
21.11.17 – 20.8.18	3%	273
21.8.18 – 29.3.20	3.25%	587
30.3.20 – 6.4.20	2.75%	8
7.4.20 – 6.1.22	2.60%	640
7.1.22 – 20.2.22	2.75%	45
21.2.22 – 4.4.22	3.00%	43
5.4.22 –	3.25%	

Digital services tax

Interest on unpaid tax

Interest runs from the date tax is due and payable until the date of payment.

Rates of interest		*Days*
14.10.20 – 6.1.22	2.60%	450
7.1.22 – 20.2.22	2.75%	45
21.2.22 – 4.4.22	3.00%	43
5.4.22 –	3.25%	

Interest on overpaid tax

Where a payment in respect of digital services tax liability for an accounting period is made before the due date, the payment carries interest at the applicable rate from the later of:

(a) the date the payment is made, and
(b) 6 months and 13 days from the start of the accounting period,

until the due date.

Rates of interest		*Days*
14.10.20 –	0.5%	

NICs Class 1A, 1B and 4, stamp duty and SDLT

Interest on unpaid tax. Interest runs from the relevant date until the date of payment. Interest is payable gross and is not tax deductible.

Rates of interest		*Days*
29.9.09 – 22.8.16	3%	2,520
23.8.16 – 20.11.17	2.75%	455
21.11.17 – 20.8.18	3%	273
21.8.18 – 29.3.20	3.25%	587
30.3.20 – 6.4.20	2.75%	8
7.4.20 – 6.1.22	2.60%	640
7.1.22 – 20.2.22	2.75%	45
21.2.22 – 4.4.22	3.00%	43
5.4.22 –	3.25%	

Interest on overpaid tax: repayment supplement

For 1996/97 onwards, interest runs from the date of payment (or, for income tax deducted at source, from 31 January following the year of assessment) to the date the repayment order is issued. See page 77 for the harmonised interest regime which now applies to income tax, capital gains tax, Class 1 NICs and SDRT.

Rates of interest		*Days*
29.9.09 –	0.5%	

Relevant dates

The relevant dates are as follows.

(a) **Class 4 NIC**
Interim payments (see page 68) – due date for payment.
Any other case – 31 January after the year of assessment or, where taxpayer gave notice of chargeability before 5 October following the year of assessment and the return was not issued until after 31 October, three months after notice to deliver the return, if later.
In practice, where a return is submitted by 30 September for calculation by HMRC of the tax due, interest runs from 30 days after notification of the liability to the taxpayer if after 31 December.

(b) **Stamp duty.** 30 days after date instrument is executed.

(c) **Class 1A NIC.** 19 July after the end of the relevant tax year.

(d) **PAYE settlement agreement.** 19 October after the end of the relevant tax year.

(e) **Class 1B NIC.** 19 October after the end of the relevant tax year.

(f) **SDLT.** 14 days (30 days before 1 March 2019) after the effective date of the transaction.

Inheritance tax

Unpaid tax

Interest is chargeable on unpaid inheritance tax from the due date for payment (see page 73) to the actual date of payment at the rates shown below. Interest is payable gross and is not deductible in computing income, profits or losses for tax purposes.

Rates of interest		*Days*
29.9.09 – 22.8.16	3%	2,520
23.8.16 – 20.11.17	2.75%	455
21.11.17 – 20.8.18	3%	273
21.8.18 – 29.3.20	3.25%	587
30.3.20 – 6.4.20	2.75%	8
7.4.20 – 6.1.22	2.60%	640
7.1.22 – 20.2.22	2.75%	45
21.2.22 – 4.4.22	3.00%	43
5.4.22 –	3.25%	

Interest on tax repaid

Any repayment of inheritance tax or interest paid carries interest from the date of payment to the date the repayment order is issued at the rates shown below. The interest is tax-free.

Rates of interest		*Days*
29.9.09 –	0.5%	

Mileage allowances car, cycling and motor cycling allowances

Car or van mileage rates (note (a))

	Mileage allowance First 10,000	Over 10,000
2011/12 onwards	45p	25p

Car or van passengers (note (b))

	Mileage allowance
2006/07 onwards	5p

Cycling allowance (note (c))

	Mileage allowance
2006/07 onwards	20p

Motorcycle allowance (note (c))

	Mileage allowance
2006/07 onwards	24p

Advisory electricity rate for company cars (note (g))

	Cost per mile
1.12.21 onwards	5p
Before 1.12.21	4p

Advisory fuel rates for company cars (notes (d), (e))

	Fuel cost per mile Petrol	Diesel	LPG
1.3.22 onwards			
Up to 1,400 cc	13p	—	8p
Up to 1,600 cc	—	11p	—
1,401–2,000 cc	15p	—	10p
1,601–2,000 cc	—	13p	—
Over 2,000 cc	22p	16p	15p
1.12.21 – 28.2.22			
Up to 1,400 cc	13p	—	9p
Up to 1,600 cc	—	11p	—
1,401–2,000 cc	15p	—	10p
1,601–2,000 cc	—	13p	—
Over 2,000 cc	22p	16p	15p
1.9.21 – 30.11.21			
Up to 1,400 cc	12p	—	7p
Up to 1,600 cc	—	10p	—
1,401–2,000 cc	14p	—	8p
1,601–2,000 cc	—	12p	—
Over 2,000 cc	20p	15p	12p
1.6.21 – 31.8.21			
Up to 1,400 cc	11p	—	8p
Up to 1,600 cc	—	9p	—
1,401–2,000 cc	13p	—	9p
1,601–2,000 cc	—	11p	—
Over 2,000 cc	19p	13p	14p
1.3.21 – 31.5.21			
Up to 1,400 cc	10p	—	7p
Up to 1,600 cc	—	9p	—
1,401–2,000 cc	12p	—	8p
1,601–2,000 cc	—	11p	—
Over 2,000 cc	18p	12p	12p

Notes

(a) The mileage allowances that can be paid free of tax and NICs to employees who use their own cars for business travel are statutory. Where employers pay less than the statutory rate, employees can claim tax relief on the difference. Employees cannot claim actual business motoring costs if these are above the statutory rates. [*ITEPA 2003, ss 229–232, 235, 236*].

(b) Tax and NIC free allowance for each fellow employee passenger carried. [*ITEPA 2003, ss 233, 234*].

(c) Employers can pay employees up to the mileage allowance tax free for using their own cycles/motorcycles for business travel. Employees can claim tax relief on the mileage allowance if their employer pays no cycle/motorcycle allowance (or on the balance up to the mileage allowance if the employer pays less than this rate). [*ITEPA 2003, ss 229–232, 235, 236*].

(d) The advisory fuel rates for company cars can be used to reimburse employees for business motoring in company cars and may be used for reimbursement by employees of fuel used for private motoring. The advisory rates will not be binding where the employer can demonstrate that the cost of business motoring is higher than the advisory rates or where a lower rate would cover the full cost of private fuel. HMRC will accept that, for one month from the date of change, employers may use either the previous or new current rates.

(e) The advisory fuel rates can also be used to reclaim VAT on fuel costs reimbursed for business travel by employees in company cars. The employer must obtain and keep a valid VAT invoice.

(f) Hybrid cars are treated as petrol or diesel cars accordingly.

(g) In August 2018 HMRC started publishing an advisory electricity rate, although electricity is not treated as a fuel for car fuel benefit purposes.

Miscellaneous levies and taxes

Aggregates levy [*FA 2001 ss 16–49, Schs 4–10*]

Aggregates levy applies to any aggregate that is subjected to commercial exploitation unless specifically exempt or previously used for construction purposes. Aggregate is rock, gravel or sand, together with whatever substances are incorporated in the rock, gravel or sand or naturally occur mixed with it. The rate of tax (apportioned on amounts less than one tonne) is:

1.4.09 onwards	£2.00 per tonne

Annual tax on enveloped dwellings [*FA 2013, ss 94–174, Schs 33–35; SI 2021 No 245; SI 2022 No 399*]

The annual tax on enveloped dwellings applies to companies, collective investment schemes and partnerships with company members which have a chargeable interest in land in the UK which consists of a dwelling at any time in a chargeable period. See also pages 18, 37.

Property value	*Annual charge* 1.4.19–31.3.20	1.4.20–31.3.21	1.4.21–31.3.22	1.4.22–31.3.23
£500,001 to £1,000,000	£3,650	£3,700	£3,700	£3,800
£1,000,001 to £2,000,000	£7,400	£7,500	£7,500	£7,700
£2,000,001 to £5,000,000	£24,800	£25,200	£25,300	£26,050
£5,000,001 to £10,000,000	£57,900	£58,850	£59,100	£60,900
£10,000,001 to £20,000,000	£116,100	£118,050	£118,600	£122,250
£20,000,001 or more	£232,350	£236,250	£237,400	£244,750

Note

(a) Where the taxpayer does not have the chargeable interest throughout the chargeable period the annual charge is reduced accordingly on a daily basis.

Bank levy [*FA 2011, s 73, Sch 19*]

Bank levy is a tax based upon the total chargeable equity and liabilities as reported in the relevant balance sheets of banks, banking and building society groups at the end of each chargeable period. The levy is collected through the corporation tax self-assessment system. The rates are as follows:

	Rate (notes (a), (b)) 1.1.16 – 31.12.16	1.1.17 – 31.12.17	1.1.18 – 31.12.18	1.1.19 – 31.12.19	1.1.20 – 31.12.20	1.1.21 onwards
Long term chargeable equity and liabilities	0.09%	0.085%	0.08%	0.075%	0.07%	0.05%
Short term chargeable liabilities	0.18%	0.17%	0.16%	0.15%	0.14%	0.1%

Notes

(a) Where the chargeable period straddles any of the above periods, the chargeable equity and liabilities are apportioned between the periods on a time basis and the levy is charged accordingly.

(b) The first £20 billion of the chargeable equity and liabilities is exempt from the levy. The £20 billion is apportioned between the long-term equity and liabilities and the short-term liabilities.

Climate change levy [*FA 2000, s 30, Sch 6; FA 2021, s 109*]

Climate change levy (CCL) is a single stage tax chargeable on taxable supplies of taxable commodities. A supply is excluded from the levy if it is for domestic use or for use by a charity otherwise than in the course or furtherance of a business. With effect from 1 April 2013 separate carbon price support rates apply outside Northern Ireland to solid fossil fuels, gas and liquid petroleum gas used in most forms of electricity generation. The rates are as follows:

Taxable commodity	*Main rates* (note (a)) 1.4.19 – 31.3.20	1.4.20 – 31.3.21	1.4.21 – 31.3.22	1.4.22 – 31.3.23
Electricity	0.847p per kWh	0.811p per kWh	0.775p per kWh	0.775p per kWh
Gas supplied by a gas utility or supplied in a gaseous state that is of a kind supplied by a gas utility	0.339p per kWh	0.406p per kWh	0.465p per kWh	0.568p per kWh
Petroleum gas or other gaseous hydrocarbon supplied in a liquid state	2.175p per kg	2.175p per kg	2.175p per kg	2.175p per kg
Coal and lignite, coke and semi-coke of coal or lignite and petroleum coke	2.653p per kg	3.174p per kg	3.640p per kg	4.449p per kg
Natural gas	0.331p per kWh	0.331p per kWh	0.331p per kWh	0.331p per kWh
Liquid petroleum gas	5.280p per kg	5.280p per kg	5.280p per kg	5.280p per kg
Coal and other taxable solid fossil fuels	154.79p per gross gigajoule	154.79p per gross gigajoule	154.79p per gross gigajoule	154.79p per gross gigajoule

Notes

(a) This is the rate at which CCL is payable if the supply is not a reduced-rate supply and the carbon price support rates do not apply.

(b) A reduction in the CCL main rates applies for energy intensive industries that have entered into a negotiated energy efficiency CCL agreement and from 1 April 2022 is generally 86% (83% from 1 April 2021 to 31 March 2022; 81% from 1 April 2020 to 31 March 2021; 78% from 1 April 2019 to 31 March 2020). The reduction is 92% for supplies of electricity on or after 1 April 2020 (93% from 1 April 2019 to 31 March 2020). The reduction is 77% for liquefied petroleum gas from 1 April 2020 (previous reduction was the same as for other commodities). Energy intensive users are those that operate a Part A process listed in *Pollution Prevention and Control (England and Wales) Regulations 2000 (SI 2000/1973), Sch 1*. From 1 April 2014 supplies of taxable commodities used in metallurgical and mineralogical processes are exempt.
Increased main rates will apply with effect from 1 April 2023: 0.672p per kWh for gas; and 5.258p per kg for coal, coke etc. The reduction for taxable commodities other than electricity and liquefied petroleum will be 88%.

Miscellaneous levies and taxes

Insurance premium tax [*FA 1994, ss 48–74, Schs 6A, 7, 7A, FA 2022, s 73*]

IPT is a tax on insurance premiums received under taxable insurance contracts. Insurance risk located in the UK is taxable unless specifically exempted by relating to one or more of (i) risks outside the UK; (ii) reinsurance; (iii) long-term business; (iv) commercial ships; (v) contracts relating to the Channel Tunnel; (vi) lifeboats and lifeboat equipment; (vii) commercial aircraft; (viii) international railway rolling stock; (ix) goods in foreign or international transit; (x) export finance related insurance; or (xi) contracts relating to motor vehicles for use by handicapped persons. The rates of tax are as follows:

	Standard rate	*Higher rate* (note (a))
From 1.6.17	12% (Tax fraction 3/28)	20% (Tax fraction 1/6)
1.10.16–31.5.17	10% (Tax fraction 1/11)	20% (Tax fraction 1/6)
1.11.15–30.9.16	9.5% (Tax fraction 19/219)	20% (Tax fraction 1/6)

Note

(a) The higher rate applies to insurance sales in three trading sectors where insurance is sold in relation to goods and services which are subject to VAT. These are (i) sales of motor cars, light vans or motorcycles; (ii) sales of electrical or mechanical domestic appliances; and (iii) sales of travel insurance.

Landfill tax [*FA 1996 ss 39–71, Sch 5; FA 2021, s 111; FA 2022, s 83*]

Landfill tax applies to all material (before 1 April 2018, waste) disposed of by way of landfill at a licensed landfill site unless the material is specifically exempt. Exemption applies to (i) material removed from inland waterways and harbours by dredging; (ii) material arising from mining and quarrying operations; (iii) pet cemeteries; and (iv) material arising from the clearance of contaminated land (where the exemption certificate application was made before 1 December 2008). From 1 April 2018 the scope of the tax is extended to disposals of material at sites operating without the appropriate licence or permit, and the exemptions above will not apply to these sites. The rates of tax are as follows:

	Active waste per tonne	*Inactive waste per tonne*
1.4.22 - 31.3.23	£98.60	£3.15
1.4.21 - 31.3.22	£96.70	£3.10
1.4.20 - 31.3.21	£94.15	£3.00
1.4.19 - 31.3.20	£91.35	£2.90
1.4.18 - 31.3.19	£88.95	£2.80
1.4.17 - 31.3.18	£86.10	£2.70
1.4.16 - 31.3.17	£84.40	£2.65

The lower rate applies to those inactive wastes listed in the *Landfill Tax (Qualifying Material) Order 2011 (SI 2011 No 1017)* and the standard rate to all other taxable waste. It does not apply to disposals of material at sites operating without the appropriate licence or permit.

Notes

(a) From 1 April 2023 the rates will be £102.10 per tonne for active waste and £3.25 per tonne for inactive waste.

(b) Landfill site operators can claim a tax credit of 90% of contributions made to approved environmental bodies, subject to a maximum percentage of the liability during the contribution year.

(c) With effect from 1 April 2015, landfill tax does not apply in Scotland. Scottish landfill tax applies with effect from that date. The standard and lower rates are the same as the landfill tax rates for active and inactive waste respectively.

(d) With effect from 1 April 2018, landfill tax does not apply in Wales. Landfill disposals tax applies with effect from that date. The standard and lower rates are the same as the landfill tax rates for active and inactive waste respectively, but there is an unauthorised disposals rate of £147.90 from 1 April 2022 (£145.05 from 1 April 2021; £141.20 from 1 April 2020; £137.00 from 1 April 2019; £133.45 from 1 April 2018).

Miscellaneous levies and taxes

Vehicle excise duty [*VERA 1994, Sch 1; FA 2009, ss 13, 14; FA 2011, ss 21, 22; FA 2021, s 104; FA 2022, ss 78, 79*]

VED ('car tax' or 'road tax') is a duty charged in respect of any mechanically-propelled vehicle which is used or kept on a public road in the UK. The duty is paid on a licence taken out by the person in whose name the vehicle is registered or by its keeper. Annual rates are as follows:

Light passenger vehicles registered on or after 1.3.01 but before 1.4.17: Standard rate (notes (a), (b))

Band	CO_2 emissions g/km	1.4.21–31.3.22	1.4.22–31.3.23
A	Up to 100	£0	£0
B	101–110	£20	£20
C	111–120	£30	£30
D	121–130	£130	£135
E	131–140	£155	£165
F	141–150	£170	£180
G	151–165	£210	£220
H	166–175	£250	£265
I	176–185	£275	£290
J	186–200	£315	£330
K (note (c))	201–225	£340	£360
L	226–255	£585	£615
M	Over 255	£600	£630

Light passenger vehicles first registered on or after 1.4.17

	CO_2 emissions g/km	1.4.21–31.3.22	1.4.22–31.3.23
See note (f)	0	£0	£0
	1–50	£10	£10
	51–75	£25	£25
	76–90	£115	£120
	91–100	£140	£150
	101–110	£160	£170
	111–130	£180	£190
	131–150	£220	£230
	151–170	£555	£585
	171–190	£895	£945
	191–225	£1,345	£1,420
	226–255	£1,910	£2,015
	Over 255	£2,245	£2,365

Light passenger vehicles registered before 1.3.01: Standard rate

Engine size below 1,550cc	£170	£180
Over 1,549cc	£280	£295
Motorcycles		
Engine size up to 150cc	£21	£22
151–400cc	£45	£47
401–600cc	£69	£73
Over 600cc	£96	£101

Light passenger vehicles first registered on or after 1.4.17: Standard rate (note (f))

CO_2 emissions g/km	1.4.21–31.3.22	1.4.22–31.3.23
0	£0	£0
1–50	£155	£165
51–75	£155	£165
76–90	£155	£165
91–100	£155	£165
101–110	£155	£165
111–130	£155	£165
131–150	£155	£165
151–170	£155	£165
171–190	£155	£165
191–225	£155	£165
226–255	£155	£165
Over 255	£155	£165

First year rate diesel vehicles (notes (d), (f))

	1.4.21–31.3.22	1.4.22–31.3.23
0	£0	£0
1–50	£25	£25
51–75	£115	£120
76–90	£140	£150
91–100	£160	£170
101–110	£180	£190
111–130	£220	£230
131–150	£555	£585
151–170	£895	£945
171–190	£1,345	£1,420
191–225	£1,910	£2,015
226–255	£2,245	£2,365
Over 255	£2,245	£2,365

Light goods vehicles registered on or after 1.3.01: Standard rate (note (e))

Standard rate	£275	£290
Euro 4 & 5	£140	£140

Notes

(a) Reduced rates apply to certain vehicles powered by alternative fuels.

(b) Duty can also be paid for a six-month licence. The charge is 55% of the equivalent annual rate. With effect from 1 October 2014 it is possible to pay the charge monthly or biannually by direct debit, subject to a 5% surcharge.

(c) Band K includes cars that have a CO_2 figure over 225g/km but were registered before 23 March 2006.

(d) First-year rates are payable for a vehicle's first licence taken out at first registration. The standard rate applies to subsequent licences.

(e) For light goods vehicles registered before 1 March 2001 the same rates apply as for light passenger vehicles registered before that date.

(f) A different banding system applies to cars registered on or after 1.4.17. There are no first-year rates for cars registered before 1.4.17. First-year rates for cars registered from 1.4.17 are still based on CO_2 emissions but a standard flat rate applies to all cars except those with zero emissions. Cars with a list price above £40,000 when new pay an additional rate of £355 per year (£335 per year before 1 April 2022; £325 per year before 1 April 2021; £320 per year before 1 April 2020) for the first 5 years in which the standard rate is paid. Alphabetical VED banding does not apply. From 1.4.18 there is a separate first-year rate for diesel cars that do not meet the Euro 6d emissions standard.

Car benefit – Cars first registered before 6 April 2020					
CO_2 emis-sions (g/km)	Electric range (miles)	% of list price		% of list price	
		Benefit for 2020/21		Benefit for 2021/22	
		Petrol	Diesel	Petrol	Diesel
0	N/A	0%	0%	1%	5%
1–50	>130	2%	6%	2%	6%
1–50	70–129	5%	9%	5%	9%
1–50	40–69	8%	12%	8%	12%
1–50	30–39	12%	16%	12%	16%
1–50	<30	14%	18%	14%	18%
51–54		15%	19%	15%	19%
55–59		16%	20%	16%	20%
60–64		17%	21%	17%	21%
65–69		18%	22%	18%	22%
70–74		19%	23%	19%	23%
75–79		20%	24%	20%	24%
80–84		21%	25%	21%	25%
85–89		22%	26%	22%	26%
90–94		23%	27%	23%	27%
95–99		24%	28%	24%	28%
100–104		25%	29%	25%	29%
105–109		26%	30%	26%	30%
110–114		27%	31%	27%	31%
115–119		28%	32%	28%	32%
120–124		29%	33%	29%	33%
125–129		30%	34%	30%	34%
130–134		31%	35%	31%	35%
135–139		32%	36%	32%	36%
140–144		33%	37%	33%	37%
145–149		34%	37%	34%	37%
150–154		35%	37%	35%	37%
155–159		36%	37%	36%	37%
160 or more		37%	37%	37%	37%

Car benefit – Cars first registered on or after 6 April 2020					
CO_2 emis-sions (g/km)	Electric range (miles)	% of list price		% of list price	
		Benefit for 2020/21		Benefit for 2021/22	
		Petrol	Diesel	Petrol	Diesel
0	N/A	0%	0%	1%	5%
1–50	>130	0%	0%	1%	5%
1–50	70–129	3%	7%	4%	8%
1–50	40–69	6%	10%	7%	11%
1–50	30–39	10%	14%	11%	15%
1–50	<30	12%	16%	13%	17%
51–54		13%	17%	14%	18%
55–59		14%	18%	15%	19%
60–64		15%	19%	16%	20%
65–69		16%	20%	17%	21%
70–74		17%	21%	18%	22%
75–79		18%	22%	19%	23%
80–84		19%	23%	20%	24%
85–89		20%	24%	21%	25%
90–94		21%	25%	22%	26%
95–99		22%	26%	23%	27%
100–104		23%	27%	24%	28%
105–109		24%	28%	25%	29%
110–114		25%	29%	26%	30%
115–119		26%	30%	27%	31%
120–124		27%	31%	28%	32%
125–129		28%	32%	29%	33%
130–134		29%	33%	30%	34%
135–139		30%	34%	31%	35%
140–144		31%	35%	32%	36%
145–149		32%	36%	33%	37%
150–154		33%	37%	34%	37%
155–159		34%	37%	35%	37%
160–164		35%	37%	36%	37%
165–169		36%	37%	37%	37%
170 or more		37%	37%	37%	37%

Benefit for 2022/23			
		% of list price	
CO_2 emissions (g/km)	Electric range (miles)	Petrol	Diesel
0	N/A	2%	N/A
1–50	>130	2%	N/A
1–50	70–129	5%	N/A
1–50	40–69	8%	N/A
1–50	30–39	12%	N/A
1–50	<30	14%	18%
51–54		15%	19%
55–59		16%	20%
60–64		17%	21%
65–69		18%	22%
70–74		19%	23%
75–79		20%	24%
80–84		21%	25%
85–89		22%	26%
90–94		23%	27%
95–99		24%	28%
100–104		25%	29%
105–109		26%	30%
110–114		27%	31%
115–119		28%	32%
120–124		29%	33%
125–129		30%	34%
130–134		31%	35%
135–139		32%	36%
140–144		33%	37%
145–149		34%	37%
150–154		35%	37%
155–159		36%	37%
160 or above		37%	37%

Notes

(a) The cash equivalent of a car benefit is treated as earnings from employment.

(b) The car benefit is linked to the car's CO_2 emissions. For all cars registered on or after 1 March 2001, the definitive CO_2 emissions figure for tax purposes is recorded on the vehicle registration document (V5). For cars first registered after 31 December 1997 and before 1 March 2001, the Vehicle Certification Agency supply CO_2 emissions and other relevant information on their website at carfueldata.direct.gov.uk. For 2020/21 onwards for all cars first registered from 6 April 2020 a new regime for calculating a car's CO_2 emissions, known as the Worldwide harmonised Light vehicles Test Procedure (WLTP) applies. This replaces emissions testing under the New European Driving Cycle (NEDC). NEDC emissions values still apply to cars first registered between 1 October 1999 and 5 April 2020 inclusive.

For cars registered after 31 December 1997 with no approved CO_2 emissions figure, for 2020/21 onwards, the tax charge is 24% of the list price for engines up to 1,400 cc, 35% for engines of 1,401 to 2,000 cc and 37% for engines above 2,000 cc or cars without a cylinder capacity.

For cars registered after 31 December 1997

(i) cars which are incapable of producing carbon dioxide engine emissions when driven are charged to tax on 2% of the list price (1% for 2021/22; 0% for 2020/21); and

(ii) automatic cars made available to disabled drivers are taxable on the equivalent manual car, if less.

(c) For cars registered before 1 January 1998, for 2020/21 onwards, the tax charge is 24% of the list price for engines up to 1,400 cc, 35% for engines of 1,401 to 2,000 cc and 37% for engines above 2,000 cc. Cars without a cylinder capacity are taxed on 37% of the car's price.

(d) The general rule is that where a car's CO_2 emissions figure is not a multiple of 5g/km, it is rounded down to the nearest 5. This rule does not apply in determining whether a car qualifies for the following rates: all rates less than the 20%/24% rates for 2020/21 and 2021/22 for cars registered before 6 April 2020; all rates less than the 18%/22% rates for 2020/21 for cars registered on or after 6 April 2020; all rates less than the 19%/23% rates for 2021/22 for cars registered on or after 6 April 2020; and all rates less than the 20%/24% rates for 2022/23. In such cases, the emissions figure must not exceed the appropriate figure shown in the table.

(e) The diesel supplement is 4%. The supplement does not apply to hybrid cars or to cars registered on or after 1 September 2017 which meet the Euro 6d emissions standards.

(f) The 'list price' is the price published by the manufacturer, importer or distributor (inclusive of delivery charges and taxes) at the time of registration. It includes any optional extras supplied with the car when first made available to the employee, together with any further accessory costing £100 or more, but does not include certain security enhancements for employees whose employment creates a threat to personal security. Where a car is converted to run on road fuel gas, the equipment is not regarded as an accessory. Where an employee makes a capital contribution to the initial cost of the car, the price of the car for the year of contribution and subsequent years is reduced by that contribution or £5,000 if less.

(g) The value of the benefit is reduced proportionately if the car is 'unavailable' for part of the year. It is unavailable before and after it is made available to the employee and on any day in a period of 30 consecutive days throughout which it is not available.

(h) The cash equivalent (after any reductions under (e) above) is reduced (or extinguished) by the amount of contributions which an employee is required to make for private use. For 2017/18 onwards, the reduction is available only if contributions are paid on or before 6 July after the tax year in which the private use is undertaken.

(i) Where a car is more than 15 years old at the end of the tax year and has a market value of at least £15,000, market value, if greater, is substituted for list price.

(j) Employers also pay Class 1A national insurance contributions on the scale charge.

[*ITEPA 2003, ss 114–148*].

Car fuel benefit – Cars first registered before 6 April 2020					
		2020/21		2021/22	
CO_2 emissions (g/km)	Electric range (miles)	Petrol (£)	Diesel (£)	Petrol (£)	Diesel (£)
0	N/A	0	0	246	1,230
1–50	>130	490	1,470	492	1,476
1–50	70–129	1,225	2,205	1,230	2,214
1–50	40–69	1,960	2,940	1,968	2,952
1–50	30–39	2,940	3,920	2,952	3,936
1–50	<30	3,430	4,410	3,444	4,428
51–54		3,675	4,655	3,690	4,674
55–59		3,920	4,900	3,936	4,920
60–64		4,165	5,145	4,182	5,166
65–69		4,410	5,390	4,428	5,412
70–74		4,655	5,635	4,674	5,658
75–79		4,900	5,880	4,920	5,904
80–84		5,145	6,125	5,166	6,150
85–89		5,390	6,370	5,412	6,396
90–94		5,635	6,615	5,658	6,642
95–99		5,880	6,860	5,904	6,888
100–104		6,125	7,105	6,150	7,134
105–109		6,370	7,350	6,396	7,380
110–114		6,615	7,595	6,642	7,626
115–119		6,860	7,840	6,888	7,872
120–124		7,105	8,085	7,134	8,118
125–129		7,350	8,330	7,380	8,364
130–134		7,595	8,575	7,626	8,610
135–139		7,840	8,820	7,872	8,856
140–144		8,085	9,065	8,118	9,102
145–149		8,330	9,065	8,364	9,102
150–154		8,575	9,065	8,610	9,102
155–159		8,820	9,065	8,856	9,102
160 or more		9,065	9,065	9,102	9,102

Cafuel benefit – Cars first registered on or after 6 April 2020					
		2020/21		2021/22	
CO_2 emissions (g/km)	Electric range (miles)	Petrol (£)	Diesel (£)	Petrol (£)	Diesel (£)
0	N/A	0	0	246	1,230
1–50	>130	0	0	246	1,230
1–50	70–129	735	1,715	984	1,968
1–50	40–69	1,470	2,450	1,722	2,706
1–50	30–39	2,450	3,430	2,706	3,690
1–50	<30	2,940	3,920	3,198	4,182
51–54		3,185	4,165	3,444	4,428
55–59		3,430	4,410	3,690	4,674
60–64		3,675	4,655	3,936	4,920
65–69		3,920	4,900	4,182	5,166
70–74		4,165	5,145	4,428	5,412
75–79		4,410	5,390	4,674	5,658
80–84		4,655	5,635	4,920	5,904
85–89		4,900	5,880	5,166	6,150
90–94		5,145	6,125	5,412	6,396
95–99		5,390	6,370	5,658	6,642
100–104		5,635	6,615	5,904	6,888
105–109		5,880	6,860	6,150	7,134
110–114		6,125	7,105	6,396	7,380
115–119		6,370	7,350	6,642	7,626
120–124		6,615	7,595	6,888	7,872
125–129		6,860	7,840	7,134	8,118
130–134		7,105	8,085	7,380	8,364
135–139		7,350	8,330	7,626	8,610
140–144		7,595	8,575	7,872	8,856
145–149		7,840	8,820	8,118	9,102
150–154		8,085	9,065	8,364	9,102
155–159		8,330	9,065	8,610	9,102
160–164		8,575	9,065	8,856	9,102
165–169		8,820	9,065	9,102	9,102
170 or more		9,065	9,065	9,102	9,102

Benefit for 2022/23			
		% of list price	
CO_2 emissions (g/km)	Electric range (miles)	Petrol	Diesel
0	N/A	506	N/A
1–50	>130	506	N/A
1–50	70–129	1,265	N/A
1–50	40–69	2,024	N/A
1–50	30–39	3,036,	N/A
1–50	<30	3,542	4,554
51–54		3,795	4,807
55–59		4,048	5,060
60–64		4,301	5,313
65–69		4,554	5,566
70–74		4,807	5,819
75–79		5,060	6,072
80–84		5,313	6,325
85–89		5,566	6,578
90–94		5,819	6,831
95–99		6,072	7,084
100–104		6,325	7,337
105–109		6,578	7,590
110–114		6,831	7,843
115–119		7,084	8,096
120–124		7,337	8,349
125–129		7,590	8,602
130–134		7,843	8,855
135–139		8,096	9,108
140–144		8,349	9,361
145–149		8,602	9,361
150–154		8,855	9,361
155–159		9,108	9,361
160 or above		9,361	9,361

Notes

(a) The cash equivalent of the benefit of car fuel is taxable as earnings.

(b) The same percentage figure on page 82 used to calculate the car benefit charge for the company car, which is directly linked to the car's CO_2 emissions, is used to calculate the benefit charge for fuel provided for private motoring. The relevant percentage figure is multiplied by £25,300 for 2022/23; £24,600 for 2021/22; and £24,500 for 2020/21.

(c) The benefit is reduced to nil if the employee is required to, and does, make good, on or before 6 July after the tax year in which the private use is undertaken, all fuel provided for private use, including journeys between home and normal place of work. There is no taxable benefit where the employer only provides fuel for business travel. The charge is proportionately reduced where the employee stops receiving free fuel part way through the tax year, but where free fuel is subsequently provided in the same tax year, the full year's charge is payable. [*ITEPA 2003, ss 151, 152*].

(d) The benefit is proportionately reduced where a car is not available or is incapable of being used for part of a year (being at least 30 days). [*ITEPA 2003, s 152*].

(e) Fuel provided for private motoring of an employee but not for a company car and all fuel provided for lower-paid minsters of religion (e.g. by paying garage bills or by use of credit tokens or vouchers) is taxable on the cost to the employer less any contributions from the employee.

(f) Employers pay Class 1A national insurance contributions on the amount of the benefit shown.

National insurance contributions Class 1

Class 1 (earnings related)		2022/23	
Lower earnings limit	— per week	£123	
	— per month	£533	
	— per year	£6,396	
Primary earnings threshold (6 April 2022–5 July 2022)	— per week	£190	
	— per month	£823	
	— per year	£9,880	
Primary earnings threshold (6 July 2022–5 April 2022) (note (h))	— per week	£242	
	— per month	£1,048	
	— per year	£12,570	
Primary earnings threshold (director) (note (i))	— per week	£229	
	— per month	—	
	— per year	£11,908	
Secondary earnings threshold	— per week	£175	
	— per month	£758	
	— per year	£9,100	
Upper earnings limit/Upper secondary threshold	— per week	£967	
	— per month	£4,189	
	— per year	£50,270	
Veterans' upper secondary threshold	— per week	£967	
	— per month	£4,189	
	— per year	£50,270	
Freeport upper secondary threshold (note (f))	— per week	£481	
	— per month	£2,083	
	— per year	£25,000	
General			
Employee (note (a))		Up to Primary threshold	Nil
		From Primary threshold to £967 pw	13.25%
		Balance above £967 pw	3.25%
Employer (notes (b), (e))		First £175 pw	Nil
		Balance above £175 pw	15.05%
Women at reduced rate			
Employee (note (a))		Up to Primary threshold	Nil
		From Primary threshold to £967 pw	7.1%
		Balance above £967 pw	3.25%

Notes

(a) For 2022/23, NICs are not payable on earnings up to and including the primary earnings threshold. Employees' rates are nil for employees of pensionable age although normal employers' contributions are still payable. Pensionable age is, in the case of a man born before 6 December 1953, 65, and in the case of a woman born before 6 April 1950, 60. For women born after 5 April 1950 and before 6 October 1954, and for men born after 5 December 1953 and before 6 October 1954, pensionable age rises on a sliding scale contained in *Pensions Act 1995, Sch 4 Pt 1*. For men and women born after 5 October 1954 and before 6 April 1960 pensionable age is 66. A sliding scale under *Sch 4 Pt 1* again applies to gradually increase the pensionable age for men and women born after 5 April 1960 and before 6 April 1961, so that for men and women born after 5 April 1961 pensionable age is 67. A further phased increase applies to those born on or after 6 April 1977 and before 6 April 1978, so that the pensionable age for those born after 5 April 1978 will be 68.

(b) For 2022/23, NICs are not payable on earnings up to and including the secondary earnings threshold. For employees below the age of 21 and apprentices under 25, NICs are not payable on earnings up to and including the upper secondary earnings threshold.

(c) See page 77 for interest on Class 1 NIC.

(d) For 2022/23, employers may claim an employment allowance of £5,000. The allowance is given effect by offset against the employer's liability for secondary Class 1 NICs. The allowance is not available to companies whose only employee is the director. From 6 April 2020 the allowance is only available to employers with a secondary Class 1 NICs liability below £100,000 in the preceding tax year. This £100,000 threshold applies cumulatively in the case of connected employers.

(e) From 6 April 2021 until 5 April 2024 employers of qualifying veterans are not required to pay Class 1 secondary NICs on earnings up to the veterans upper secondary threshold during the first year of their civilian employment. For 2021/22 employers must still pay the NIC as normal and claim it back retrospectively from April 2022 onwards.

(f) From 6 April 2022 employers in designated tax sites in Freeports will no longer be required to pay Class 1 secondary NICs on earnings up to the freeport upper secondary threshold for eligible new employees in the first 3 years of employment. The employer must elect to apply the relief in circumstances where they may also qualify for NIC relief for under 21s, under 25 apprentices or armed forces veterans.

(g) All Class 1, 1A, 1B and Class 4 NIC rates are increased by 1.25% for 2022/23 only in preparation for the introduction of the health and social care levy for 2023/24 onwards. The 1.25% levy will be payable on an amount of earnings or profits on which an employee, employer or self-employed individual is already liable to pay a qualifying NIC (Class 1, 1A, 1B and 4 NICs). For administrative purposes, the levy will operate in the same way as NICs. Individuals over state pensionable age will be liable to the levy. NIC rates will revert to the 2021/22 levels for 2023/24 onwards.

(h) At the Spring Statement on 23 March 2022, the Chancellor announced that the Class 1 primary threshold would increase from 6 July 2022 to align with the income tax personal allowance.

(i) Primary thresholds for 2022/23 for weekly and annual earnings periods for directors subject to SI 2001 No 1004, Reg 8.

National insurance contributions Class 1

Class 1 (earnings related)		2021/22		2020/21	
Lower earnings limit	— per week	£120		£120	
	— per month	£520		£520	
	— per year	£6,240		£6,240	
Primary earnings threshold	— per week	£184		£183	
	— per month	£797		£792	
	— per year	£9,568		£9,500	
Secondary earnings threshold	— per week	£170		£169	
	— per month	£737		£732	
	— per year	£8,840		£8,788	
Upper earnings limit/Upper secondary threshold	— per week	£967		£962	
	— per month	£4,189		£4,167	
	— per year	£50,270		£50,000	
General					
Employee (note (a))		First £184 pw	Nil	First £183 pw	Nil
		From £184 pw to £967 pw	12%	From £183 pw to £962 pw	12%
		Balance above £967 pw	2%	Balance above £962 pw	2%
Employer (notes (b), (e))		First £170 pw	Nil	First £169 pw	Nil
		Balance above £170 pw	13.8%	Balance above £169 pw	13.8%
Women at reduced rate					
Employee (note (a))		First £184 pw	Nil	First £183 pw	Nil
		From £184 pw to £967 pw	5.85%	From £183 pw to £962 pw	5.85%
		Balance above £967 pw	2%	Balance above £962 pw	2%

Notes

(a) For 2020/21 and 2021/22, NICs are not payable on earnings up to and including the primary earnings threshold. Employees' rates are nil for employees of pensionable age although normal employers' contributions are still payable. Pensionable age is, in the case of a man born before 6 December 1953, 65, and in the case of a woman born before 6 April 1950, 60. For women born after 5 April 1950 and before 6 October 1954, and for men born after 5 December 1953 and before 6 October 1954, pensionable age rises on a sliding scale contained in *Pensions Act 1995, Sch 4 Pt 1*. For men and women born after 5 October 1954 and before 6 April 1960 pensionable age is 66. A sliding scale under *Sch 4 Pt 1* again applies to gradually increase the pensionable age for men and women born after 5 April 1960 and before 6 April 1961, so that for men and women born after 5 April 1961 pensionable age is 67. A further phased increase applies to those born on or after 6 April 1977 and before 6 April 1978, so that the pensionable age for those born after 5 April 1978 will be 68.

(b) For 2020/21 and 2021/22, NICs are not payable on earnings up to and including the secondary earnings threshold. For employees below the age of 21 and apprentices under 25, NICs are not payable on earnings up to and including the upper secondary earnings threshold.

(c) See page 77 for interest on Class 1 NIC.

(d) For 2020/21 and 2021/22, employers may claim an employment allowance of £4,000. The allowance is given effect by offset against the employer's liability for secondary Class 1 NICs. The allowance is not available to companies whose only employee is the director. From 6 April 2020 the allowance is only available to employers with a secondary Class 1 NICs liability below £100,000 in the preceding tax year. This £100,000 threshold applies cumulatively in the case of connected employers.

(e) From 6 April 2021 until 5 April 2024 employers of qualifying veterans will no longer be required to pay Class 1 secondary NICs on earnings up to the upper secondary threshold during the first year of their civilian employment. For 2021–22 employers must still pay the NIC as normal and claim it back retrospectively from April 2022 onwards.

National insurance contributions Class 1

Class 1 (earnings related)		2019/20		2018/19	
Lower earnings limit	— per week	£118		£116	
	— per month	£512		£503	
	— per year	£6,136		£6,032	
Primary earnings threshold	— per week	£166		£162	
	— per month	£719		£702	
	— per year	£8,632		£8,424	
Secondary earnings threshold	— per week	£166		£162	
	— per month	£719		£702	
	— per year	£8,632		£8,424	
Upper earnings limit/Upper secondary threshold	— per week	£962		£892	
	— per month	£4,167		£3,863	
	— per year	£50,000		£46,350	
General					
Employee (note (a))		First £166 pw	Nil	First £162 pw	Nil
		From £166 pw to £962 pw	12%	From £162 pw to £892 pw	12%
		Balance above £962 pw	2%	Balance above £892 pw	2%
Employer (notes (b), (e))		First £166 pw	Nil	First £162 pw	Nil
		Balance above £166 pw	13.8%	Balance above £162 pw	13.8%
Women at reduced rate					
Employee (note (a))		First £166 pw	Nil	First £162 pw	Nil
		From £166 pw to £962 pw	5.85%	From £162 pw to £892 pw	5.85%
		Balance above £962 pw	2%	Balance above £892 pw	2%

Notes

(a) For 2018/19 and 2019/20, NICs are not payable on earnings up to and including the primary earnings threshold. Employees' rates are nil for employees of pensionable age although normal employers' contributions are still payable. Pensionable age is, in the case of a man born before 6 December 1953, 65, and in the case of a woman born before 6 April 1950, 60. For women born after 5 April 1950 and before 6 October 1954, and for men born after 5 December 1953 and before 6 October 1954, pensionable age rises on a sliding scale contained in *Pensions Act 1995, Sch 4 Pt 1*. For men and women born after 5 October 1954 and before 6 April 1960 pensionable age is 66. A sliding scale under *Sch 4 Pt 1* again applies to gradually increase the pensionable age for men and women born after 5 April 1960 and before 6 April 1961, so that for men and women born after 5 April 1961 pensionable age is 67. A further phased increase applies to those born on or after 6 April 1977 and before 6 April 1978, so that the pensionable age for those born after 5 April 1978 will be 68.

(b) For 2018/19 and 2019/20, NICs are not payable on earnings up to and including the secondary earnings threshold. For employees below the age of 21 and apprentices under 25, NICs are not payable on earnings up to and including the upper secondary earnings threshold.

(c) See page 77 for interest on Class 1 NIC.

(d) For 2018/19 and 2019/20, employers may claim an employment allowance of £3,000. The allowance is given effect by offset against the employer's liability for secondary Class 1 NICs. The allowance is not available to companies whose only employee is the director.

National insurance contributions Class 1

Class 1 (earnings related)		2017/18		2016/17	
Lower earnings limit	— per week	£113		£112	
	— per month	£490		£486	
	— per year	£5,876		£5,824	
Primary earnings threshold	— per week	£157		£155	
	— per month	£680		£672	
	— per year	£8,164		£8,060	
Secondary earnings threshold	— per week	£157		£156	
	— per month	£680		£676	
	— per year	£8,164		£8,112	
Upper earnings limit/Upper secondary threshold	— per week	£866		£827	
	— per month	£3,750		£3,583	
	— per year	£45,000		£43,000	
General					
Employee (note (a))		First £157 pw	Nil	First £155 pw	Nil
		From £157 pw to £866 pw	12%	From £155 pw to £827 pw	12%
		Balance above £866 pw	2%	Balance above £827 pw	2%
Employer (notes (b), (e))		First £157 pw	Nil	First £156 pw	Nil
		Balance above £157 pw	13.8%	Balance above £156 pw	13.8%
Women at reduced rate					
Employee (note (a))		First £157 pw	Nil	First £155 pw	Nil
		From £157 pw to £866 pw	5.85%	From £155 pw to £827 pw	5.85%
		Balance above £866 pw	2%	Balance above £827 pw	2%

Notes

(a) For 2016/17 and 2017/18, NICs are not payable on earnings up to and including the primary earnings threshold. Employees' rates are nil for employees of pensionable age although normal employers' contributions are still payable. Pensionable age is, in the case of a man born before 6 December 1953, 65, and in the case of a woman born before 6 April 1950, 60. For women born after 5 April 1950 and before 6 October 1954, and for men born after 5 December 1953 and before 6 October 1954, pensionable age rises on a sliding scale contained in *Pensions Act 1995, Sch 4 Pt 1*. For men and women born after 5 October 1954 and before 6 April 1960 pensionable age is 66. A sliding scale under *Sch 4 Pt 1* again applies to gradually increase the pensionable age for men and women born after 5 April 1960 and before 6 April 1961, so that for men and women born after 5 April 1961 pensionable age is 67. A further phased increase applies to those born on or after 6 April 1977 and before 6 April 1978, so that the pensionable age for those born after 5 April 1978 will be 68.

(b) For 2016/17 and 2017/18, NICs are not payable on earnings up to and including the secondary earnings threshold. For employees below the age of 21 and apprentices under 25, NICs are not payable on earnings up to and including the upper secondary earnings threshold.

(c) See page 77 for interest on Class 1 NIC.

(d) Employers may claim an employment allowance of £3,000 for 2017/18 and 2016/17. The allowance is given effect by offset against the employer's liability for secondary Class 1 NICs. For 2016/17 onwards the allowance is not available to companies whose only employee is the director.

National insurance contributions Classes 1A, 1B, 2, 3 and 4

	2022/23	2021/22	2020/21	2019/20	2018/19	2017/18	2016/17
Class 1A (note (a))	15.05%	13.8%	13.8%	13.8%	13.8%	13.8%	13.8%
Class 1B (PSAs) (note (b))	15.05%	13.8%	13.8%	13.8%	13.8%	13.8%	13.8%
Class 2 (self-employed, flat rate) (note (e))							
Small profits threshold/small earnings exemption—per year	£6,725	£6,515	£6,475	£6,365	£6,205	£6,025	£5,965
Contributions —per week	£3.15	£3.05	£3.05	£3.00	£2.95	£2.85	£2.80
Share fishermen	£3.80	£3.70	£3.70	£3.65	£3.60	£3.50	£3.45
Volunteer development workers	£6.15	£6.00	£6.00	£5.90	£5.80	£5.65	£5.60
Class 3 (voluntary contributions)							
Contributions —per week	£15.85	£15.40	£15.30	£15.00	£14.65	£14.25	£14.10
Class 4 (self-employed, profits related) (note (c))							
Lower annual limit	£11,908	£9,568	£9,500	£8,632	£8,424	£8,164	£8,060
Upper annual limit	£50,270	£50,270	£50,000	£50,000	£46,350	£45,000	£43,000
Percentage rate between lower and upper annual limits	10.25%	9%	9%	9%	9%	9%	9%
Percentage rate above upper annual limit	3.25%	2%	2%	2%	2%	2%	2%
Maximum contributions (note (d))							
Class 1 or Class 1/Class 2	£5,182.60	£4,979.88	£4,954.44	£5,062.56	£4,642.80	£4,509.24	£4,273.92
Class 4 limiting amount	£4,099.05	£3,824.83	£3,806.65	£3,882.12	£3,569.69	£3,466.29	£3,293.00

Notes

(a) **Class 1A contributions.** Class 1A contributions are payable by employers on the provision of cars and private fuel to employees and most other benefits in kind provided by employers. Employees' contributions are not payable. The income tax rules are used to determine the chargeable amount (see pages 84 to 86). Contributions are payable by 19 July following the tax year to which they relate. If private fuel is provided for use in an employee's own car, Class 1A contributions do not apply but there may be a liability for both employer's and employee's Class 1 contributions depending upon how the fuel is provided.
For the provisions relating to interest on unpaid and overpaid Class 1A contributions, see page 79.

(b) **Class 1B contributions.** Class 1B contributions are payable by employers by reference to the value of any items included in a PAYE settlement agreement (PSA) which would otherwise be earnings for Class 1 or Class 1A, including the amount of tax paid.
Employees' contributions are not payable. Income tax and Class 1B contributions on a PSA are payable by 19 October following the end of the tax year to which the PSA applies.

(c) **Class 2 and Class 4 contributions.** The provisions relating to interest on unpaid tax and interest on overpaid tax also apply to Class 2 and 4 contributions. See page 79.
Where Class 2 and 4 contributions are due, the same penalties for failure to make a return within the required period or making an incorrect return apply as for income tax purposes. See page 97.

(d) **Maximum contributions.** Where an earner is employed in more than one employment (whether employed earners' employments or self-employments) liability for Class 1 or Class 1 and Class 2 contributions cannot exceed a maximum figure. For 2022/23, the weekly primary threshold is taken to be £229 for the purposes of this calculation. Similarly, where Class 4 contributions are payable in addition to Class 1 and/or Class 2 contributions, liability for Class 4 contributions cannot exceed a limiting amount.
Subject to below, the Class 1/Class 2 maximum is the equivalent of 53 primary Class 1 contributions at the maximum standard rate. The Class 4 maximum is such amount as, when added to the Class 1/Class 2 contributions payable (after applying the maximum if appropriate), equals the limiting amount shown above (this being the maximum Class 4 contributions payable at 10.25% (9% for 2021/22 and earlier years) plus 53 Class 2 contributions).
Because of the open-ended Class 1 and Class 4 contributions at 3.25% (2% for 2021/22 and earlier years), each person has, in effect, their own 'personalised maximum'. Further adjustments to the figures quoted in the table above are required for any contributions payable at the 3.25% rate (2% for 2021/22 and earlier years) on earnings over the upper earnings limit and profits over the upper annual limit.

(e) For 2022/23, Class 2 NICs are not payable where an individual's profits fall between the small profits threshold and the Class 4 lower annual profits limit. The individual is treated as having paid Class 2 NICs for the purposes of benefits entitlement.

PAYE

PAYE thresholds

2022/23	£242 per week	£1,048 per month

Payment by quarterly instalments

Employers whose average monthly liability for PAYE and NIC is less than £1,500 can choose to pay quarterly instead. Payments are due 14 days after the end of the relevant quarter (extended to 17 days where payment is made by electronic means).

PAYE codes

Code suffix	*Meaning*
C	Income taxed at the Welsh rate of income tax
L	Personal allowance
M	Marriage allowance transferred from spouse or civil partner
N	Marriage allowance transferred to spouse or civil partner
S	Income taxed at the Scottish rate of income tax
T	Other calculations included to work out the personal allowance
K	Total allowances in the code are less than total deductions
D0	Tax to be deducted at higher rate
SD0	Income taxed at the Scottish rate of income tax: tax to be deducted at intermediate rate
CD0	Income taxed at the Welsh rate of income tax: tax to be deducted at higher rate
D1	Tax to be deducted at additional rate
SD1	Income taxed at the Scottish rate of income tax: tax to be deducted at higher rate
CD1	Income taxed at the Welsh rate of income tax: tax to be deducted at additional rate
SD2	Income taxed at the Scottish rate of income tax: tax to be deducted at top rate
BR	Tax to be deducted at basic rate; no allowances given
SBR	Income taxed at the Scottish rate of income tax: tax to be deducted at basic rate; no allowances given
CBR	Income taxed at the Welsh rate of income tax: tax to be deducted at basic rate; no allowances given
NT	No tax to be deducted
0T	No allowances available; tax to be deducted at appropriate rate
S0T	Income taxed at the Scottish rate of income tax: no allowances available; tax to be deducted at appropriate rate
C0T	Income taxed at the Welsh rate of income tax: no allowances available; tax to be deducted at appropriate rate
M1	Tax to be deducted on a month 1 basis
W1	Tax to be deducted on a week 1 basis

Penalties—P11D

Failure to submit returns. For returns not submitted by 6 July following the tax year

(a) a penalty of up to £300 per form;

(b) if failure continues after penalty under (a) imposed, continuing penalty of up to £60 per form per day.

Gross pay for PAYE and NIC purposes (HMRC Guide CWG2 (2022))

The following payments should be entered as pay on the employee's payroll record/deduction working sheet (as opposed to being returned at the year end or included in a PAYE settlement agreement).

Childcare vouchers not meeting the qualifying conditions (NIC only).

Christmas boxes in cash.

Clothing or uniforms—(i) Payments to employees for non-durable items such as tights or stockings (PAYE only); and (ii) other payments to employees to purchase clothing or uniforms whether this can be worn at any time or (for PAYE only) only at work.

Council tax paid on employee's living accommodation except where the value does not have to be included on form P11D (NICs only).

Credit cards, charge cards, etc.—employees' use of an employer's card for expenditure, *other than* goods or services bought on the employer's behalf, on readily convertible assets (see below), and (for NICs) where no reimbursement made.

Credit card reward payments for detecting/withdrawing lost/stolen cards made by employer.

Damages or similar payments made to an employee injured at work if there is a contractual liability to make it.

Directors' remuneration, salary, bonuses, fees etc. including any advance or anticipatory payments paid, voted or credited.

Employment income provided through third parties when taxable under disguised remuneration rules in *ITEPA 2003, Pt 7A*.

Employment Tribunal awards under an order for re-instatement or re-engagement or for continuation of employment, or a protective award.

Guarantee payments under *Employment Rights Act 1996*.

Honoraria

Incentive awards made by cash or vouchers exchangeable for cash.

Inducement payments such as 'golden hellos' to recruit or retain employees.

Loans written off (NICs only.)

Long service awards in cash or cash vouchers.

Lost time payments other than those made by, or by the employer on behalf of, a third party.

Maternity suspension payments made under the *Employment Rights Act 1996*.

Meal allowances and vouchers comprising (i) cash payments for meals; and (ii) vouchers redeemable for food and drink or cash alternative (but not vouchers redeemable for food and drink only or for food and drink on business premises for any canteen where meals are generally provided for employer's staff).

Medical suspension payments made under the *Employment Rights Act 1996*.

Mortgage payments (for NICs only) on a contract between the employee and mortgagee.

Payments in kind (other than readily convertible assets for which see below) which can be turned into cash *by surrender*, e.g. premium bonds.

Payments made to an employee pursuing a claim for *damages against a third party* for loss of earnings following an accident if the employee is not required to repay the employer.

Pensions (PAYE only)

Personal bills paid for goods and services supplied to employees and directors, club memberships, etc. where the payments are made or reimbursed direct to the employee, and (for NICs only) where made direct to the provider or via an overdrawn director's loan account into which director's earnings normally paid.

Prize money paid in cash to employees for competitions the employer runs in connection with its business and which are not open to the public.

Readily convertible assets i.e. assets which are (i) capable of being sold on a recognised investment exchange, London Bullion market or New York Stock Exchange (other than shares under an approved scheme); (ii) a right over a money debt; (iii) subject to a fiscal warehousing regime; (iv) give rise to a right to enable an employee to obtain money; (v) subject to trading arrangements; (vi) already owned by the employee and whose value is enhanced by the employer.

Relocation payments that are non-qualifying.

Round sum allowances (PAYE only) if includes a profit element, and (NICs only) if business expense cannot be identified.

Sickness, maternity and other absence from work payments.

Statutory adoption (SAP), **maternity** (SMP), **paternity** (SPP), **shared parental** (ShPP), **parental bereavement** (SPBP), **sick pay** (SSP).

Subscriptions or fees to professional bodies: (i) paid directly by the employer but not allowable under *ITEPA 2003, ss 343, 344* (NIC only); (ii) reimbursed by the employer and allowable under *ITEPA 2003, ss 343, 344* (PAYE only) or not so allowable.

Suggestion scheme awards to employees (see *ITEPA 2003, s 321* for exemption).

Telephone bills — NICs on full amount of rental and on private calls where telephone used for business and private calls, the employee is the subscriber and the employer pays for the calls and/or rental. See also *Personal bills* above where the telephone is used exclusively for private calls.

Termination payments — part treated as 'Post-Employment Notice Pay'.

Tips and service charges where a scheme is operated by the employer (if separate organised arrangements exist, for example, employees are paid out of a tronc, then the troncmaster is responsible for operating PAYE but not for NICs).

Training payments (for course fees, books, etc.) unless the training is work-related or is encouraged or required by the employer in connection with the employee's work.

Travelling time payments.

Trivial commutations from registered pension schemes (PAYE only)

Vouchers which can be redeemed or exchanged for (i) goods and cash or cash alone; (ii) goods alone or transport services (NICs only) or (iii) readily convertible assets.

Wages, salaries, fees, overtime, bonuses, commission, etc.

PAYE settlement agreements (PSAs) [*ITEPA 2003, ss 703–707; F(No 2)A 2017, s 6; SI 2003 No 2682 Pt 6; HMRC SP 5/96*]

PSAs cover arrangements under which employers can settle, in a single payment, the tax and Class 1B NICs (see page 93) liability on certain benefits in kind and expense payments. Expenses payments and benefits can be included in a PSA if they are minor or payable on an irregular basis or in circumstances where it is impracticable to apply PAYE or apportion the value of particular benefits which have been shared by employees.

The scope of the PSA must be finalised by 6 July, and any tax paid by 22 October (19 October if paying by post), following the tax year to which the PSA applies. From 2018/19 the requirement for employers to agree annually with HMRC which employee expenses and benefits may be included is removed. Employers will now be able to create an enduring agreement with HMRC which will remain in place for subsequent tax years unless varied or cancelled by the employer or HMRC.

Personal service companies etc. [*ITEPA 2003, ss 48–61; FA 2017, s 6, Sch 1*]

These provisions are commonly known under the name 'IR35' and apply where personal services are provided to a client through an intermediary – normally the worker's personal service company. The effect of the legislation is to treat the worker as an employee of the client for working out the 'deemed employment payment'.

Subject to the revised rules for public sector engagements from April 2017 and the rules for engagements with medium-sized and large businesses from April 2021, the provisions operate as follows. The computation involves taking into account all payments and benefits, including those paid direct to the worker for a tax year other than by the intermediary for his services. Certain, restricted, allowable expenses, are deducted from 'earnings'. Finally, any payments or benefits received by the worker from the intermediary are deducted. Tax (under PAYE) and NIC is calculated and the amounts due are payable by the worker and his company. The provisions also apply to office holders.

For public sector engagements from April 2017 the liability to pay the correct employment taxes moves from the worker's own company to the public sector body or agency/third party paying the company, and the amount will be deducted from the amount paid to the company. The normal 5% flat rate deduction from payments for the worker's services cannot be made in computing the deemed employment payment.

From April 2021 the public sector rules are extended to engagements between an intermediary and medium-sized and large businesses in the private sector. The liability to pay the correct employment taxes moves from the worker's own company to the private sector business, and the amount will be deducted from the amount paid to the company.

Managed service companies [*ITEPA 2003, ss 61A–61J; FA 2007, s 25, Sch 3*]

Where a worker provides his services through an intermediary which is a managed service company (as defined), all payments received by him from the company which are not otherwise employment income are deemed to be employment income. The company must operate PAYE and, from 6 August 2007, pay NICs on each such payment. PAYE and NIC debts which cannot be recovered from a managed service company will be collectible from certain other persons, primarily the company's director or the person who provided the company to the worker.

These rules do not apply to an engagement within the personal service company rules as they apply to public sector engagements from April 2017 or engagements with medium-sized and large businesses from April 2021.

Apprenticeship levy

Apprenticeship levy is introduced with effect from 6 April 2017. It is set at a rate of 0.5% of an employer's pay bill and paid by the employer through PAYE. Each employer will receive an allowance of £15,000 to offset against their levy payment so that the levy will only be paid on any pay bill in excess of £3 million. The pay bill is the total of employee earnings subject to Class 1 secondary Contributions, as if disregarding the secondary and upper secondary thresholds.

Student loan repayments *[SI 2009 No 470]*

Student loan repayments of employees are collected through the PAYE system. The employer must calculate and deduct student loan repayments due each pay period, based on the employee's earnings for that period. The deduction is 9% of earnings in excess of the relevant threshold in the table below. If total earnings for a tax year do not exceed the yearly threshold, the employee can claim a refund of any repayments deducted in that tax year. Repayments must also be made by reference to other income (from self-employment, savings and investments etc.) through the self-assessment system where total income exceeds the yearly threshold.

Year	*Percentage*	*Threshold*		
Plan 1				
		Per week	**Per month**	**Per year**
2022/23	9%	£388.36	£1,682.91	£20,195.00
2021/22	9%	£382.59	£1,657.91	£19,895.00
2020/21	9%	£372.88	£1,615.83	£19,390.00
2019/20	9%	£364.13	£1,577.91	£18,935.00
2018/19	9%	£352.50	£1,527.50	£18,330.00
2017/18	9%	£341.00	£1,481.00	£17,775.00
Plan 2 (course started on or after 1 September 2012, England and Wales only)				
2022/23	9%	£524.90	£2,274.58	£27,295.00
2021/22	9%	£524.90	£2,274.58	£27,295.00
2020/21	9%	£511.05	£2,214.58	£26,575.00
2019/20	9%	£494.71	£2,143.75	£25,725.00
2018/19	9%	£480.76	£2,083.83	£25,000.00
2017/18	9%	£403.00	£1,750.00	£21,000.00
Plan 4 (redesignation of Plan 1 loans taken out by students who studied in Scotland and applied for the loans through the Student Awards Agency for Scotland. Applies from 6 April 2021 to allow for increase to the re-payment threshold introduced by the Scottish Government)				
2022/23	9%	£487.98	£2,114.58	£25,375.00
2021/22	9%	£480.76	£2,083.33	£25,000.00
Postgraduate loans				
2019/20 onwards	6%	£403.84	£1,750.00	£21,000.00

National minimum wage/national living wage

Hourly rate *Age of worker*	*Apprentice rate*	*Under 18*	*18–20*	*21–22*	*23 and over* (note (a))
1.4.22 onwards	£4.81	£4.81	£6.83	£9.18	£9.50
1.4.21–31.3.22	£4.30	£4.62	£6.56	£8.36	£8.91
Age of worker	*apprentice rate*	*Under 18*	*18–20*	*21–24*	*25 or over* (note (a))
1.4.20–31.3.21	£4.15	£4.55	£6.45	£8.20	£8.72
1.4.19–31.3.20	£3.90	£4.35	£6.15	£7.70	£8.21
1.4.18–31.3.19	£3.70	£4.20	£5.90	£7.38	£7.83

Note

(a) The national living wage applies for employees aged 23 and over (25 or over before 1 April 2021).

Offence	Penalty
Error in taxpayer's document [*FA 2007, Sch 24 para 1*] Careless or deliberate error in document amounting to or leading to understatement of liability, overstatement or loss or false or inflated claim to repayment of tax. Applies to IT (including Cl), CIS, CGT, CT, VAT, IHT and SDLT. Applies to annual tax on enveloped dwellings, apprenticeship levy, and disposals of UK land. Also, applies to digital services tax where the tax liability arises on or after 1 April 2020.	Deliberate and concealed action or omission: 100% of potential lost revenue. Deliberate but not concealed action or omission: 70% of potential lost revenue. Careless action or omission: 30% of potential lost revenue. *Reductions.* A statutory reduction in the amount of the penalty is made for disclosure of an inaccuracy. For an unprompted disclosure, a 100% penalty may be reduced to no less than 30%, a 70% penalty to no less than 20% and a 30% penalty to any percentage, including 0%. For a prompted disclosure, a 100% penalty may be reduced to no less than 50%, a 70% penalty to no less than 35% and a 30% penalty to no less than 15%. HMRC can also reduce a penalty in special circumstances. In December 2017 HMRC announced a restriction on quality of disclosure penalty reductions where taxpayers 'a significant period (normally 3 years) to correct or disclose the inaccuracy'. They will restrict the penalty range by 10% above the minimum before working out the reductions. It is not clear when the 3-year period starts. *Offshore evasion.* See page 99 for the increase in the amount of the penalty where the error involves an offshore matter.
Error in taxpayer's document attributable to another person [*FA 2007, Sch 24 para 1A*] Deliberately supplying false information to, or deliberately withholding information from, a person giving a document within the above provisions to HMRC resulting in document containing an inaccuracy amounting to or leading to understatement of liability, overstatement of loss or false or inflated claim to repayment of tax.	100% of potential lost revenue, subject to the same reductions as above for disclosure or in special circumstances.
Failure to notify HMRC of error in assessment [*FA 2007, Sch 24 para 2*] Failure to take reasonable steps to notify HMRC of an under-assessment within the 30 days beginning with the date of the assessment. Applies to IT, CT, CGT, VAT, IHT, SDLT and ATED.	30% of potential lost revenue, subject to the same reductions as above for disclosure or in special circumstances.
Failure to comply with notification obligations and VAT offences [*FA 2008, Sch 41*] Failure to comply with any of the following obligations: • to notify chargeability to IT or CGT within six months of tax year • to notify chargeability to CT within one year of accounting period • to notify chargeability to Diverted Profits Tax • to notify chargeability to Digital Services Tax (DST) for obligations arising on or after 1 April 2020 • to notify liability to register for VAT • to notify acquisition of goods from another member state (for VAT purposes) Issue of invoice showing VAT by person not authorised to do so. Applies also to similar obligations in relation to insurance premium tax, diverted profits tax, aggregates levy, climate change levy, landfill tax, air passenger duty and certain other types of duty.	Deliberate and concealed failure: 100% of potential lost revenue. Deliberate but unconcealed failure: 70% of potential lost revenue. Any other case: 30% of potential lost revenue. *Reductions.* A statutory reduction in the amount of the penalty is made for disclosure of a failure. For an unprompted disclosure, a 100% penalty may be reduced to no less than 30%, a 70% penalty to no less than 20% and a 30% penalty to any percentage, including 0%, unless HMRC do not become aware of the failure until twelve months after the time tax first became unpaid because of the failure, in which case the penalty may be reduced to no less than 10%. For a prompted disclosure, a 100% penalty may be reduced to no less than 50%, a 70% penalty to no less than 35% and a 30% penalty to no less than 10% (20% where HMRC do not become aware of the failure until twelve months after the time tax first became unpaid because of the failure). HMRC can also reduce a penalty in special circumstances. In December 2017 HMRC announced a restriction on quality of disclosure penalty reductions where taxpayers 'a significant period (normally 3 years) to correct or disclose the inaccuracy'. They will restrict the penalty range by 10% above the minimum before working out the reductions. It is not clear when the 3-year period starts. *Offshore evasion.* See page 99 for the increase in the amount of the penalty where the failure to comply with an obligation involves an offshore matter.

Penalties general

Offence	Penalty
Failure to comply with HMRC investigatory powers [*FA 2008, Sch 36 paras 39, 40*] Failure to comply with an information notice within *FA 2008, Sch 36 Pt 1* or deliberately obstructing an HMRC officer in the course of an inspection of premises under *FA 2008, Sch 36 Pt 2* which has been approved by the First-tier Tribunal. Applies to (a) IT, CT, CGT, VAT and certain foreign taxes; (b) IHT and SDLT; (c) ATED (see page 81); (d) pension scheme registration applications; (e) diverted profits tax from 1 April 2015; (f) digital Services Tax from 1 April 2020.	(i) initial penalty of £300. (ii) if failure/obstruction continues, a further penalty up to £60 per day. (iii) if failure/obstruction continues after penalty under (i) imposed, daily penalty can be increased to a maximum of £1,000. In addition, a tax-related amount can be determined by the Upper Tribunal.
HMRC investigatory powers: inaccurate information etc [*FA 2008, Sch 36 para 40A*] Providing inaccurate information or document carelessly or deliberately or failing to take reasonable steps to notify HMRC of an inaccuracy discovered later. One penalty for each inaccuracy.	Up to £3,000
HMRC investigatory powers: breach of non-disclosure requirement [*FA 2008, Sch 36 para 51A*] Breach of non-disclosure requirement in relation to a third party notice or financial institution notice under FA 2008 Sch 36 para 51A. Applies from 10 June 2021.	£1,000
Late filing of returns [*FA 2009, Sch 55*] Failure to make a return or deliver a specified document on or before the filing date. Applies to income tax (and CGT) returns and documents; pension scheme returns; construction industry scheme returns; annual tax on enveloped dwellings returns; PAYE real time information monthly returns; and Class 2 NICs for 2015/16 onwards. Applies also to NRCGT returns (although the £10 daily penalty does not apply) and disposals of UK land returns from 6 April 2019. Penalties for returns of UK land disposals were suspended for disposals completed between 6 April 2020 and 30 June 2020, provided return was filed by 31 July 2020. Interest continued to accrue on unpaid tax. To be extended over a number of years to other taxes. A points-based system of late filing penalties will come into effect for income tax self-assessment for accounting periods beginning on or after 6 April 2024 for taxpayers within the Making Tax Digital regime (those with business or property turnover of over £10,000 per year) and 6 April 2025 for other self-assessment taxpayers. It applies for VAT for accounting periods beginning on or after 1 January 2023 (see page 127).	(i) initial penalty of £100. If the 2019/20 return was filed by 28 February 2021 no £100 late filing penalty was issued. Similarly, if the 2020/21 return was filed by 28 February 2022, no £100 late filing penalty was issued. (ii) if failure continues two months after penalty date a penalty of £200 (CIS only). (iii) if failure continues three months after penalty date and HMRC give notice, a further penalty of £10 per day for each day failure continues in 90-day period beginning with date specified in notice. Penalty does not apply to CIS returns. Daily penalties were not charged in respect of late 2018/19 tax returns. (iv) if failure continues six months after penalty date, a further penalty of the greater of 5% of the tax liability and £300. (v) for returns other than CIS returns, if failure continues 12 months after penalty date and the withholding of information is deliberate and concealed a further penalty of the greater of 100% of the tax liability and £300; if the withholding is deliberate and not concealed, the greater of 70% of the liability and £300; or otherwise, greater of 5% of the liability and £300. (vi) for CIS returns, if failure continues 12 months after penalty date and the withholding of information is deliberate and concealed a further penalty of the greater of 100% of the tax liability and £3,000; if the withholding is deliberate and not concealed, the greater of 70% of the liability and £1,500; or otherwise, greater of 5% of the liability and £300. Where the information required in the return relates only to persons registered for gross payment, and the withholding of information is deliberate and concealed the penalty is £3,000; if the withholding is deliberate but not concealed the penalty is £1,500. For the first CIS return made by a contractor (together with any returns with an earlier filing date), the total fixed penalties cannot exceed £3,000 and any tax-geared penalty which would otherwise be the greater of £300 and 5% of the tax due is instead 5%. *Real time information.* No penalty for first failure in a tax year. Each subsequent failure: £100 for employer with 1–9 employees, £200 for 10–49 employees, £300 for 50–249 employees, £400 for 250 or more employees. Further penalty where failure continues for more than three months: 5% of tax due. No penalty for new employer for return received within 30 days of making the first payment to employee(s). *Reductions.* A statutory reduction in the amount of the penalty is made for disclosure of a failure. For an unprompted disclosure, a 100% penalty may be reduced to no less than 30% and a 70% penalty to no less than 20%. For a prompted disclosure, a 100% penalty may be reduced to no less than 50% and a 70% penalty to no less than 35%. HMRC can also reduce a penalty in special circumstances. In December 2017 HMRC announced a restriction on quality of disclosure penalty reductions where taxpayers 'a significant period (normally 3 years) to correct or disclose the inaccuracy'. They will restrict the penalty range by 10% above the minimum before working out the reductions. It is not clear when the 3-year period starts. *Offshore evasion.* See below.

Offence	Penalty
Tax agents: dishonest conduct [*FA 2012, Sch 38 para 26; SI 2013 No 279*] HMRC also have the power to publish the names and details of tax agents who incur a penalty exceeding £5,000.	Up to £50,000 (minimum £5,000) although HMRC have the discretion to apply a special reduction to a £5,000 penalty to reflect the quality of the disclosure and compliance with any access notice.
Tax agents: failure to comply with file access notice [*FA 2012, Sch 38 paras 22, 23*]	(i) initial penalty of £300. (ii) if failure continues, a further penalty up to £60 per day.
Failure to make payments on time [*FA 2009 Sch 56*] Applies to IT, CGT, NICs, ATED, SDRT and diverted profits tax. Applies to apprenticeship levy from 16.9.16, to pension schemes overseas transfer charge from 6.3.17, and to disposals of UK land from 2019/20. To be extended over a number of years to other taxes. A new system of late payment penalties based on a percentage of the outstanding amount will come into effect for income tax self-assessment for accounting periods beginning on or after 6 April 2024 for taxpayers within the Making Tax Digital regime (those with business or property turnover of over £10,000 per year) and 6 April 2025 for other self-assessment taxpayers. It applies for VAT for accounting periods beginning on or after 1 January 2023 (see page 127).	*In-year payments.* The first failure in a tax year does not count as a default. If there are one, two or three defaults during a tax year, penalty of 1% of total amount of defaults. If four, five or six defaults during a tax year, penalty of 2%; if seven, eight or nine defaults, penalty of 3%; if ten or more defaults in one tax year penalty 4%. If tax remains unpaid six months after penalty date a penalty of 5% of the unpaid amount applies; a further 5% penalty applies if tax is still unpaid after a further six months. *IT, CGT, Class 1A, 1B, 2, 4 NICs.* A 5% penalty applies if full amount not paid within 30 days of due date. If amount remains unpaid six months after due date a penalty of 5% applies; a further 5% penalty applies if amount is still unpaid after a further six months. If the 2019/20 self-assessment tax due was either paid or a time to pay arrangement was in place by 1 April 2021, the first late payment penalty was not charged. A similar rule applies to tax for 2020/21 by reference to 1 April 2022.
Failure by the lead trustee to register a trust before the trust deadline, or to tell HMRC about any changes to the registration.	(i) £100 if registered within up to 3 months of deadline. (ii) £200 if registered between 3 to 6 months of deadline. (iii) higher of £300 or 5% of total tax liability in relevant year if registered more than 6 months after deadline. Note: Penalties not issued automatically and to be reviewed on a case by case basis. Penalties relating to notification of changes will only apply once facility to notify has been set up.
Enabling offshore tax evasion or non-compliance [*FA 2016, Sch 20; SI 2016 No 1249*] With effect from 1 January 2017, enabling another person (Q) to carry out offshore tax evasion or non-compliance which has resulted in conviction of a relevant offence or liability to a relevant penalty. Applies to IT, CGT and IHT.	Where Q liable to offshore asset move penalty: the higher of £3,000 and 50% of the potential lost revenue from the original tax non-compliance In all other cases: the higher of £3,000 and 100% of the potential lost revenue Reductions apply for disclosure
Asset-based penalty for offshore inaccuracies and failures [*FA 2016, Sch 22; SI 2017 No 277*] For periods beginning after 5 April 2016 (or, for IHT purposes, for transfers of value made on or after 1 April 2017), applies to a person already liable to a CGT, IHT or asset-based IT penalty under *FA 2007, Sch 24 para 1, FA 2008, Sch 41*, or *FA 2009, Sch 55* for a deliberate action or failure involving an offshore matter or transfer for a tax year in which the potential lost revenue exceeds £25,000.	The lower of 10% of the asset value and 10 times the offshore potential lost revenue Reductions apply for disclosure and in special circumstances
Failure to correct offshore non-compliance Failure to correct on or by 30 September 2018 irregularities in relation to undeclared past UK IT, CGT and IHT liabilities involving offshore interests which exist at 5 April 2017.	200% of the offshore potential lost revenue (PLR) Reductions apply for disclosure but minimum penalty will be 100% of PLR

Offence	Penalty
Offshore evasion [*FA 2010, Sch 10; FA 2015, Sch 20; FA 2016, s 163, Sch 21; SI 2017 No 259*] Penalties in respect of income tax or CGT under *FA 2007, Sch 24 para 1, FA 2008, Sch 41 para 1* and *FA 2009, Sch 55* are increased where the error or failure is linked to an offshore matter. For transfers of value made on or after 1 April 2016, the increased penalty under *FA 2007, Sch 24 para 1* is extended to IHT. For documents, returns and assessments relating to periods beginning after 5 April 2016 (or, for IHT purposes, for transfers of value made on or after 1 April 2017), the increased penalties apply also where the error or failure is linked to an offshore transfer. The offshore matter or transfer must relate to a territory within category 2 or 3. No increase is made in relation to category 1 territories. With effect from a date to be fixed, the territory classification system will be updated to reflect the jurisdictions that adopt the new global standard of automatic tax information exchange; and to have four categories. The current categories are: **1:** Anguilla; Aruba; Australia; Belgium; Bulgaria; Canada; Cayman Islands; Cyprus; Czech Republic; Denmark (excluding Faroe Islands and Greenland); Estonia; Finland; France; Germany; Greece; Guernsey; Hungary; Ireland; Isle of Man; Italy; Japan; Latvia; Liechtenstein (after 23 July 2013); Lithuania; Malta; Montserrat; Netherlands (excluding Bonaire, Sint Eustatius and Saba); New Zealand (excluding Tokelau); Norway; Poland; Portugal; Romania; Slovakia; Slovenia; South Korea; Spain; Sweden; Switzerland (after 23 July 2013); USA (excluding overseas territories and possessions). **2:** All territories (except the UK) not within categories 1 or 3. **3:** Albania; Algeria; Andorra; Bonaire, Sint Eustatius and Saba; Brazil; Cameroon; Cape Verde; Colombia; Republic of the Congo; Cook Islands; Costa Rica; Curaçao; Cuba; Democratic People's Republic of Korea; Dominican Republic; Ecuador; El Salvador; Gabon; Guatemala; Honduras; Iran; Iraq; Jamaica; Kyrgyzstan; Lebanon; Macau; Marshall Islands; Federated States of Micronesia; Monaco; Nauru; Nicaragua; Niue; Palau; Panama; Paraguay; Peru; Seychelles; Sint Maarten; Suriname; Syria; Tokelau; Tonga; Trinidad and Tobago; UAE; Uruguay. The following territories were in category 3 before 24 July 2013: Antigua and Barbuda, Armenia, Bahrain, Barbados, Belize, Dominica, Grenada, Mauritius, San Marino, Saint Kitts and Nevis, Saint Lucia, and Saint Vincent and the Grenadines.	*Category 2 territories*. The amount of the penalty is increased by 50%. Reductions for disclosure vary. *Category 3 territories*. The amount of the penalty is increased by 100%. Reductions for disclosure vary.
Offshore asset move [*FA 2015, Sch 21; SI 2015 No 866; SI 2017 No 989*] Offshore asset moved on or after 27 March 2015 from a specified territory to a non-specified territory where IT, CGT or IHT penalty under *FA 2007, Sch 24 para 1, FA 2008, Sch 41*, or *FA 2009, Sch 55* above already applies for a deliberate failure. The specified territories are: (before 3 November 2017) Albania, Andorra, Anguilla, Antigua and Barbuda, Argentina, Aruba, Australia, Austria, The Bahamas, Bahrain (after 2 November 2017), Barbados, Belgium, Belize, Bermuda, Brazil, British Virgin Islands, Brunei Darussalam, Bulgaria, Canada, Cayman Islands, Chile, China, Colombia, Cook Islands (after 2 November 2017), Costa Rica, Croatia, Curaçao, Cyprus, Czech Republic, Denmark, Dominica, Estonia, Faroe Islands, Finland, France, Germany, Ghana (after 2 November 2017), Gibraltar, Greece, Greenland, Grenada, Guernsey, Hong Kong, Hungary, Iceland, India, Indonesia, Ireland, Isle of Man, Israel, Italy, Japan, Jersey, Korea (South), Kuwait (after 2 November 2017), Latvia, Lebanon (after 2 November 2017), Liechtenstein, Lithuania, Luxembourg, Macau, Malaysia, Malta, Marshall Islands, Mauritius, Mexico, Monaco, Montserrat, Nauru (after 2 November 2017), Netherlands (including Bonaire, Sint Eustatius and Saba) New Zealand (not including Tokelau), Niue, Norway, Panama (after 2 November 2017), Poland, Portugal, Qatar, Romania, Russia, Saint Kitts and Nevis, Saint Lucia, Saint Vincent and the Grenadines, Samoa, San Marino, Saudi Arabia, Seychelles, Singapore, Sint Maarten, Slovak Republic, Slovenia, South Africa, Spain, Sweden, Switzerland, Trinidad and Tobago, Turkey, Turks and Caicos Islands, United Arab Emirates, (before 3 November 2017) United States of America (not including overseas territories and possessions), Uruguay, Vanuatu (after 2 November 2017).	50% of amount of original penalty
Uncertain tax treatment [*FA 2022, Sch 17*] Failure by large business to make notification of uncertain tax treatment in corporation tax, income tax, PAYE or VAT return (FA 2022 Sch 17). Applies to returns required to be made on or after 1 April 2022.	£5,000 for first failure, £25,000 for second failure, £50,000 for any further failure. In determining whether a failure is the first, second or a further failure, only the period of three years prior to the period for which the affected return is made and the tax in question are considered.

Penalties income tax, capital gains tax and corporation tax

Offence	Penalty
Failure to maintain records [*TMA 1970, s 12B; FA 2013, Sch 33; FA 2020, Sch 8 para 55*]	
Failure to keep and preserve appropriate records supporting personal, trustees' or partnership returns	Up to £3,000
Failure to keep and preserve records supporting ATED return (see page 81).	
Failure to keep and preserve records to enable delivery of a DST return.	
Failure to render return [*FA 1998, Sch 18 paras 17, 18; FA 2020, Sch 8 paras 52, 53*]	
(a) Corporation tax	(i) £100 if up to 3 months late (£500 if previous two returns also delivered late); (ii) £200 if over 3 months late (£1,000 if previous two returns also late);
Failure continuing at later of final day for delivery of return and 18 months after return period	Further penalty of 10% of tax unpaid 18 months after return period (20% of tax unpaid at that date if return not made within 2 years of return period)
(b) Digital Services Tax	(i) £100 if up to 3 months late; (ii) £200 in any other case; (iii) increased to £500 and £1,000 respectively for third successive failure; (iv) If not delivered within 18 months of accounting period end, tax-geared penalties apply of: (a) 10% of unpaid tax if delivered within 2 years; (b) 20% in any other case.
Negligence or fraud	Up to amount of tax underpaid by reason of incorrectness for
Negligently or fraudulently making an incorrect statement in connection with a claim to reduce payments on account [*TMA 1970, s 59A*]	Up to the amount (or additional amount) payable on account if a correct statement had been made
Other returns, etc. [*TMA 1970, ss 98, 98A*]	
Failure to comply with a notice to deliver any return or other document, to furnish any particulars, to produce any document or record, to make anything available for inspection or give any certificate under the provisions listed in *TMA 1970, s 98*	(i) up to £300 (£3,000 in certain specified cases) (ii) if failure continues after penalty under (i) imposed, continuing penalty of up to £60 (£600) per day
Failure to submit PAYE returns (P14, P35, P38 and P38A) or returns of sub-contractors in the construction industry	See under PAYE (page 89) which provisions also apply to returns of sub-contractors
Sub-contractors in the Construction Industry Scheme	
Fraudulent attempt by sub-contractor to obtain or misuse a sub-contractor's certificate (pre-6 April 2007 scheme) [*ICTA 1988, s 561(10), (11)*]	Up to £3,000
Making false statements etc. for the purpose of becoming registered for gross payment (post-5 April 2007 scheme) [*FA 2004, s 72*]	Up to £3,000

Penalties income tax, capital gains tax and corporation tax

Offence	Penalty
Certificates of non-liability to income tax [*TMA 1970, s 99A*] Fraudulently or negligently giving such a certificate in connection with receiving bank or building society interest gross or failing to comply with an undertaking in the certificate	Up to £3,000
Refusal to allow deduction of income tax at source [*TMA 1970, s 106*]	£50
Falsification of documents [*TMA 1970, s 20BB*] Intentionally falsifying, concealing or destroying documents	On summary conviction, a penalty not exceeding the statutory maximum (currently £5,000). On conviction on indictment, imprisonment for up to 2 years or a fine or both
Advance pricing agreements [*TIOPA 2010, s 227; FA 1999, s 86*] Fraudulently or negligently making a false or misleading statement in the preparation of, or application to enter into, any advance pricing agreement	Up to £10,000
Enablers of Defeated Tax Avoidance Arrangements [*F(No 2)A 2017, s 65, Sch 16*] Enabling the use of abusive tax avoidance arrangements which are later defeated.	The amount of consideration received or receivable by enabler for enabling the tax avoidance arrangements.
Failure to provide loan charge information for income provided through third parties [*F(No 2)A 2017, Schs 11 and 12*]	(i) an initial penalty of £300; (ii) if failure continues, a further penalty up to £60 per day up to a maximum of 90 days
Inaccuracy in information or document relating to loan charge for income provided through third parties [*F(No 2)A 2017, Schs 11 and 12*]	Up to £3,000 per inaccuracy
Failure to amend a company tax return in relation to corporate interest restriction [*TIOPA 2010, Sch 7A*]	£500

Penalties inheritance tax and stamp duty land tax

Offence	Penalty
Failure to deliver inheritance tax account [*IHTA 1984, s 245*] Failure to deliver an account within 12 months of death	(i) An initial penalty of £100 (or tax payable if less); (ii) A further penalty up to £60 for each day on which the failure continues (where failure is declared by court, tribunal or Special Commissioners); (iii) If failure continues after six months after the date on which account is due, and proceedings under (ii) not commenced, a further penalty of £100 (or tax payable if less); (iv) If failure continues one year after end of the period in which account is due, and tax is payable, a penalty up to £3,000
Failure to notify instrument varying disposition on death [*IHTA 1984, s 245A(1A), (1B)*] Failure to notify HMRC within six months after the date of the instrument (where additional tax is payable)	(i) An initial penalty up to £100; (ii) A further penalty up to £60 for each day on which the failure continues (where failure is declared by court, tribunal or Special Commissioners); (iii) If failure continues one year after end of the period in which notification is due, a penalty up to £3,000
Negligence or fraud (IHT) [*IHTA 1984, s 247*] Person other than taxpayer negligently or fraudulently furnishing or producing incorrect information or document	Up to £3,000
Failure to deliver SDLT return [*FA 2003, Sch 10 paras 3, 4*] Failure to deliver return within 14 days (30 days before 1 March 2019) after the effective date of the land transaction	(i) £100 if return delivered within three months of filing date, otherwise £200; (ii) If return not delivered within 12 months after filing date, a penalty up to the tax chargeable
Failure to comply with notice to deliver SDLT return [*FA 2003, Sch 10 para 5*] Failure to comply within period specified in notice	Up to £60 for each day on which the failure continues after notification of penalty decision by tribunal or General or Special Commissioners
Failure to keep and preserve records [*FA 2003, Sch 10 para 11, Sch 11 para 6*] Failure to keep and preserve such records as may be needed to enable delivery of correct return or certificate for required period	Up to £3,000 unless information is provided by other documentary evidence

Pensions

Registered pension schemes *[FA 2004, ss 149–284, Schs 28–36; FA 2013, ss 47–49; F(No 2)A 2015, Sch 4; FA 2016, ss 19–22, Schs 4, 5; F(No 2)A 2017, s 7, FA 2021, s 28]*

Individual contributions. An individual may make unlimited contributions but tax relief is only available on contributions up to the higher of 100% of relevant earnings and £3,600 gross (provided the scheme operates tax relief at source). There is no provision for the carry-back or carry-forward of contributions to tax years other than the year of payment.

Employer contributions are deductible for tax purposes, with exceptionally large contributions being spread over a period of up to 4 years. The contributions are not treated as taxable income of the employee (although this exemption does not extend to contributions for the benefit of family members).

'Tax-free' lump sum. The maximum 'tax-free' lump sum that can be paid out is 25% of the fund, subject to an overriding maximum of 25% of the lifetime allowance. There is transitional protection of lump sum rights accrued before 6 April 2006.

Lifetime allowance. Each individual has a lifetime allowance as follows.

2022/23	£1,073,100	2020/21	£1,073,100	2018/19	£1,030,000
2021/22	£1,073,100	2019/20	£1,055,000	2017/18	£1,000,000

If benefits are withdrawn in excess of the allowance, tax is charged on the excess at 55% if taken as a lump sum and at 25% if used to buy a pension. Any tax due may be deducted from the individual's benefits.

Annual allowance. Each individual has an annual allowance for maximum 'pension inputs' (i.e. contributions paid to money purchase schemes and/or increases in accrued benefits under final salary schemes) as follows.

2022/23	£40,000	2020/21	£40,000	2018/19	£40,000
2021/22	£40,000	2019/20	£40,000	2017/18	£40,000

If pension inputs exceed the annual allowance, the excess is chargeable at the individual's marginal tax rate. The individual is liable for the tax subject to an election for the scheme to pay the charge if it exceeds £2,000 (in which event scheme benefits are proportionately reduced). An individual can carry forward unused annual allowance for up to three tax years. There are special rules for taxpayers who flexibly access a money purchase arrangement. Such taxpayers are, in certain circumstances, restricted to a £4,000 annual allowance (£10,000 before 6 April 2017) in respect of money purchase pension savings. If this 'money purchase annual allowance' (MPAA) limit is exceeded, the taxpayer has a reduced £36,000 annual allowance (£30,000 before 6 April 2017) for the remainder of their pension savings (in addition to the MPAA).

For 2020/21 onwards, the annual allowance is reduced for individuals whose annual income (including pension contributions) exceeds £240,000 (£150,000 for 2017/18 to 2019/20). The allowance is reduced by £1 for every £2 of income over £240,000 (£150,000 for 2017/18 to 2019/20) down to a minimum allowance of £4,000 (£10,000 for 2017/18 to 2019/20). The reduction does not normally apply where annual income excluding pension contributions is less than £200,000 (£110,000 for 2017/18 to 2019/20) (subject to anti-avoidance provisions).

Minimum pension age. The minimum pension age is 55 with earlier retirement permitted on ill-health grounds. Those with existing contractual rights to draw a pension earlier have those rights protected and there is special protection for members of pre-6 April 2006 approved schemes with early retirement ages. The available lifetime allowance for these protected groups is, however, reduced. From 6 April 2028, the minimum pension age will increase to 57.

Retired members of the police, fire service and other uniformed services will not lose their protected pension age should they have returned to work with the same employer or an employer connected to that employer, in the same field from which they retired, whether or not there is a break between the date they retired and the date they were re-employed, if they did so as part of the Government's response to the coronavirus (COVID-19) pandemic.

Maximum benefit age. There is no maximum age at which benefits must be taken.

Everyone aged 55 or over with defined contribution pension savings is able to access them as they wish, regardless of the total amount of their pension savings, and are charged to income tax as pension income at their marginal rate for the tax year of access.

Retail price index Capital gains—indexation

Year	Jan	Feb	Mar	Apr	May	Jun	Jul	Aug	Sep	Oct	Nov	Dec
1982	78.7	78.8	79.44	81.04	81.62	81.85	81.88	81.90	81.85	82.26	82.66	82.51
1983	82.61	82.97	83.12	84.28	84.64	84.84	85.30	85.68	86.06	86.36	86.67	86.89
1984	86.84	87.20	87.48	88.64	88.97	89.20	89.10	89.94	90.11	90.67	90.95	90.87
1985	91.20	91.94	92.80	94.78	95.21	95.41	95.23	95.49	95.44	95.59	95.92	96.05
1986	96.25	96.60	96.73	97.67	97.85	97.79	97.52	97.82	98.30	98.45	99.29	99.62
1987	100.0	100.4	100.6	101.8	101.9	101.9	101.8	102.1	102.4	102.9	103.4	103.3
1988	103.3	103.7	104.1	105.8	106.2	106.6	106.7	107.9	108.4	109.5	110.0	110.3
1989	111.0	111.8	112.3	114.3	115.0	115.4	115.5	115.8	116.6	117.5	118.5	118.8
1990	119.5	120.2	121.4	125.1	126.2	126.7	126.8	128.1	129.3	130.3	130.0	129.9
1991	130.2	130.9	131.4	133.1	133.5	134.1	133.8	134.1	134.6	135.1	135.6	135.7
1992	135.6	136.3	136.7	138.8	139.3	139.3	138.8	138.9	139.4	139.9	139.7	139.2
1993	137.9	138.8	139.3	140.6	141.1	141.0	140.7	141.3	141.9	141.8	141.6	141.9
1994	141.3	142.1	142.5	144.2	144.7	144.7	144.0	144.7	145.0	145.2	145.3	146.0
1995	146.0	146.9	147.5	149.0	149.6	149.8	149.1	149.9	150.6	149.8	149.8	150.7
1996	150.2	150.9	151.5	152.6	152.9	153.0	152.4	153.1	153.8	153.8	153.9	154.4
1997	154.4	155.0	155.4	156.3	156.9	157.5	157.5	158.5	159.3	159.5	159.6	160.0
1998	159.5	160.3	160.8	162.6	163.5	163.4	163.0	163.7	164.4	164.5	164.4	164.4
1999	163.4	163.7	164.1	165.2	165.6	165.6	165.1	165.5	166.2	166.5	166.7	167.3
2000	166.6	167.5	168.4	170.1	170.7	171.1	170.5	170.5	171.7	171.6	172.1	172.2
2001	171.1	172.0	172.2	173.1	174.2	174.4	173.3	174.0	174.6	174.3	173.6	173.4
2002	173.3	173.8	174.5	175.7	176.2	176.2	175.9	176.4	177.6	177.9	178.2	178.5
2003	178.4	179.3	179.9	181.2	181.5	181.3	181.3	181.6	182.5	182.6	182.7	183.5
2004	183.1	183.8	184.6	185.7	186.5	186.8	186.8	187.4	188.1	188.6	189.0	189.9
2005	188.9	189.6	190.5	191.6	192.0	192.2	192.2	192.6	193.1	193.3	193.6	194.1
2006	193.4	194.2	195.0	196.5	197.7	198.5	198.5	199.2	200.1	200.4	201.1	202.7
2007	201.6	203.1	204.4	205.4	206.2	207.3	206.1	207.3	208.0	208.9	209.7	210.9
2008	209.8	211.4	212.1	214.0	215.1	216.8	216.5	217.2	218.4	217.7	216.0	212.9
2009	210.1	211.4	211.3	211.5	212.8	213.4	213.4	214.4	215.3	216.0	216.6	218.0
2010	217.9	219.2	220.7	222.8	223.6	224.1	223.6	224.5	225.3	225.8	226.8	228.4
2011	229.0	231.3	232.5	234.4	235.2	235.2	234.7	236.1	237.9	238.0	238.5	239.4
2012	238.0	239.9	240.8	242.5	242.4	241.8	242.1	243.0	244.2	245.6	245.6	246.8
2013	245.8	247.6	248.7	249.5	250.0	249.7	249.7	251.0	251.9	251.9	252.1	253.4
2014	252.6	254.2	254.8	255.7	255.9	256.3	256.0	257.0	257.6	257.7	257.1	257.5
2015	255.4	256.7	257.1	258.0	258.5	258.9	258.6	259.8	259.6	259.5	259.8	260.6
2016	258.8	260.0	261.1	261.4	262.1	263.1	263.4	264.4	264.9	264.8	265.5	267.1
2017	265.5	268.4	269.3	270.6	271.7	272.3	272.9	274.7	275.1	275.3	275.8	278.1

Notes

(a) The index was re-referenced in January 1987 from 394.5 to 100. The figures above which relate to months before January 1987 have been recomputed from the new base.
(b) Details provided for the purposes of calculating indexation allowance. The figures are reproduced up to December 2017 when indexation allowance was frozen. See page 20.

Weekly rates from weeks commencing	11.4.22	12.4.21	6.4.20	8.4.19	9.4.18	10.4.17	11.4.16
Retirement pensions (note (a))	£	£	£	£	£	£	£
Retirement on or after 6 April 2016	185.15	179.60	175.20	168.60	164.35	159.55	155.65
Retirement before 6 April 2016							
—category A or B	141.85	137.60	134.25	129.20	125.95	122.30	119.30
—category B (lower)	85.00	82.45	80.45	77.45	75.50	73.30	71.50
—category C or D (non-contributory)	85.00	82.45	80.45	77.45	75.50	73.30	71.50
—increase for adult dependant (note (b))	—	—	—	70.00	68.35	66.35	65.70
—age addition (over 80)	0.25	0.25	0.25	0.25	0.25	0.25	0.25
Bereavement benefit: deaths before 6 April 2017 (notes (a), (m))							
Widowed parent's allowance	126.35	122.55	121.95	119.90	117.10	113.70	112.55
Bereavement allowance (standard rate) (note (c))	126.35	122.55	121.95	119.90	117.10	113.70	112.55
Carer's allowance (previously invalid care allowance) (note (a))							
Basic	69.70	67.60	67.25	66.15	64.60	62.70	62.10
Increase for adult dependant (note (b))	—	—	—	38.90	38.00	36.90	36.55
Employment and support allowance (notes (f), (g), (k))							
Under 25	61.05	59.20	58.90	57.90	57.90	57.90	57.90
25 or over	77.00	74.70	74.35	73.10	73.10	73.10	73.10
Incapacity benefit (notes (a), (f), (h), (i))							
Long term (after 52 weeks)	118.25	114.70	114.15	112.25	109.60	106.40	105.35
—increase for adult dependant	68.70	66.65	66.30	65.20	63.65	61.80	61.20
Increase of long term benefit for age							
—higher rate (under 35)	12.55	12.15	12.10	11.90	11.60	11.25	11.15
—lower rate (35 to under 45)	6.95	6.75	6.70	6.60	6.45	6.25	6.20
Short term (over pension age)							
—higher rate (from week 29 to 52) (note (f))	118.25	114.70	114.15	112.25	109.60	106.40	105.35
—increase for adult dependant	66.10	64.10	63.80	62.75	61.30	59.50	58.90
Short term (under pension age)							
—higher rate (from week 29 to 52)	105.55	102.40	101.90	100.20	97.85	95.00	94.05
—increase for adult dependant	53.50	51.90	51.65	50.80	49.60	48.15	47.65
Industrial death benefit (deaths before 11.4.88 only) (note (a))							
Widow's pension (higher permanent rate)	141.85	137.60	134.25	129.20	125.95	122.30	119.30
Widow's pension (lower permanent rate)	42.56	41.28	40.28	38.76	37.79	36.69	35.79
Widower's pension	141.85	137.60	134.25	129.20	125.95	122.30	119.30
Statutory adoption pay (note (d))							
Higher rate— 9/10ths of average weekly earnings	Varies	Varies	Varies	Varies	Varies	Varies	Varies
Standard rate (note (j))	156.66	151.97	151.20	148.68	145.18	140.98	139.58
Earnings threshold	123.00	120.00	120.00	118.00	116.00	113.00	112.00

Social security taxable benefits

Weekly rates from weeks commencing	11.4.22	12.4.21	6.4.20	8.4.19	9.4.18	10.4.17	11.4.16
Statutory maternity pay (note (d))	£	£	£	£	£	£	£
Higher rate— 9/10ths of average weekly earnings	Varies	Varies	Varies	Varies	Varies	Varies	Varies
Standard rate (note (j))	156.66	151.97	151.20	148.68	145.18	140.98	139.58
Earnings threshold	123.00	120.00	120.00	118.00	116.00	113.00	112.00
Statutory paternity pay (note (d))							
Standard rate (note (j))	156.66	151.97	151.20	148.68	145.18	140.98	139.58
Earnings threshold	123.00	120.00	120.00	118.00	116.00	113.00	112.00
Statutory shared parental pay (note (d))							
Standard rate (note (j))	156.66	151.97	151.20	148.68	145.18	140.98	139.58
Earnings threshold	123.00	120.00	120.00	118.00	116.00	113.00	112.00
Statutory parental bereavement pay (note (d))							
Standard rate (note (j))	156.66	151.97	151.20	—	—	—	—
Earnings threshold	123.00	120.00	120.00	—	—	—	—
Statutory sick pay (note (d))							
Standard rate	99.35	96.35	95.85	94.25	92.05	89.35	88.45
Earnings threshold	123.00	120.00	120.00	118.00	116.00	113.00	112.00
Invalidity allowances when paid with retirement pensions (note (f))							
Higher rate (under 40 when first taken ill)	24.15	23.40	23.30	22.90	22.35	21.70	21.50
Middle rate (40–49 when first taken ill)	15.50	15.00	14.90	14.70	14.40	14.00	13.90
Lower rate (50 to pension age when first taken ill)	7.75	7.50	7.45	7.35	7.20	7.00	6.95
Jobseekers allowance (notes (e), (k))							
Single —under 25	61.05	59.20	58.90	57.90	57.90	57.90	57.90
—25 or over	77.00	74.70	74.35	73.10	73.10	73.10	73.10
Couple —both under 18	61.05	59.20	58.90	57.90	57.90	57.90	57.90
—both under 18, with child responsibility	92.20	89.45	89.00	87.50	87.50	87.50	87.50
—one under 18, one 18–24	61.05	59.20	58.90	57.90	57.90	57.90	57.90
—one under 18, one over 25	77.00	74.70	74.35	73.10	73.10	73.10	73.10
—both over 18	121.05	117.40	116.80	114.85	114.85	114.85	114.85

Notes

(a) Any increase for a child dependant paid with retirement pension, bereavement benefit, carer's allowance, incapacity benefit and higher rate industrial death benefit is non-taxable.

(b) Adult dependency increases to state pension and carer's allowance were not available to new retirees or new carer's allowance claimants from 6 April 2010 and were withdrawn completely on 5 April 2020.

(c) Reduced rates apply if the claimant aged below 55 at the time of spouse's death.

(d) Rates for statutory sick pay, statutory maternity pay, statutory paternity pay, statutory shared parental pay, statutory adoption pay, and statutory parental bereavement pay apply from 6 April each year.

(e) Jobseekers allowance applies to claimants who are required to be both available for and actively seeking employment. Where the amount of a jobseekers allowance paid exceeds the figure shown above, the excess is not taxable.

(f) Employment and support allowance replaces incapacity benefit for new claimants on or after 27 October 2008. Existing claimants continue to receive incapacity benefit. Incapacity benefit itself replaced invalidity allowance from April 1995: invalidity allowances still payable are for a transitional period.

(g) Only contributory employment and support allowance is taxable. Income related allowance is not taxable.

(h) Incapacity benefit is taxable except for benefits paid in the first 28 weeks of incapacity and benefits paid to persons already receiving invalidity benefit on 13 April 1995 so long as they remain incapable of work.

(i) The short-term, higher rate of incapacity benefit for over pension age is not a taxable benefit for those eligible to receive the benefit before 13 April 1995.

(j) 9/10ths of average weekly earnings, if less.

(k) Income support, income-based jobseeker's allowance, income based employment and support allowance, housing benefit, child tax credits and working tax credits are being replaced by universal credit (see page 109). It is intended that by 2024, all claimants currently receiving the legacy benefits will be automatically transferred to universal credit. In the interim the natural migration to universal credit will continue through new claims and changes in the circumstances of claimants.

(l) A cap applies to limit the total amount of benefit that most people aged 16 to 64 can receive. The cap applies to the total amount that the individuals in a household receive from specified benefits. Initially, the cap operates by reducing the amount of housing benefit paid by local authorities. From October 2013 the cap applies directly to all new claims to universal credit including those migrated from existing benefits. From 7 November 2016, the cap is £384.62 a week or £442.31 in Greater London for couples and for single parents whose children live with them and £257.69 a week or £296.35 in Greater London for single adults with no children or whose children do not live with them. Where the cap is applied directly to universal credit, the restriction is made on a monthly basis: £1,667 a month or £1,917 in Greater London for couples and for single parents, and £1,117 a month or £1,284 in Greater London for single adults without children.

(m) For deaths on or after 6 April 2017 non-taxable bereavement support payments apply. A first payment of £3,500 for those with children under 20 in full-time education is followed by monthly payments of £350. For those without children under 20 in full-time education the first payment is £2,500 and monthly payments are £100. Monthly payments paid for up to 18 months.

Social security taxable benefits

Total benefit if received for full tax year (52 weeks)	2022/23	2021/22	2020/21	2019/20	2018/19	2017/18	2016/17
Retirement pensions	£	£	£	£	£	£	£
Retirement on or after 6 April 2016	9,627	9,339	9,110	8,767	8,546	8,296	8,093
Retirement before 6 April 2016							
—category A or B	7,376	7,155	6,981	6,718	6,549	6,359	6,203
—category B (lower)	4,420	4,287	4,183	4,027	3,926	3,811	3,718
—category C or D (non-contributory)	4,420	4,287	4,183	4,027	3,926	3,811	3,718
—increase for adult dependant	—	—	—	3,640	3,554	3,450	3,416
—age addition (over 80)	13	13	13	13	13	13	13
Bereavement benefit: deaths before 6 April 2017 (see note (e))							
Widowed parent's (mother's) allowance	6,570	6,372	6,341	6,234	6,089	5,912	5,852
Bereavement allowance (widow's pension)	6,570	6,372	6,341	6,234	6,089	5,912	5,852
Carer's allowance (previously invalid care allowance)							
Basic	3,624	3,515	3,497	3,439	3,359	3,260	3,229
Increase for adult dependant	—	—	—	2,022	1,976	1,918	1,900
Incapacity benefit							
Long term (after 52 weeks)	6,149	5,964	5,935	5,837	5,699	5,532	5,478
—increase for adult dependant	3,572	3,465	3,447	3,390	3,309	3,213	3,182
Increase of long term benefit for age							
—higher rate (under 35)	652	631	629	618	603	585	579
—lower rate (35 to under 45)	361	351	348	343	335	325	322
Industrial death benefit (deaths before 11.4.88 only)							
Widow's pension (higher permanent rate)	7,376	7,155	6,981	6,718	6,549	6,359	6,203
Widow's pension (lower permanent rate)	2,213	2,146	2,094	2,015	1,965	1,907	1,861
Widower's pension	7,376	7,155	6,981	6,718	6,549	6,359	6,203
Invalidity allowances when paid with retirement pensions							
Higher rate	1,255	1,216	1,211	1,190	1,162	1,128	1,118
Middle rate	806	780	774	764	748	728	722
Lower rate	403	390	387	382	374	364	361

Notes

(a) See notes on previous page.

(b) All figures are exclusive of additional benefits in respect of graduated pension, additional pension, etc. which vary with the individual. Certain benefits may be subject to reduction or withdrawal occasioned by earnings of the individual or of an adult dependant. See note (d) below for the basis of assessment.

(c) Retirement pension may be deferred. The following rules apply to those reaching state pension age before 6 April 2016. For periods of deferral after 5 April 2005, subject to conditions, either the benefit finally payable is increased or a taxable lump sum is payable. Increased benefit is calculated by adding 0.2% of the pension otherwise payable for each full week of deferral, subject to a minimum deferral of 5 weeks. The lump sum is equal to the pension that would have been payable in the deferral period plus interest at a rate at least 2% above the Bank of England base rate, subject to a minimum deferral of 12 months.

(d) Benefits are assessed on the 'accruals' basis rather than on a receipts basis. HMRC consider that where a person is entitled to receive 53 weekly payments within a single tax year, the taxable amount is 53 times the weekly amount, rather than the amount shown in the above table. This applies also where the benefit is paid four-weekly and 14 payments are made in the tax year.

(e) For deaths on or after 6 April 2017 non-taxable bereavement support payments apply. A first payment of £3,500 for those with children under 20 in full-time education is followed by monthly payments of £350. For those without children under 20 in full-time education the first payment is £2,500 and monthly payments are £100. Monthly payments paid for up to 18 months.

Social security non-taxable benefits

Weekly rates from weeks commencing		11.4.22	12.4.21
Attendance allowance		£	£
Higher rate (day and night)		92.40	89.60
Lower rate (day or night)		61.85	60.00
Bereavement support payments (see notes (m) on p 104 and (e) on p 105)			
Child benefit (see note (a))			
Eldest child		21.80	21.15
Each subsequent child		14.45	14.00
Child dependency addition			
Paid with retirement pension, bereavement benefit, carer's allowance, incapacity benefit, severe disablement unemployability supplement		11.35	11.35
Disability living allowance (DLA)/personal independence payment			
Care/daily living component	higher rate	92.40	89.60
	middle rate	61.85	60.00
	lower rate (DLA only)	24.45	23.70
Mobility component	higher rate	64.50	62.55
	lower rate	24.45	23.70
Guardian's allowance		18.55	18.00
Housing benefit (income related) (note (b))		Varies	Varies
Incapacity benefit (short-term)			
Over pension age—lower rate (first 28 weeks)		113.45	110.05
—increase for adult dependant		66.10	64.10
Under pension age—lower rate (first 28 weeks)		89.25	86.55
—increase for adult dependant		53.50	51.90
Income support (income related) (note (b))		Varies	Varies
Non-taxable in hands of those not available for employment and not involved in a trade dispute			

Weekly rates from weeks commencing		11.4.22	12.4.21
Industrial injuries disablement benefit			
Standard rate	Disablement %	£	£
	100%	188.60	182.90
	90%	169.74	164.61
	80%	150.88	146.32
	70%	132.02	128.03
	60%	113.16	109.74
	50%	94.30	91.45
	40%	75.44	73.16
	30%	56.58	54.87
	20%	37.72	36.58
Unemployability supplement		116.60	113.10
— increase for early incapacity:			
higher rate		24.15	23.40
middle rate		15.50	15.00
lower rate		7.75	7.50
Constant attendance allowance			
— exceptional rate		151.00	146.40
— intermediate rate		113.25	109.80
— normal maximum rate		75.50	73.20
— part-time rate		37.75	36.60
Exceptionally severe disablement allowance		75.50	73.20
Maternity allowance (where SMP not available)			
Standard rate		156.66	151.97
MA threshold		30.00	30.00
Severe disablement allowance			
Basic rate		83.75	81.25
Age-related addition	under 40	12.55	12.15
—(age when disabled)	under 50	6.95	6.75
	under 60	6.95	6.75
Increase for adult dependant		41.20	39.95

Notes

(a) **High income child benefit charge.** An income tax charge (the 'high income child benefit charge') is imposed on an individual whose adjusted net income exceeds £50,000 in a tax year and who is, or whose partner is, in receipt of child benefit. In the event that both partners have an adjusted net income that exceeds £50,000, the charge applies only to the partner with the highest income. The amount of the charge is 1% of the amount of the child benefit for every £100 of income above £50,000. If the individual's adjusted net income exceeds £60,000, the charge is the full amount of the child benefit. '*Adjusted net income*' is, broadly, taxable income before deducting personal reliefs but adjusted by deducting the gross equivalent of any gift aid donations or any pension contributions paid net of basic rate tax. A person (P) who is entitled to child benefit for one or more children can elect not to receive that benefit if P reasonably expects that, in the absence of an election, P or another person would be liable to a high income child benefit charge.

(b) Income support, income-based jobseeker's allowance, income based employment and support allowance, housing benefit, child tax credits and working tax credits are being replaced by universal credit (see page 109). It is intended that by 2024, all claimants currently receiving the legacy benefits will be automatically transferred to universal credit. In the interim the natural migration to universal credit will continue through new claims and changes in the circumstances of claimants.

(c) A cap applies to limit the total benefits that most people aged 16 to 64 can receive. The cap applies to the total amount that the individuals in a household receive from specified benefits. Initially, the cap operates by reducing the amount of housing benefit. From October 2013 the cap applies directly to all new claims to universal credit. From 7 November 2016 the cap is £384.62 a week or £442.31 in Greater London for couples and for single parents whose children live with them, and £257.69 a week or £296.35 in Greater London for single adults with no children or whose children do not live with them. Where the cap is applied directly to universal credit, the restriction is made on a monthly basis: £1,667 a month or £1,917 in Greater London for couples and for single parents, and £1,117 a month or £1,284 in Greater London for single adults without children.

(d) Severe disablement allowance has been replaced with employment and support allowance except for those who reached retirement age before 6 April 2014.

Social security tax credits and universal credit

Tax Credits	2022/23	2021/22
Child tax credit per annum	£	£
Family element (see note (b))	545	545
Child element (see note (a))	2,935	2,845
Disabled child additional element	3,545	3,435
Enhanced disabled child additional element	1,430	1,390
Working tax credit per annum/weekly equivalents		
Basic element (see note (c))	2,070	2,005
Additional couple's and lone parent element	2,125	2,060
30 hour element	860	830
Disabled worker element	3,345	3,240
Enhanced disabled adult element	1,445	1,400
Childcare element (weekly)		
— maximum eligible cost	300	300
— maximum eligible cost for 1 child	175	175
— percent of eligible costs covered	70%	70%
Common features		
Income threshold	6,770	6,565
Withdrawal rate	41%	41%
Income threshold for those entitled to child tax credit only	17,005	16,480
Income rise disregard	2,500	2,500
Income fall disregard	2,500	2,500
Pension credit (weekly amounts)		
Standard minimum guarantee		
— claimant with partner	278.70	270.30
— other claimants	182.60	177.10
Additional amounts for severely disabled		
— single	69.40	67.30
— couple (one qualifies)	69.40	67.30
— couple (both qualify)	138.80	134.60
Additional amount for carers	38.85	37.70
Capital disregarded	10,000	10,000

Universal Credit	2022/23	2021/22
Monthly rates	£	£
Standard allowance		
Single under 25 (see note (e))	265.31	344.00
Single 25 or over (see note (f))	334.91	411.51
Joint claimants both under 25	416.45	490.60
Joint claimants, one or both 25 or over	525.72	596.98
Child element (see note (a))		
First child	290.00	282.50
Second/subsequent child	244.58	237.08
Disabled child additions		
—higher rate	414.88	402.41
—lower rate	132.89	128.89
Childcare element		
— maximum for 1 child	646.35	646.35
— maximum for 2 or more children	1,108.04	1,108.04
Limited capability for work element	132.89	128.89
Limited capability for work and work-related activity element	354.28	343.63
Carer element	168.81	163.73
Non-dependants' housing cost contributions	77.87	75.53
Work allowances		
Higher (no housing element) (note (g))		
— single, one or more children	573.00	557.00
— single, limited capability for work	573.00	557.00
— joint, one or more children	573.00	557.00
— joint, limited capability for work	573.00	557.00
Lower (note (h))		
— single, one or more children	344.00	335.00
— single, limited capability for work	344.00	335.00
— joint, one or more children	344.00	335.00
— joint, limited capability for work	344.00	335.00

Notes

(a) Universal credit is being phased in nationally. It is intended that by 2024, all claimants currently receiving the legacy benefits will be automatically transferred to universal credit. In the interim the natural migration to universal credit will continue through new claims and changes in the circumstances of claimants.

(b) The child element is no longer awarded for third and subsequent children born after 5 April 2017. This also applies to families claiming universal credit for the first time after April 2017. The restriction does not apply to disabled children and multiple births.

(c) Only one family element per family. It is not payable to those starting a family after 5 April 2017.

(d) The Government made a one-off payment in April 2021 of £500 to eligible working tax credit claimants across the UK.

(e) Includes a temporary increase for assessment periods ending on or after 6th April 2021 and before 6th October 2021 of £86.67 per assessment period. Reduced to £257.33 from 6 October 2021.

(f) Includes a temporary increase for assessment periods ending on or after 6th April 2021 and before 6th October 2021 of £86.67 per assessment period. Reduced to £324.84 from 6 October 2021.

(g) Increased from £515.00 to £557.00 from 24 November 2021.

(h) Increased from £293.00 to £335.00 from 24 November 2021.

Stamp duty land tax

Land transactions from 1 April 2021 onwards (note (a))

Residential property (notes (b), (c), (f), (g), (h))

Consideration (rates apply to consideration in each slice)	**Main rate for residents**	**Main rate for non-residents**	**Higher rate for residents**	**Higher rate for non-residents**
1.4.21–30.6.21				
Up to £500,000	Nil	2%	3%	5%
£500,001–£925,000	5%	7%	8%	10%
£925,001–£1,500,000	10%	12%	13%	15%
£1,500,001 or more	12%	14%	15%	17%

Consideration (rates apply to consideration in each slice)	**Main rate for residents**	**Main rate for non-residents**	**Higher rate for residents**	**Higher rate for non-residents**
1.7.21–30.9.21				
Up to £250,000	Nil	2%	3%	5%
£250,001–£925,000	5%	7%	8%	10%
£925,001–£1,500,0000	10%	12%	13%	15%
£1,500,001 or more	12%	14%	15%	17%

Consideration (rates apply to consideration in each slice)	**Main rate for residents**	**Main rate for non-residents**	**Higher rate for residents**	**Higher rate for non-residents**
1.10.21–				
Up to £125,000	Nil	2%	3%	5%
£125,001–£250,000	2%	4%	5%	7%
£250,001–£925,000	5%	7%	8%	10%
£925,001–£1,500,000	10%	12%	13%	15%
£1,500,001 or more	12%	14%	15%	17%

Non-residential or mixed property

Consideration (rates apply to consideration in each slice)	**Rate**
1.4.21–	
Up to £150,000	Nil
£150,001–£250,000	2%
£250,001 or more	5%

Land transactions before 1 April 2021 (note (a))

Residential property (notes (b), (c), (f) (g), (h))

Consideration (rates apply to consideration in each slice)	**Rate**
4.12.14–31.3.16	
Up to £125,000	Nil
£125,001–£250,000	2%
£250,001–£925,000	5%
£925,001–£1,500,000	10%
£1,500,001 or more	12%

Consideration (rates apply to consideration in each slice)	**Main rate**	**Higher rate**
1.4.16–7.7.20		
Up to £125,000	Nil	3%
£125,001–£250,000	2%	5%
£250,001–£925,000	5%	8%
£925,001–£1,500,000	10%	13%
£1,500,001 or more	12%	15%

Consideration (rates apply to consideration in each slice)	**Main rate**	**Higher rate**
8.7.20–31.3.21		
Up to £500,000	Nil	3%
£500,001–£925,000	5%	8%
£925,001–£1,500,000	10%	13%
£1,500,001 or more	12%	15%

Non-residential or mixed property

Consideration (rates apply to consideration in each slice)	**Rate**
4.12.14–16.3.16	
Up to £150,000	Nil
£150,001–£250,000	1%
£250,001–500,000	3%
£500,001 or more	4%

Consideration (rates apply to consideration in each slice)	**Rate**
17.3.16–	
Up to £150,000	Nil
£150,001–£250,000	2%
£250,001 or more	5%

Notes

(a) Stamp duty land tax does not apply to transactions in land in Scotland with an effective date on or after 1 April 2015. See page 113 for Land and buildings transaction tax. Stamp duty land tax does not apply in Wales from 1 April 2018, when Landfill disposals tax applies, see page 113.

(b) The **higher rate** of SDLT applies to certain transactions in residential property with an effective date on or after 1 April 2016, except, broadly, where the contract was entered into and substantially performed before 26 November 2015. The rate applies to purchases of additional residential property by individuals and to purchases of residential property by companies and certain trusts. It does not apply to transactions under £40,000. There is provision for relief where an individual's main residence is replaced and there is a gap in ownership of such a residence, or an overlap in ownership, not exceeding 3 years. Relief is available in certain circumstances when someone gets divorced, exchanges a property with a spouse, adds to an existing interest in their main residence or is a child whose affairs are subject to the Court of Protection. For purchases on or after 1 January 2017, a taxpayer will still be able to obtain a refund if HMRC is satisfied that they were unable to sell the previous residence within 3 years due to 'exceptional circumstances'.

(c) **Residential property acquired by non-natural person.** Where a residential property is purchased by a non-natural person (such as a company, collective investment scheme or a partnership of which a company or such a scheme is a member), a rate of stamp duty land tax of 15% (for residents) and 17% (for non-residents from 1 April 2021 (see note (h) below)) applies if the consideration exceeds £500,000 (£2 million where the contract is entered into before 20 March 2014). The rate applies to the whole of the consideration despite the change to a 'slice' basis for residential property generally from 4 December 2014. Exclusions apply for certain corporate trustees, property developers and other businesses.

(d) Interest on unpaid SDLT runs from 14 days (30 days before 1 March 2019) after the effective date of the transaction, or the date of a disqualifying event, until the tax is paid. In the case of a deferred payment, interest runs from the date payment is due until the tax is paid. Interest is added to repayments of overpaid SDLT and runs from the date the tax was paid or an amount was lodged with HMRC to the date the order for repayment is issued. For rates of interest see page 79.

(e) **First-time buyer relief.** With effect from 22 November 2017, residential property purchases by first-time buyers attract a nil rate of SDLT for purchase consideration up to £300,000. Purchase consideration over £300,000 up to and including £500,000 attracts 5% SDLT, though the 2% non-resident surcharge applies from 1 July 2021. Therefore the lower rates from 1 July 2021 for non-residents are 2% and 7% respectively. Where the purchase consideration is in excess of £500,000, no relief is due and standard rates above apply. These provisions were temporarily suspended whilst the nil rate band was increased to £500,000 for transactions with an effective date between 8 July 2020 and 30 June 2021 inclusive.

(f) **Other SDLT exemptions and reliefs.** No SDLT is chargeable on: (i) gifts inter vivos; (ii) transfers to beneficiaries under a Will or an intestacy; (iii) certain transfers on divorce or dissolution of a civil partnership; (iv) transfers to charities for use for charitable purposes; (v) transfers to bodies established for national purposes or (where the effective date is on or after 17 July 2012) certain National Health Service bodies; (vi) land transfers within groups of companies; (vii) land transferred for shares on company reconstructions and acquisitions; (viii) transfers of intellectual property; (ix) certain transfers to registered providers of social housing; (x) certain leases granted by registered providers of social housing; (xi) (from 15 September 2016), transfer of property into an property authorised investment fund or co-ownership authorised contractual scheme in return for an issue of units, within an initial seeding period of up to three years (xii) (from 12 February 2019), certain transfers of securities, property and land from a failed institution to the appointed temporary holding entity under a Bank of England stabilisation power, and on transfers of securities to bondholders following exercise of the bail-in stabilisation power; and (xiii) certain acquisitions of land situated in freeport tax sites from the date a freeport tax site is formally designated until 30 September 2026. See *SI 2021 Nos 1193*, *1194*, *1195* and *1389* for details of the current freeport tax sites.
A a relief applies where more than one residential property is purchased from the same vendor. SDLT is charged on the mean consideration for each property, subject to a minimum rate of 1%.

(g) **Temporary increase in nil rate threshold.** For transactions with an effective date between 8 July 2020 and 30 June 2021 inclusive, the nil rate band for residential property was increased from £125,000 to £500,000 with an additional temporary relief for transactions with an effective date between 1 July 2021 and 30 September 2021 inclusive, by a reduction from £500,000 to £250,000. The nil rate band reverted to the previous threshold of £125,000 from 1 October 2021.

(h) A 2% surcharge applies from 1 April 2021 on purchases of residential property made by non-residents (as defined for SDLT purposes only), including certain UK resident companies controlled by non-residents.

Premiums (note (a))

Lease rentals after 1 April 2021	**On net present value of rent over term of lease (applying a discount rate of 3.5%)** (rates apply to the amount of npv in the slice)				**Rate for residents**	**Rate for non-residents**
		1.4.21–30.6.21	**1.7.21–30.9.21**	**1.10.21–**		
Residential property		Up to £500,000	Up to £250,000	Up to £125,000	Nil	2%
		£500,001 or more	£250,001 or more	£125,001 or more	1%	3%
		1.4.21–			**Rate for residents**	
Non-residential or mixed property		Up to £150,000			Nil	
		£150,001–£5,000,000			1%	
		£5,000,001 or more			2%	

Premiums (note (a))

Lease rentals before 1 April 2021	**On net present value of rent over term of lease (applying a discount rate of 3.5%)** (rates apply to the amount of npv in the slice — but see notes (a), (b))				**Rate**
		22.3.12–16.3.16	17.3.16–7.7.20	7.7.20–31.3.21	
Residential property		Up to £125,000	Up to £125,000	Up to £500,000	Nil
		£125,001 or more	£125,001 or more	£500,001 or more	1%
Non-residential or mixed property		Up to £150,000	Up to £150,000	Up to £150,000	Nil
		£150,001 or more	£150,001–£5,000,000	£150,001–£5,000,000	1%
			£5,000,001 or more	£5,000,001 or more	2%

Notes

(a) The same tax is payable for a premium granted as for a land transaction. For transactions with an effective date before 17 March 2016, special rules apply to a premium in respect of non-residential property where the rent exceeds £1,000 p.a.

(b) For transactions with an effective date between 8 July 2020 and 30 June 2021 inclusive, the nil rate band for residential property was increased from £125,000 to £500,000 with an additional temporary relief for transactions with an effective date between 1 July 2021 and 30 September 2021 inclusive, with a reduction from £500,000 to £250,000. The nil rate band reverted to the previous threshold of £125,000 from 1 October 2021.

Land and buildings transaction tax (Scotland)

Land transactions

Residential property

Consideration (rates apply to consideration in each slice)	Rate (notes (b), (c))
15.7.20–31.3.21	
Up to £250,000	Nil
£250,001–£325,000	5%
£325,001–£750,000	10%
£750,001 or more	12%
1.4.15–14.7.20 and from 1.4.21	
Up to £145,000	Nil
£145,001–£250,000	2%
£250,001–£325,000	5%
£325,001–£750,000	10%
£750,001 or more	12%

Non-residential or mixed property

Consideration (rates apply to consideration in each slice)	Rate (note (b))
25.1.19–	
Up to £150,000	Nil
£150,001–£250,000	1%
£250,001 or more	5%
1.4.15–25.1.19	
Up to £150,000	Nil
£150,001–£350,000	3%
£350,001 or more	4.5%

Land transaction tax (Wales)

Land transactions

Residential property

Consideration (rates apply to consideration in each slice)	Main rate	Higher rate (note (g))
1.7.21–		
Up to £180,000	Nil	4%
£180,001–£250,000	3.5%	7.5%
£250,001–£400,000	5%	9%
£400,001–£750,000	7.5%	11.5%
£750,001–£1,500,000	10%	14%
£1,500,001 or more	12%	16%
22.12.20–30.6.21		
Up to £180,000	Nil	4%
£180,001–£250,000	Nil	7.5%
£250,001–£400,000	5%	9%
£400,001–£750,000	7.5%	11.5%
£750,001–£1,500,000	10%	14%
£1,500,001 or more	12%	16%
27.7.20–21.12.20		
Up to £180,000	Nil	3%
£180,001–£250,000	Nil	6.5%
£250,001–£400,000	5%	8%
£400,001–£750,000	7.5%	10.5%
£750,001–£1,500,000	10%	13%
£1,500,001 or more	12%	15%
1.4.18–26.7.20		
Up to £180,000	Nil	3%
£180,001–£250,000	3.5%	6.5%
£250,001–£400,000	5%	8%
£400,001–£750,000	7.5%	10.5%
£750,001–£1,500,000	10%	13%
£1,500,001 or more	12%	15%

Non-residential or mixed property

Consideration (rates apply to consideration in each slice)	Rate
22.12.20–	
Up to £225,000	Nil
£225,001–£250,000	1%
£250,001–£1,000,000	5%
£1,000,001 or more	6%
1.4.18–21.12.20	
Up to £150,000	Nil
£150,001–£250,000	1%
£250,001–1,000,000	5%
£1,000,001 or more	6%

Notes

(a) Land and buildings transaction tax (LBTT) applies to transactions in land in Scotland with an effective date on or after 1 April 2015. Land transaction tax (LTT) applies to transactions in land in Wales with an effective date on or after 1 April 2018. Stamp duty land tax does not apply to such transactions.

(b) For land transactions with an effective date on or after 25 January 2019 (other than where contracts were entered into before 12 December 2018), an additional amount of LBTT of 4% (previously 3% for transactions with an effective date on or after 1 April 2016 where contracts were entered into after 27 January 2016) of the consideration applies to transactions which consist of or include the acquisition of an additional dwelling by individuals or which consist of or include the acquisition of a dwelling by certain businesses, companies and trusts. The charge does not apply to purchases of property under £40,000. There is provision for relief from the higher rate where an individual's main residence is replaced and there is a gap in ownership of such a residence, or an overlap in ownership, not exceeding 18 months. For transactions with an effective date between 24 September 2018 and 24 March 2020 inclusive, the period is extended from 18 months to 36 months. From 30 June 2017 relief is available in certain circumstances when two buyers jointly buy a new dwelling and previously lived together as a married couple, civil partners or cohabitants in a dwelling owned by either one of them solely. The revised rates from 25 January 2019 apply only to contracts entered into from 12 December 2018. With effect for contracts entered into after 8 February 2018, where the effective date of the transaction is after 29 June 2018 **relief for first-time buyers** applies a nil rate to the first £175,000 of purchase consideration resulting in first-time buyers benefiting from the relief up to a maximum of £600. Note, however, that there was a temporary increase in the overall nil rate band to £250,000 from 15 July 2020 to 31 March 2021.

(c) For LBTT transactions with an effective date between 15 July 2020 and 31 March 2021 inclusive, the nil rate band for residential property was increased from £145,000 to £250,000. It reverted to £145,000 from 1 April 2021.

(d) **Leases — Scotland.** LBTT applies to non-residential leases but only to certain very long residential leases. Before 7 February 2020, where a lease is chargeable the amount of tax payable is 1% of the amount of net present value (NPV) of the rent above £150,000. For transactions with an effective date on or after 7 February 2020, where contracts were entered into on or after that date and subject to some exceptions for further returns, the rate is 1% of the NPV between £150,000 and £2m, and 2% above £2m (rates apply to the amount of NPV in the slice, not the whole value). The same tax is payable for a premium in respect of a lease within the charge as for a land transaction. Special rules apply to a premium in respect of non-residential property where the rent exceeds £1,000 a year.

(e) There are various exemptions and reliefs from LBTT, see 'LBTT3010 - Tax Reliefs' and 'LBTT3002 - Exempt Transactions' at www.revenue.scot. Penalties apply for late returns, late payment and inaccuracies in documents. Interest is charged on late payments and is payable on overpayments.

(f) There are various exemptions and reliefs from LTT, see Land Transaction Tax and Anti-avoidance of Devolved Taxes (Wales) Act 2017 Schs 3, 9–22. Penalties apply for late returns, late payment and inaccuracies in documents. Interest is charged on late payments and is payable on overpayments.

(g) A higher rate of LTT of 4% (3% for transactions with an effective date between 1 April 2018 and 21 December 2020) applies broadly to purchases of additional residential property by individuals, and to purchases of residential property by companies and trusts other than bare trusts and interest in possession trusts. It does not apply to purchases of property under £40,000. If there is a period of overlap in ownership of a main residence, a refund of the higher rate can be obtained if the previous main residence is sold within 36 months following the purchase of the new. Relief is also available where immediately before the purchase the buyer's spouse or civil partner owns a major interest in the same dwelling and that dwelling will be the buyer's only or main residence immediately before and after the purchase.

(h) For LTT transactions with an effective date between 27 July 2020 and 30 June 2021 inclusive, the nil rate band for residential property was increased from £180,000 to £250,000. It reverted to the previous threshold of £180,000 from 1 July 2021.

(i) **Leases — Wales.** LTT is applied to non-residential leases and the amount of tax payable for transactions with an effective date between 1 April 2018 and 21 December 2020 is 1% of the amount of net present value of the rent between £150,000 and £2m, 2% above £2m. For transactions with an effective date on or after 22 December 2020 the rate is 1% of the amount of net present value (NPV) of the rent between £225,000 and £2m, and 2% above £2m (rates apply to the amount of NPV in the slice, not the whole value). The same tax is payable for a premium in respect of a lease within the charge as for a land transaction. Special rules apply to a premium in respect of non-residential property where the rent exceeds £13,500 a year on or after 4 February 2021 (£9,000 before 4 February 2021).

Stamp taxes

Stamp duty

Shares, etc.	
Shares converted into depositary receipts or put into duty free clearance systems (note (n))	1.5%
Purchase of own shares by company	0.5%
Transfers of stock or marketable securities	0.5%
Takeovers, mergers, demergers, schemes of reconstruction and amalgamation (except where no real change of ownership)	0.5%

Stamp duty reserve tax

Agreements to transfer chargeable securities for money or money's worth (e.g. renounceable letters of allotment)	0.5%
Chargeable securities converted into depository receipts or put into clearance services (notes (m), (n))	1.5%
Dealings before 30 March 2014 in units of unit trusts and shares in OEICs	0.5%

Notes

(j) Stamp duty applies only to shares and marketable securities and to the transfer of an interest in a partnership holding stock or marketable securities.

(k) Stamp duty is not chargeable where the amount or value of the consideration is £1,000 or under.

(l) **Stamp duty exemptions and reliefs.** No stamp duty is chargeable on:
- (i) gifts inter vivos;
- (ii) transfers to charities for use for charitable purposes;
- (iii) transfers to bodies established for national purposes;

An exemption from stamp duty and stamp duty reserve tax applies with effect, broadly, from 28 April 2014 for transfers of securities admitted to trading on recognised growth markets. From April 2014 transfers of units in exchange traded funds will similarly be exempt.

(m) Following the Tribunal decision in *HSBC Holdings plc and Bank of New York Mellon Corporation v HMRC* FTT, [2012] UKFTT 163 (TC), the 1.5% stamp duty reserve tax charge is no longer applicable to issues of UK shares and securities to clearance services or depositary receipt issuers anywhere in the world. The charge continues to apply to transfers of such shares or securities to clearance services or depositary receipt issuers. See HMRC Notice, 27 April 2012.

(n) For options entered into on or after 25 November 2015 and exercised on or after 16 March 2016, where UK securities are deposited with a depositary receipt issuer or clearance service following the exercise of an option, the 1.5% rate applies to the higher of the market value or the option strike price at the date the instrument is executed (stamp duty) or the date of transfer (SDRT).

Time limits claims and elections

	Provision	Time limit
General		
TMA 1970, s 43(1)	Under self-assessment for individuals etc., unless otherwise prescribed	4 years after end of tax year.
FA 1998, Sch 18 para 55	For companies, unless otherwise prescribed	4 years after end of accounting period.
	Listed below are the more important *prescribed* time limits. Unless otherwise stated, time limits run from the end of the chargeable period	
Income tax		
ITA 2007, s 202	**Enterprise investment scheme relief**	5th anniversary of 31 January following tax year in which shares issued
ITEPA 2003, Sch 5 para 44	**Enterprise management incentives**—notification of grant of options to HMRC	92 days after grant of option
ITTOIA 2005, ss 222, 222A, 225	**Farming**—averaging of profits	1 year after 31 January following second or fifth tax year to which claim relates
ITA 2007, s 426	**Gift aid**—election to treat donations as made in the previous tax year	On or before date the donor delivers his tax return for the previous tax year but no later than 31 January following the end of that tax year
	Losses set off against other income	
ITA 2007, s 124	(a) Property business losses	1 year after 31 January following tax year of loss
ITA 2007, s 64	(b) Trading losses	1 year after 31 January following tax year of loss
ITA 2007, s 72	(c) Trading losses in any of the first 4 tax years	1 year after 31 January following tax year of loss
ITA 2007, s 132	(d) Losses on disposal of shares in unlisted trading companies	1 year after 31 January following tax year of loss
ITA 2007, s 96	**Post-cessation expenditure**—set off against income	1 year after 31 January following tax year of payment
ITTOIA 2005, s 257	**Post-cessation receipts** received within, broadly, 6 years of date of discontinuance to be treated as received on that date	1 year after 31 January following tax year of receipt
ITTOIA 2005, s 818	**Qualifying care receipts**—election to tax on the alternative method of calculating profits	1 year after 31 January following tax year
ITTOIA 2005, ss 799, 800	**Rent a room relief**—(a) relief not to apply; (b) relief to apply to gross income in excess of limit; or (c) withdrawal of claim under (a) or (b)	1 year after 31 January following tax year
ITA 2007, s 257EA	**Seed enterprise investment scheme relief**	5th anniversary of 31 January following tax year in which shares issued
ITTOIA 2005, ss 271A	**Simplified cash basis for unincorporated property businesses**—cash basis *not* to apply	1 year after 31 January following tax year
ITA 2007, s 257P	**Social investment relief**	5th anniversary of 31 January following tax year in which investment made
ITTOIA 2005, ss 783AL, 783AM, 783BJ, 783BK	**Trading or property allowance**—full relief not to apply; partial relief to apply	1 year after 31 January following tax year
ITTOIA 2005, s 185	**Trading stock**—work in progress on discontinuance valued at cost	1 year after 31 January following tax year of cessation;
Income tax and corporation tax		
CTA 2009, s 122 *ITTOIA 2005, s 124*	**Herd basis**	2 years after first accounting period in which herd kept (CT) or 1 year after 31 January following first year of assessment for which herd kept in basis year (IT)
CTA 2009, s 178(6) *ITTOIA 2005, s 194(6)*	**Know-how** used in trade—sale not to be treated as goodwill	2 years from date of disposal
CTA 2009, ss 914(5), 917(4); *ITTOIA 2005, ss 590(6), 591(3)*	**Patents**—capital sums to be treated (a) by UK residents as charged in period received, or (b) by non-residents as spread over 6 years	1 year after 31 January following tax year of receipt (IT); 2 years after accounting period of receipt (CT)

	Provision	Time limit
CTA 2009, s 268(6); ITTOIA 2005, s 326(6)	**Rents etc**	1 year after 31 January following tax year (IT)
	Furnished holiday lettings—averaging provisions	2 years after accounting period (CT)
CTA 2009, s 1275(5); ITTOIA 2005, s 842(5)	**Unremittable overseas income** to be excluded from liability to tax	1 year after 31 January following tax year in which income arises (IT); 2 years after accounting period in which income arises (CT)
Corporation tax		
FA 2000, Sch 15 para 68	**Corporate venturing**—relief for losses on disposal of shares against income	2 years
TMA 1970, Sch 3ZB para 1	**Exit charge payment plans**—application for	9 months from end of accounting period of migration
FA 1998, Sch 18 para 83W	**Film, television, video games, theatre, museum and gallery exhibition and orchestra tax reliefs**—claims to be made, amended or withdrawn in the company tax return	1 year from filing date for the return
FA 1998, Sch 18 para 74	**Group relief and group relief for carried forward losses**	The latest of: (i) 1 year from the filing date of the claimant company's return for the accounting period for which the claim is made; (ii) 30 days after the end of an enquiry into the return; (iii) if HMRC amend the return after an enquiry, 30 days after the issue of notice of assessment;(iv) if an appeal is made against the amendment, 30 days after the determination of the appeal; (or such later date as HMRC allow). (NB filing date is generally 1 year after end of accounting period)
	Intangible assets	
CTA 2009, s 730(3)	(a) Election to replace accounts depreciation with fixed WDA of 4%	2 years
CTA 2009, s 816(2)	(b) Election to exclude certain expenditure on computer software	2 years
FA 2013, s 60	(c) Disincorporation relief (transfer before 1 April 2018 only)	2 years beginning with date of transfer
	Losses set off against other income	
CTA 2010, s 37(7)	(a) Trading losses	2 years
CTA 2010, s 70(4)	(b) Losses by an investment company on disposal of shares in unlisted trading companies	2 years
CTA 2009, s 458(2)	(c) Non-trading deficit on loan relationships	2 years
	Post-1 April 2017 losses carried forward	
CTA 2010, s 45A(7)	(a) Trading losses to be offset against *total* profits of a later accounting period	2 years
CTA 2010, s 45B(6)	(b) Trading losses *not* to be carried forward against *trade* profits of the next accounting	2 years
CTA 2010, s 62(5C)	(c) Property losses to be carried forward against *total* profits	2 years
CTA 2009, s 463G	(d) Non-trading deficit on loan relationships to be carried forward against *total* profits	2 years
CTA 2010, s 357G(3)	**Patent box**	1 year from filing date for the return for the first accounting period for which the election is to apply
FA 1998, Sch 18 para 83E	**Research and development**—tax relief claims to be made, amended or withdrawn in the company tax return	1 year from filing date for the return
Capital allowances	(NB: A 'chargeable period' for capital allowances purposes is an accounting period of a company or a period of account of an individual.)	
CAA 2001, s 3(2),(3)(b); FA 1998, Sch 18 para 82	**Companies**—claims for capital allowances (including variations and withdrawals)	1st anniversary of filing date for claimant company's tax return but deferred in cases of HMRC enquiry (NB: filing date is generally 1 year after accounting period)
	Connected persons	
CAA 2001, s 266	(a) Successions to trades between connected persons: machinery or plant treated as transferred at tax written down value	2 years from date of succession
CAA 2001, s 570(5)	(b) Sales between persons under common control treated as being at tax written down value	2 years from date of sale

Time limits claims and elections

	Provision	Time limit
CAA 2001, s 177(5)	**Equipment leasing**—fixtures treated as belonging to lessor	1 year after 31 January following tax year in which ends lessor's chargeable period in which expenditure incurred (IT); 2 years after that chargeable period (CT)
CAA 2001, s 260(6)	**Excess capital allowances**—set-off against other income of companies	2 years
	Plant and machinery	
CAA 2001, s 183(2)	Fixture on land subsequently let to be treated as belonging to lessee	2 years after lease takes effect
	Oilfields	
CAA 2001, s 164(2)	General decommissioning expenditure	2 years
	Ships	
CAA 2001, s 130(4)	(a) Postponement, disclaimer or reduction of first year allowances or writing down allowances	1 year after 31 January following tax year in which chargeable period ends (IT); 2 years after chargeable period (CT)
CAA 2001, s 129(2)	(b) 'Single ship pool' provisions not to apply	1 year after 31 January following tax year in which chargeable period ends (IT); 2 years after chargeable period (CT)
	Short life assets	
CAA 2001, s 85(2)	(a) Plant or machinery to be treated as short life asset	1 year after 31 January following tax year in which chargeable period ends (IT); 2 years after chargeable period (CT)
CAA 2001, s 89(6)	(b) Transfer of short life asset to connected person at tax wdv	2 years after chargeable period
Chargeable gains		
	Assets held on 6 April 1965	
TCGA 1992, Sch 2 para 4	(a) All disposals of quoted securities to be treated as acquired at market value on that date	2 years after end of accounting period in which first relevant disposal after 5 April 1985. CT only
TCGA 1992, Sch 2 para 17	(b) Disposals of other assets computed by reference to market value on that date	2 years after end of accounting period of disposal. CT only
	Assets held on 31 March 1982	
TCGA 1992, s 35(5)(6)	(a) Universal re-basing	2 years after end of accounting period in which first relevant disposal after 5 April 1988. CT only
TCGA 1992, Sch 4 para 9	(b) 50% reduction in taxing deferred gains arising from assets acquired before 31 March 1982	2 years after end of accounting period of disposal or in which gain treated as accruing. CT only
TCGA 1992, ss 169H–169S	**Business asset disposal relief (formerly known as entrepreneurs' relief)**	1 year after 31 January following tax year of qualifying business disposal
TCGA 1992, s 187(1)	**Companies ceasing to be UK resident before 1 January 2019**—postponement of charge on deemed disposal where 75% subsidiary of UK company	2 years after ceasing to be UK resident
FA 2013, s 60	**Disincorporation relief** (transfer before 1 April 2018 only)	2 years beginning with date of transfer
TCGA 1992, s 162A	**Incorporation relief**—election to disapply incorporation relief under *TCGA 1992, s 162* on a transfer of a business	2 years after 31 January following tax year in which transfer takes place (reduced by 1 year where transferor disposes of all shares received in exchange by end of the tax year following that in which transfer takes place
TCGA 1992, s 253(3), (3A)	**Loans to traders** becoming irrecoverable	2 years
TCGA 1992, s 24(2)	**Negligible value securities**	2 years after end of chargeable period of deemed sale and reacquisition
TCGA 1992, s 222	**Private residences**—determination of main residence	2 years after acquisition of second residence
TCGA 1992, s 261B	**Trading losses** to be relieved against gains	1 year after 31 January following tax year of loss

	Provision	Time limit
Inheritance tax		
	Death	
IHTA 1984, s 125	(a) Valuation of woodlands	2 years after death
IHTA 1984, ss 8A, 8B	(b) Transfer of unused nil-rate band to spouse or civil partner	2 years after end of month of survivor's death or, if later, 3 months after personal representatives first act
IHTA 1984, s 57	**Termination of interest in possession**—notice to trustees of available exemptions on termination	6 months after termination
IHTA 1984, ss 30, 78	**National Heritage property**—property transferred to be designated as such, and thus exempt	2 years after transfer or other chargeable event after 16 March 1998

Annual accounting scheme

A business may, subject to conditions, complete one VAT return each year. It can join the scheme if taxable supplies in the next tax year are not expected to exceed

1.4.06 onwards	£1,350,000

but must leave at the end of any accounting year in which yearly taxable supplies exceed

1.4.06 onwards	£1,600,000

Quarterly or monthly payments on account may be required.

Capital goods scheme [*SI 1995 No 2518, Regs 112–116*]

The scheme applies to capital items within the list below which the owner (or person who holds an interest) uses in the course of, and for the purpose of, a business carried on by him. Input tax adjustments are required where, during the adjustment period, there is a change in the extent of the taxable use of the item.

Item	Minimum value	Adjustment period
Land	£250,000	10 years
Building (or part)	£250,000	10 years
Civil engineering work (or part of such a work)	£250,000	10 years
Computer or computer equipment	£50,000	5 years
Aircraft	£50,000	5 years
Ship, boat or other vessel	£50,000	5 years

Where the minimum value would otherwise be £250,000 it is reduced to £1 where the owner, or a person to whom the owner has granted an interest, uses the item to make a grant falling within *VATA 1994 Sch 9 Group1 Item 1(ka)* (self-storage facilities) and decides, before 1 April 2013, to treat the item as a capital item within the scheme. A written record of the decision must be kept.

Aircraft, ships, boats and other vessels are within the scheme only where the item is acquired on or after 1 January 2011. The adjustment period is shortened in certain cases where, at the time of the owner's first use of the item, the number of yearly intervals in the adjustment period exceeds the number of complete years that his interest in the item has to run or where the owner already owned the item prior to VAT registration. The adjustment formula is:

$$\frac{\text{Total VAT on item}}{\text{Length of adjustment period}} \times \text{adjustment percentage}$$

where the 'adjustment percentage' is the percentage change in the extent to which the item is used (or treated as used) in making taxable supplies between the time at which the original entitlement to deduction of the input tax was determined and the adjustment period interval in question. For goods acquired on or after 1 January 2011 total input tax includes any non-business VAT.

Cash accounting scheme

A business may, subject to conditions, account for and pay VAT on the basis of cash paid and received. It can join the scheme if taxable supplies in the next year are not expected to exceed

1.4.07 onwards	£1,350,000

but must leave if taxable supplies in the previous year have exceeded

1.4.07 onwards	£1,600,000

Deregistration

(i) UK taxable supplies

A registered taxable person ceases to be liable to be registered if, at any time, HMRC are satisfied that the value of his taxable supplies in the year then beginning will not exceed the following limits

Effective date	£	Effective date	£
1.4.22	83,000	1.4.19	83,000
1.4.21	83,000	1.4.18	83,000
1.4.20	83,000	1.4.17	83,000

unless the reason the value of taxable supplies will not exceed the limit is that in the period in question the person will cease making taxable supplies or will suspend making them for a period of 30 days or more

(ii) Supplies from EU countries ('distance selling')

NOTE: These rules only apply to registration for supplies into Northern Ireland from the EU from 1 January 2021. In addition, the UK distance selling threshold referenced below was abolished and replaced with an EU-wide threshold (applying also to Northern Ireland) of EUR 10,000 with effect from 1 July 2021. A person registered under these provisions ceases to be liable to be registered if, at any time

(a) his relevant supplies in the year ended 31 December last before that time did not exceed the following limits; and

(b) HMRC are satisfied that the value of his relevant supplies in the year immediately following that year will not exceed the following limits

Effective date	£
1.1.93–30.6.21	70,000

(iii) Acquisitions from EU countries

NOTE: These rules only apply in respect of registration for bringing goods into Northern Ireland from the EU from 1 January 2021. The concept of acquisitions was broadly abolished in the rest of the UK from that date. A person registered under these provisions ceases to be liable to be registered if, at any time

(a) his relevant acquisitions in the year ended 31 December last before that time did not exceed the following limits; and

(b) HMRC are satisfied that the value of his relevant acquisitions in the year immediately following that year will not exceed the following limits

Effective date	£	Effective date	£
1.4.22	85,000	1.4.19	85,000
1.4.21	85,000	1.4.18	85,000
1.4.20	85,000	1.4.17	85,000

EU country codes

Any registration number contained in a VAT invoice provided to a registered person in another EU country must include the appropriate country code as listed below. Country codes are also needed for the completion of EU sales lists.

Country	Code	Country	Code
Austria	AT	Latvia	LV
Belgium	BE	Lithuania	LT
Bulgaria	BG	Luxembourg	LU
Croatia	HR	Malta	MT
Cyprus	CY	Netherlands	NL
Czech Republic	CZ	Northern Ireland	XI
Denmark	DK	Poland	PL
Estonia	EE	Portugal	PT
Finland	FI	Romania	RO
France	FR	Slovak Republic	SK
Germany	DE	Slovenia	SI
Greece	GR	Spain	ES
Hungary	HU	Sweden	SE
Ireland	IE		
Italy	IT		

EU sales lists [*SI 1995 No 2518, Regs 21–23*]

Before 1 January 2021, all businesses registered for VAT in the UK which:

(a) made supplies of goods to traders registered for VAT in an EU country;
(b) transferred its own goods from the UK to an EU country;
(c) was the intermediary in triangular transactions between VAT-registered traders in an EU country; or
(d) made supplies of services to a person in an EU country which are subject to the reverse charge in the customer's country,

had to submit to HMRC statements ('EU sales lists') containing particulars of the transactions involved. Such lists may be submitted electronically or using Form VAT 101. With effect from 1 January 2021 the circumstances in which returns are required are reduced and apply only to VAT-registered businesses trading or operating under the Northern Ireland protocol. From 1 January 2021 the requirement for returns is as follows:

Type of supply		Frequency
Goods only	Where the value of supplies subject to acquisition tax in an EU member state exceeds £35,000 in the current or four previous quarters	Calendar monthly
	Where the value of supplies subject to acquisition tax in an EU member state does not exceed £35,000 in the current or four previous quarters	Quarterly (i.e. for each calendar quarter ending 31 March, 30 June, 30 September and 31 December)
Goods supplied by a business completing annual VAT returns	Total annual taxable turnover does not exceed £145,000; annual value of supplies to EU member states not more than £11,000 (and do not include *New Means of Transport*)	On application — annual on agreed due date
Goods only supplied	Total annual taxable turnover does not exceed the VAT registration threshold plus £25,500; annual value of supplies to EU member states not more than £11,000 (and do not include *New Means of Transport*)	On application — annual in simple format on agreed due date

The requirement for returns until 31 December 2020 is as follows:

Type of supply		Frequency
Goods	Supplies of goods are in excess of £35,000 in any of the current or last four quarters	Calendar monthly
	Supplies of goods are below £35,000 per quarter in the current and previous four quarters	Quarterly (i.e. for each calendar quarter ending 31 March, 30 June, 30 September and 31 December)
Services supplied to a business where the place of supply is where the customer belongs		Quarterly as above
Goods and services where a business is required to submit monthly lists for goods		Monthly for all supplies, or monthly for goods and quarterly for services
Goods or services supplied by a business completing annual VAT returns	Total annual taxable turnover does not exceed £145,000; annual value of supplies to other EU countries not more than £11,000 (and do not include *New Means of Transport*)	On application — annual on agreed due date
Goods only supplied	Total annual taxable turnover does not exceed the VAT registration threshold plus £25,500; annual value of supplies to other EU countries not more than £11,000 (and do not include *New Means of Transport*)	On application — annual in simple format on agreed due date

If an ESL is completed online it must be submitted within 21 days after the end of the reporting period. In other cases the list must be submitted within 14 days after the end of the reporting period.

Value added tax Exempt supplies and flat-rate scheme for small businesses

Exempt supplies [*VATA 1994, Sch 9*]

A supply of goods or services is an exempt supply if falling within one of the Groups listed below. Where a supply falls within one of the Groups but is also covered by the zero-rating provisions, the latter takes priority.

Group 1	Land
Group 2	Insurance
Group 3	Postal services
Group 4	Betting, gaming, dutiable machine games and lotteries
Group 5	Finance
Group 6	Education
Group 7	Health and welfare
Group 8	Burial and cremation
Group 9	Subscriptions to trade unions, professional and other public interest bodies
Group 10	Sport, sports competitions and physical education
Group 11	Works of art, etc.
Group 12	Fund-raising events by charities and other qualifying bodies
Group 13	Cultural services, etc.
Group 14	Supplies of goods where input tax cannot be recovered
Group 15	Investment gold
Group 16	Supplies of services by groups involving cost sharing

Flat-rate scheme for small businesses

An eligible business which expects its taxable supplies (excluding VAT) in the next year to be no more than £150,000 can opt to join a flat-rate scheme. It can then calculate net VAT due by applying the appropriate flat-rate percentage from the list below to total turnover generated, including exempt income.

From 1 April 2017 a 16.5% rate applies to a 'limited cost trader', that is a trader whose VAT-inclusive expenditure on goods used for business purposes (excluding capital expenditure, food and drink for consumption by the business or its employees, and certain vehicles, vehicle parts and fuel) is less than 2% of turnover, or greater than 2% of turnover but less than £1,000 per year. Any trader which is not a limited cost trader continues to use the flat rate based on the categories of business detailed below.

Category of business	*Appropriate %* *4.1.11 onwards* *(except temporary rates)*
Accountancy or book-keeping	14.5
Advertising	11
Agricultural services	11
Any other activity not listed elsewhere	12
Architect, civil and structural engineer or surveyor	14.5
Boarding or care of animals	12
Business services that are not listed elsewhere	12
Catering services, including restaurants and takeaways before 15 July 2020 and from 1 April 2022	12.5
Catering services, including restaurants and takeaways from 15 July 2020 to 30 September 2021	4.5
Catering services, including restaurants and takeaways from 1 October 2021 to 31 March 2022	8.5
Computer and IT consultancy or data processing	14.5
Computer repair services	10.5
Entertainment (excluding film, radio, television or video production, see below) or journalism	12.5
Estate agency or property management services	12
Farming or agriculture that is not listed elsewhere	6.5
Film, radio, television or video production	13
Financial services	13.5
Forestry or fishing	10.5
General building or construction services (note (a))	9.5
Hairdressing or other beauty treatment services	13
Hiring or renting goods	9.5
Hotel or accommodation before 15 July 2020 and from 1 April 2022	10.5
Hotel or accommodation from 15 July 2020 to 30 September 2021	0
Hotel or accommodation from 1 October 2021 to 31 March 2022	5.5
Investigation or security	12
Labour-only building or construction services (note (a))	14.5
Laundry or dry-cleaning services	12
Lawyers or legal services	14.5
Library, archive, museum or other cultural activities	9.5
Management consultancy	14
Manufacturing fabricated metal products	10.5
Manufacturing food	9
Manufacturing that is not listed elsewhere	9.5
Manufacturing yarn, textiles or clothing	9
Membership organizations	8
Mining or quarrying	10
Packaging	9
Photography	11
Post offices	5
Printing	8.5
Publishing	11
Pubs before 15 July 2020 and from 1 April 2022	6.5
Pubs from 15 July 2020 to 30 September 2021	1
Pubs from 1 October 2021 to 31 March 2022	4
Real estate activities not listed elsewhere	14
Repairing personal or household goods	10
Repairing vehicles	8.5
Retailing food, confectionery, tobacco, newspapers or children's clothing	4
Retailing pharmaceuticals, medical goods, cosmetics or toiletries	8
Retailing that is not listed elsewhere	7.5
Retailing vehicles or fuel	6.5

Category of business	*Appropriate %* *4.1.11 onwards* *(except temporary rates)*
Secretarial services	13
Social work	11
Sport or recreation	8.5
Transport or storage, including couriers, freight, removals and taxis (note (b))	10
Travel agency	10.5
Veterinary medicine	11
Wholesaling agricultural products	8
Wholesaling food	7.5
Wholesaling that is not listed elsewhere	8.5

Notes

(a) 'Labour-only building or construction services' means building or construction services where the value of materials supplied is less than 10% of relevant turnover from such services; any other building or construction services are 'general building or construction services'.

(b) Once in the scheme a business may continue to use it until its total business income exceeds £230,000, and if income does exceed this limit, the business can still remain in the scheme if the income in the following year is estimated not to exceed £191,500. The £230,000 threshold is normally compared to total income (including VAT but excluding sales of capital assets) in the year to the anniversary of the start date (of using the flat rate scheme). However it is also necessary to leave the scheme when there are reasonable grounds to believe the total value of income in the next 30 days will exceed £230,000.

Interest

Default Interest [*VATA 1994, s 74; FA 2021, Sch 29*]

Interest runs on the amount of any VAT assessed (or the amount of any VAT paid late by voluntary disclosure) from the reckonable date (normally the latest date on which a return is required for the period in question) until the date of payment (although in practice it runs to the date shown on the notice of assessment or notice of voluntary disclosure if paid within 30 days of that date). The period of interest cannot commence more than three years before the date of assessment or payment. The rates of interest are as follows.

The VAT late payment interest rules will change, and will be similar to those that already apply for income tax self-assessment for accounting periods beginning on or after 1 January 2023. See page 77 for the harmonised interest regime.

29.9.09–22.8.16	3%
23.8.16–20.11.17	2.75%
21.11.17–20.8.18	3%
21.8.18–29.3.20	3.25%
30.3.20–6.4.20	2.75%
7.4.20–6.1.22	2.60%
7.1.22–20.2.22	2.75%
21.2.22–4.4.22	3.00%
5.4.22–	3.25%

Interest in cases of official error [*VATA 1994, s 78*]

Where VAT has been overpaid or underclaimed due to an error by HMRC, then on a claim HMRC must pay interest from the date they receive payment (or authorise a repayment) for the return period in question until the date on which they authorise payment of the amount on which interest is due. This provision does not require HMRC to pay interest on an amount on which repayment supplement is due. The rates of interest are as follows.

29.9.09–	0.5%

Repayment supplement — VAT [*VATA 1994, s 79; FA 2021, Sch 29*]

Where a person is entitled to a repayment of VAT, the payment due is increased by a supplement of the greater of (i) 5% of that amount; or (ii) £50 provided

(a) the return or claim is received by HMRC not later than the last day on which it is required to be made;
(b) HMRC do not issue a written instruction making the refund within the relevant period; and
(c) the amount shown on the return or claim does not exceed the amount due by more than 5% of that amount or £250 whichever is the greater.

The '*relevant period*' is 30 days beginning with the receipt of the return or claim or, if later, the day after the last day of the VAT period to which the return or claim relates.

The VAT repayment interest rules will change, and will be similar to those that already apply for income tax self assessment for accounting periods beginning on or after 1 January 2023. See p 74 for the harmonised interest regime.

Partial exemption

A registered person who makes taxable and exempt supplies is partly exempt and may not be able to deduct (or reclaim) all his input tax. Where, however, the input tax attributable to exempt supplies in a prescribed accounting period or tax year is within certain de minimis limits, all such input tax is treated as attributable to taxable supplies and recoverable (subject to the normal rules). The de minimis limits are

Exempt input tax not exceeding	£625 per month on average: and 50% of all input tax for the period concerned

Rates

Standard rate	4.1.11 onwards	20%	VAT fraction 1/6
Reduced rate		5%*	1/21
Flat-rate scheme for farmers		4% flat-rate addition to sale price	

*A temporary reduced rate of 12.5% applied to VATA 1994 Sch 7A Groups 14–16 from 1 October 2021 to 31 March 2022.

For the flat-rate scheme for farmers, from 1 January 2021 there are entry and exit thresholds for the scheme of £150,000 and £230,000 respectively. These thresholds are the same as those applying to the flat-rate scheme for small businesses on p 117.

Reduced rate supplies [*VATA 1994, Sch 7A*]

A supply of goods or services is charged at the reduced rate if falling within one of the following Groups.

Group 1	Domestic fuel and power
Group 2	Installation of energy-saving materials (zero-rated in Great Britain from 1 April 2022 to 31 March 2027; reduced rate continuing in Northern Ireland)
Group 3	Grant-funded installation of heating equipment or security goods or connection of a gas supply
Group 4	Women's sanitary products (zero-rated from 11pm on 31 December 2020)
Group 5	Children's car seats and bases
Group 6	Residential conversions
Group 7	Residential renovations and alterations
Group 8	Contraceptive products
Group 9	Welfare advice or information
Group 10	Installation of mobility aids for the elderly
Group 11	Smoking cessation products
Group 12	Caravans
Group 13	Cable-suspended transport systems
Group 14	Course of catering (5% from 15 July 2020 to 30 September 2021 and 12.5% from 1 October 2021 to 31 March 2022)
Group 15	Holiday accommodation etc (5% from 15 July 2020 to 30 September 2021 and 12.5% from 1 October 2021 to 31 March 2022)
Group 16	Shows and certain other attractions (5% from 15 July 2020 to 30 September 2021 and 12.5% from 1 October 2021 to 31 March 2022)

Registration

(i) UK taxable supplies

A person who makes taxable supplies is liable to be registered

(a) at the end of any month if the value of taxable supplies in the year then ending has exceeded the limit in column A below; or

(b) at any time, if there are reasonable grounds for believing that the value of taxable supplies in the next 30 days will exceed the limit in column A below

except that a person does not become liable to be registered under (a) above if HMRC are satisfied that the value of taxable supplies in the year beginning at the time he would be liable to be registered will not exceed the limit in column B below. With effect from 1 December 2012 a non-UK established business is required to register for VAT regardless of the value of taxable supplies in the UK.

Effective date	*A (£)*	*B (£)*
1.4.22	85,000	83,000
1.4.21	85,000	83,000
1.4.20	85,000	83,000
1.4.19	85,000	83,000
1.4.18	85,000	83,000
1.4.17	85,000	83,000

(ii) Supplies from EU countries ('distance selling')

NOTE: These rules only apply to registration in Northern Ireland from 1 January 2021 to 31 June 2021 (they ceased to apply to the rest of the UK after 31 December 2020). From 1 July 2021 this threshold was abolished and replaced with an EU-wide threshold (applying also to Northern Ireland) of EUR 10,000. A business person in an EU country not registered or liable to be registered in Northern Ireland (before 1 January 2021 the UK) under (i) above is liable to be registered on any day if, in the period beginning with 1 January in that year, he has made, and is responsible for the delivery of, supplies to non-taxable persons in Northern Ireland (before 1 January 2021 the UK) exceeding the following limits

Effective date	£
1.1.93–30.6.21	70,000

(iii) Acquisitions from EU countries

NOTE: These rules only apply to registration for bringing goods into Northern Ireland from the EU from 1 January 2021. The concept of acquisitions was broadly abolished in the rest of the UK from that date. A person not registered or liable to be registered under (i) or (ii) above is liable to be registered

(a) at the end of any month if, in the period beginning with 1 January in that year, he has made acquisitions of taxable goods for business purposes (or for non-business purposes if a public body, charity, club, etc.) from suppliers in EU countries whose value exceeds the following limits; or

(b) at any time, if there are reasonable grounds for believing that the value of such acquisitions in the next 30 days will exceed the following limits

Effective date	£	Effective date	£
1.4.22	85,000	1.4.19	85,000
1.4.21	85,000	1.4.18	85,000
1.4.20	85,000	1.4.17	85,000

Returns and payment of VAT

Subject to below, a completed VAT return must be sent to HMRC, and any VAT due paid, not later than one month after the end of the return period. This is subject to a relaxation as a result of the COVID-19 pandemic. Businesses were not required to make a VAT payment during the period from 20 March 2020 until 30 June 2020. They could instead pay any liabilities which accumulated during the deferral period in full by 31 March 2021 and interest and penalties were not charged on any amounts that were deferred. Alternatively, businesses could pay in interest-free instalments if they opted-in between March and June 2021 or sought specific help from HMRC. Penalties were due if none of the options were taken by 30 June 2021.

For VAT accounting periods beginning on or after 1 April 2019, with limited exceptions, all VAT-registered taxpayers have to keep, maintain and preserve an electronic account of specified information using 'functional compatible software', and submit the return and make payment electronically, unless taxable supplies are below the VAT threshold in the previous year. From April 2022 the requirement is extended to VAT-registered taxpayers trading below the VAT threshold. Before 1 April 2019 all businesses (subject to limited exceptions in the case of insolvency or religious objection) had to submit returns online using the eVAT service.

Where returns are sent electronically, any VAT due must also be paid electronically. Otherwise, payment can be made by post to VAT Central Unit at Southend-on-Sea, by debit card or, subject to a fee, by credit card, or electronically by Bank Giro Credit transfer, BACS or CHAPS.

Where payment is made electronically, a business automatically receives a 7-day extension for the submission of the return and payment of VAT. The concession cannot be used (i) by businesses required to make payments on account unless it makes monthly returns; (ii) by businesses using the annual accounting scheme; or (iii) to make VAT payments other than VAT return payments (e.g. assessments).

Businesses with an annual VAT liability of £2.3m or more must make interim payments on account (POAs) at the end of the second and third months of each VAT quarter with a balancing payment for the quarter with the VAT return. All POAs and balancing payments must be made by electronic transfer.

Digital services — VAT mini one-stop shop (VAT MOSS). The following rules no longer apply from 1 January 2021. From 1 January 2015 the place of supply for business-to-consumer (B2C) supplies of broadcasting, telecommunications and e-services (digital services) was determined by the location of the consumer unless, between 1 January 2019 and 31 December 2020, such annual supplies across the EU were less than €10,000. This applies to all businesses that supply digital services above that threshold to consumers (ie private individuals), whether or not they are registered for UK VAT. Any business supplying digital services above the €10,000 limit to a consumer in another member state therefore was required to charge VAT on the supply in that member state and register for VAT in that member state. Supplies of digital services to businesses only (including the self-employed) are not affected by these rules. To avoid having to register for VAT in every EU member state where digital services were supplied, it was possible (prior to 1 January 2021) for a business to opt to use the VAT Mini One Stop Shop online service (VAT MOSS). Using the VAT MOSS online service meant a business was able to submit a single calendar quarterly VAT MOSS return and payment covering all its EU digital service supplies.

Zero-rated supplies [*VATA 1994, Sch 8*]

A supply of goods or services is a zero-rated supply if falling within one of the following Groups. Such a supply is a taxable supply with a nil rate of tax

Group 1	Food
Group 2	Sewerage services and water
Group 3	Books, etc including e-publications from 1 May 2020.
Group 4	Talking books for the blind and disabled and wireless sets for the blind
Group 5	Construction of buildings, etc.
Group 6	Protected buildings
Group 7	International services
Group 8	Transport
Group 9	Caravans and houseboats
Group 10	Gold
Group 11	Bank notes
Group 12	Drugs, medicines, aids for disabled, etc.
Group 13	Imports, exports, etc.
Group 15	Charities, etc.
Group 16	Clothing and footwear
Group 18	European Research Infrastructure Consortia
Group 19	Women's sanitary products (from 11pm on 31 December 2020)
Group 20	*Personal protective equipment (coronavirus) (from 1 May 2020 to 31 October 2020)*
Group 21	Online marketplaces (deemed supply) (from 11pm on 31 December 2020)
Group 22	Free zones (from 8 November 2021)
Group 23	Installation of energy-saving materials (from 1 April 2022 to 31 March 2027; Northern Ireland excluded)

Value added tax car fuel scale rates

CO_2 emissions	Scale charge		
	Yearly returns	Quarterly returns	Monthly returns
g/km	£	£	£
Return periods beginning after 30.4.20			
120 or below	581	144	48
125	870	218	72
130	930	231	76
135	986	246	81
140	1,047	261	87
145	1,103	275	91
150	1,163	290	96
155	1,219	305	101
160	1,279	319	106
165	1,335	334	111
170	1,396	348	115
175	1,452	362	120
180	1,512	377	125
185	1,568	392	130
190	1,628	406	135
195	1,684	421	140
200	1,745	436	144
205	1,801	450	149
210	1,861	464	154
215	1,917	479	159
220	1,977	493	164
225 or more	2,033	508	168

CO_2 emissions	Scale charge		
	Yearly returns	Quarterly returns	Monthly returns
g/km	£	£	£
Return periods beginning after 30.4.21			
120 or below	585	145	48
125	875	219	72
130	936	233	77
135	992	247	82
140	1,053	262	87
145	1,109	277	91
150	1,170	292	97
155	1,226	306	102
160	1,287	321	106
165	1,343	336	111
170	1,404	350	116
175	1,460	364	121
180	1,521	379	126
185	1,577	394	130
190	1,638	409	136
195	1,694	423	141
200	1,755	438	145
205	1,811	453	150
210	1,872	467	155
215	1,928	481	160
220	1,989	496	165
225 or more	2,045	511	169

CO_2 emissions	Scale charge		
	Yearly returns	Quarterly returns	Monthly returns
g/km	£	£	£
Return periods beginning after 30.4.22			
120 or below	700	174	58
125	1,048	262	87
130	1,121	279	92
135	1,188	296	98
140	1,261	314	104
145	1,329	332	110
150	1,401	349	116
155	1,469	367	122
160	1,542	385	127
165	1,609	402	133
170	1,682	419	139
175	1,749	437	145
180	1,822	454	151
185	1,889	472	156
190	1,962	490	163
195	2,030	507	169
200	2,102	525	174
205	2,170	543	180
210	2,242	559	185
215	2,310	577	192
220	2,383	595	198
225 or more	2,450	612	203

Notes

(a) Subject to (d) below, a taxable person is required to account for output tax where fuel is supplied for private motoring to either himself or his employees. The scale charges set out above can be used to represent the tax-inclusive value of the fuel supplied and apply separately to supplies to each individual in any prescribed accounting period in respect of any one vehicle. Where there is a choice between using the scale charge and another method of determining the value, if a taxable person opts to use the scale charge it must be used for all cars in which business fuel is made available for private use.

(b) The rules apply to all cars but not to other vehicles such as vans, motorcycles and invalid cars. They do not apply to pooled cars or cars used exclusively for business purposes. Travel between home and work is regarded as a private rather than business journey.

(c) Where the above scale rates are used, a taxable person can reclaim input tax on all fuel purchased, even if used for private motoring.

(d) Where the CO_2 emissions figure of a vehicle is not a multiple of five, the figure is rounded down to the next multiple of five to determine the level of charge. For bi-fuel vehicles, the lower CO_2 emissions figure is used. Vehicles which are too old to have a CO_2 emissions figure are treated as having an emissions figure of 140 g/km for vehicles with an engine capacity of 1,400 cc or less, 175 g/km for vehicles with an engine capacity between 1,401 cc and 2,000 cc and 225 or more g/km for vehicles with an engine capacity of more than 2,000 cc.

(e) Employers can use HMRC's advisory fuel rates to reclaim VAT on fuel costs reimbursed for business travel by employees in company cars. The employer must obtain and keep a valid VAT invoice. See page 80.

	Nature of offence	Penalty
Default surcharge [*VATA 1994, s 59*] The default surcharge penalty is replaced by a harmonised system of penalties for late filing and late payment for accounting periods beginning on or after 1 January 2023 (see below and page 77).	Failure to furnish a return in time or pay the VAT shown on it as due. Where no VAT is due or the VAT due is paid on time but the return is submitted late, although HMRC record the default there is no *liability* to a surcharge The provisions also apply to the Payments on Account Scheme	The greater of £30 or the following percentages of outstanding VAT 1st default in surcharge period 2% 2nd default in surcharge period 5% 3rd default in surcharge period 10% 4th default in surcharge period 15% 5th default in surcharge period 15% Further defaults 15%
Late return [*FA 2021, Sch 24*] For accounting periods beginning on or after 1 January 2023	Failure to make return on time where maximum number of penalty points have been awarded.	£200
Late payment [*FA 2021, Sch 26*] For accounting periods beginning on or after 1 January 2023	(a) First penalty if failure is between 16 days and 30 days and '15-day time to pay condition' is not met	2% of amount outstanding after 15 days
	(b) If failure is more than 30 days and '30-day time to pay condition' is not met	Penalty above plus 2% of amount outstanding after 30 days
	Second penalty if failure is more than 30 days (but subject to any time to pay arrangements in place)	4% per annum for period outstanding
Incorrect zero-rating [*VATA 1994, s 62*]	Issuing an incorrect certificate stating that certain supplies fall to be zero-rated or taxed at the reduced rate	Difference between the VAT which should have been charged and the VAT actually charged
EU sales lists (ESL)/reverse charge	(a) Submission of reverse charge statement or an ESL containing a material inaccuracy. [*VATA 1994, s 65, Sch 9ZA para 73*]	£100 for each material inaccuracy within two years following a penalty notice from HMRC identifying an earlier material inaccuracy
	(b) Failure to submit a reverse charge statement or an ESL. [*VATA 1994, s 66, Sch 9ZA para 73*]	Greater of £50 or a daily penalty (maximum 100 days) of £5, £10 or £15 depending upon whether the statement or list is the first, second, or third or subsequent statement or list in a default period specified by HMRC
Import VAT [*FA 2003, ss 24–41*]	(a) Non-compliance in cases of 'occasional serious error' involving at least £10,000 duty and/or VAT; persistent failure to comply with regulatory obligations; and failure to correct deficiencies in systems, etc.	£2,500 maximum
	(b) Evasion penalty (as an alternative to criminal prosecution)	Up to the amount of duty and/or VAT sought to be evaded

Value added tax civil penalties

	Nature of offence	Penalty
Electronic returns *[SI 1995 No 2518, Reg 25A]*	Failure to make return electronically by person required to do so	*Annual VAT exclusive turnover* — *Penalty* £100,000 or less — £100 £100,001–£5,600,000 — £200 £5,600,001–£22,800,000 — £300 £22,800,001 or more — £400
Breach of walking possession agreement *[VATA 1994, s 68]*	Breach of agreement under which property distrained remains in possession of a person who has failed to pay VAT	One half of the VAT due or amount recoverable
Records (including digital records) *[VATA 1994, ss 69, 69B]*	Failure to preserve for six years or such lesser period as HMRC allow	£500
	Failure to preserve records specified in HMRC direction	£200 for each day of failure (maximum 30 days)
Breaches of regulatory provisions *[VATA 1994, s 69]*	Failure to notify end of liability or entitlement to be registered, failure to keep records or failure to comply with any regulations, order or rules made under *VATA 1994*	Greater of £50 or a daily penalty (maximum 100 days) of No of failures in previous two years — Daily rate 0 — £5* 1 — £10* 2 — £15* * or, where the failure consists of not paying VAT or not making a return in the required time, 1/6, 1/3 and 1/2 of 1% of the VAT due respectively, if greater
VAT fraud *[VATA 1994, ss 69C–69E]*	Transactions connected with fraudulent evasion of VAT	30% of potential lost VAT
Investment gold *[VATA 1994, s 69A]*	Failure to comply with key requirements of the investment gold scheme	17½% of the value of the transaction concerned
Use of avoidance schemes *[VATA 1994, Sch 11A paras 10, 11]*	*Businesses with supplies over £600,000 — failure to disclose the use of an avoidance scheme included in a statutory list published by HMRC.* **Replaced from 1 January 2018, see below**	*15% of the VAT avoided*
	Businesses with supplies over £10 million — failure to disclose use of certain schemes within 30 days of the due date for the first VAT return affected (unless the promoter of the scheme has already registered it with HMRC). **Replaced from 1 January 2018, see below**	*£5,000*
Use of avoidance schemes *[F(No 2)A 2017, Sch 17]*	Failure from 1 January 2018 to notify details of, or notify use of, a notifiable proposal which enables a person to obtain a tax advantage within 31 days of the making of the proposal	Penalty up to £600 per day in 'initial period' A continuing penalty not exceeding £600 for each day on which the failure continues after imposition of initial penalty (but a tribunal can determine a higher penalty up to £1 million)
	Failure from 1 January 2018 to provide HMRC with the reference number and related information in relation to notifiable arrangements above	Penalty not exceeding £5,000 in respect of each scheme to which the failure relates For second failure within three years of first, penalty not exceeding £7,500 in respect of each scheme For subsequent failures within three years of previous, penalty not exceeding £10,000 in respect of each scheme

Index

Entries printed in bold type are main subject headings

Index

Index

Index